The Romantic Hero and his Heirs
in French Literature

American University Studies

Series II
Romance Languages and Literature

Vol. 10

PETER LANG
New York · Berne · Frankfort on the Main · Nancy

Lloyd Bishop

The Romantic Hero
and his Heirs
in French Literature

PETER LANG
New York · Berne · Frankfort on the Main · Nancy

Library of Congress Cataloging in Publication Data

Bishop, Lloyd, 1933–
   The Romantic Hero and his Heirs in French Literature.

   (American University Studies. Series II, Romance
Languages and Literature, ISSN 0740-9257; vol. 10)
   Bibliography: p.
   Includes index.
   1. French Literature – 19th Century – History and
Criticism.   2. Romanticism – France.   3. Heroes in
Literature.   4. French Literature – 20th Century – History
and Criticism.   I. Title.   II. Series.
PQ287.B57   1984   840'.9'145   83-49351
ISBN 0-8204-0096-3

CIP-Kurztitelaufnahme der Deutschen Bibliothek

Bishop, Lloyd:
The Romantic Hero and his Heirs in French
Literature / Lloyd Bishop. – New York; Berne;
Frankfort on the Main; Nancy: Lang, 1984.
   (American University Studies: Ser. 2, Romance
   Languages and Literature; Vol. 10)
   ISBN 0-8204-0096-3

NE: American University Studies / 02

© Peter Lang Publishing, Inc., New York 1984

Printed by Lang Druck, Inc., Liebefeld/Berne (Switzerland)

To my mother --

a romantic soul

Acknowledgments

I gratefully acknowledge the help and encouragement of several colleagues, especially Professor Robert Denommé of the University of Virginia, Professor James McNab of Guilford College and Professor B. F. Bart of the University of Pittsburg. Special thanks are owed to Anita Malebranche and to Lisa Neill for their expert technical assistance.

In another form, parts of this book have appeared in The French Review, Nineteenth-Century French Studies, and in an earlier book of mine, In Search of Style. I wish to thank the copyright holders for permission to reprint portions of "Jesus as Romantic Hero in Le Mont des Oliviers," © 1973 by the American Association of Teachers of French, in The French Review, special issue no. 5, Spring 1973, 41-48; "Romantic Irony in Musset's Namouna," © 1979 by T. H. Goetz in Nineteenth-Century French Studies, 7 (1979), 181-91; "Romantic Irony in Le Rouge et le Noir," © 1982 by the Rector and Visitors of the University of Virginia in In Search of Style: Essays in French Literary Stylistics, 46-63.

Permission to quote from works protected by copyright has been generously granted by:

Editions Gallimard for a quotation from "Le grand combat" in L'Espace du dedans by Henri Michaux (Copyright © 1966 by Editions Gallimard); for a quotation from Plume by Henri Michaux (Copyright c 1963 by Editions Gallimard).

The Institute of Psycho-Analysis and the Hogarth Press for a quotation from Civilization and its Discontents in The Standard Edition of the Complete Psychological Works of Sigmund Freud by Sigmund Freud (Copyright © 1961 by the Hogarth Press).

Grove Press, for the entire text of "Breath" in First Love and Other Shorts by Samuel Beckett (Copyright © 1969 by Samuel Beckett).

CONTENTS

chapter one

PORTRAIT OF A HERO

Everyone talks about the romantic hero, but few write
about him. Some fifty years ago, Mario Praz, limiting himself
to a discussion of the erotic sensibility, catalogued his pathological tendencies in The Romantic Agony. More recently, George
Ross Ridge, in The Hero of French Romantic Literature, provided
a composite view of his dominant characteristics without attempting an exhaustive survey. These two books, and a few essays
scattered in periodicals and book chapters, are really all
we have on the subject. Frederick Garber has correctly asserted
that "although the bibliography of individual figures is,
of course, extensive, studies of wider aspects of the tradition
of the romantic hero are comparatively rare."[1] And Raney
Stanford has justifiably complained that "our contemporary
view of the romantic hero has been blurred by infrequently
examined assumptions."[2] The purpose of The Romantic Hero and his
Heirs is two-fold: I first want to supplement Ridge's solid work
by looking closely at some of the important romantic heroes
of French literature and enlarge upon the general portrait
drawn by Ridge. Then I shall attempt to trace the romantic
hero's literary heirs from the romantic period to the middle
of the twentieth century--and beyond. I believe and shall
try to prove that the romantic hero, when joined with his legitimate heirs, is the chief hero of modern French literature.
The book is not a puerile reductio ad romanticism but a serious
attempt to trace a literary lineage. I support the thesis
not only by examining the internal evidence of primary sources
but also by establishing a surprisingly large corpus of opinion
on the part of distinguished literary critics and historians. By
bringing together my own findings and those of other scholars
I shall establish the fact that a consensus has by now developed
concerning the centrality of the romantic hero in modern

French literature. The romantic hero did not die with the romantic period; he lives on in his progeny. The descendants are not carbon copies, of course, but despite the inevitable (and significant) permutations, the family resemblance is unmistakable. Indeed the most striking thing I have discovered about the romantic hero is his persistence; he recurs with the insistence of myth. If literature, even more than philosophy, reflects the temper of an age, it is in an age's literary hero that one should look for its chief emblem. This book, then, is a description and the genealogy of a literary hero. It is also a description of the modern sensibility.

Who _is_ the romantic hero? and where can we find a full-length portrait of him? Most histories of literature offer a sketchy picture at best. A good place to start looking is Ridge's book. The romantic hero's basic trait according to Ridge--and he presents a very good case--is acute self-consciousness.[3] The discovery and portrayal of the unique self is indeed the dominant characteristic of the first wave of French romanticism--up to 1830--which, among other things, was an explosion of individualism in literature. Presenting the self as something quasi-divine is one of the two romantic "heresies" (the other is Nature worship). Ridge asserts, and he is right again, that the romantic hero is self-conscious mainly because he is aware of the fundamental difference (or the "pathos of distance") between himself and the "herdmen." The latter go about their daily round of activities without questioning the basic assumptions of their society or the basic ground of their being. Not so the romantic hero. He conforms in this respect to Ortega y Gasset's idea of heroes: "They refuse to repeat the gestures that custom, tradition, or biological instincts force them to make. These men we call heroes because to be a hero means to be one out of many, to be oneself . . . . This will to be oneself is heroism."[4]

The French romantic hero, especially in fiction, is introspective, and is the first to marvel at his strange uniqueness. This introspection usually makes of him a man of moods

more often than a man of action. His self-consciousness
seems more marked than that found in heroes of other romantic
literatures. As Walter L. Reed says, in his _Meditations
on the Hero_: "The heroes of French Romanticism are more
prone to self-consciousness themselves, more passive than active.
As with Constant's Adolphe and Musset's _enfant de notre siècle_,
they exhibit the disease of the age rather than provide its
remedy."[5] In _Either/Or_ Kierkegaard has noticed the peculiar
self-consciousness of modern heroes:

> In ancient tragedy the action itself has an epic moment
> in it; it is as much event as action. The reason for this
> naturally lies in the fact that the ancient world did not
> have subjectivity fully self-conscious and reflective. Even
> if the individual moved freely, he still rested in the substantial
> categories of state, family, and destiny. This substantial
> category is exactly the fatalistic element in Greek tragedy,
> and its exact peculiarity. The hero's destruction is, therefore,
> not only a result of his own deeds, but is also a suffering,
> whereas in modern tragedy the hero's destruction is not really
> suffering, but is action. In modern times, therefore, situation
> and character are really predominant. The tragic hero, conscious
> of himself as a subject, is fully reflective, and this reflection
> has not only reflected him out of every immediate relation
> to state, race, and destiny, but has often reflected him out
> of his own preceding life.[6]

Kierkegaard's statement about ancient heroes moving
within the "substantial categories of state, family and destiny"
is echoed by Lukács' view of ancient society as "bounded"
and well integrated whereas modern society is unbounded and
its literary heroes all lonely wanderers and questors. No
god plots the modern hero's path or walks ahead of him.
As David H. Miles comments, Lukács believes that "the farther we
travel from the unselfconsciousness of the Greeks, the more
we suffer from the burden of consciousness itself, and the
novel hero becomes emblematic of this suffering."[7] And Kierkegaard's observation about the modern tragic hero's self-
consciousness reflecting him out of every immediate relation
to state, race and destiny is echoed in Erich Heller's analysis
of the modern artist's "journey to the interior" or toward
self-absorbed contemplation resulting in "the disinherited mind."

The romantic hero does not enjoy the ancient hero's sense of belonging with regard to his "home" or his world. Homelessness, or rootlessness, is his basic situation; his wanderlust it not so much a retreat _from_ but a futile search _for_ a true home.

The romantic hero, then, is a solitary hero, the very antithesis of the ideal man of seventeenth-century classicism: the eminently sociable honnête homme. Sartre, we recall, has noted that self-consciousness is basically a "nihilating" consciousness, it is the consciousness of not being anything else in one's phenomenal field. But the original romantic hero at least is not the emblem of a negative ontology. He is solitary because he is superior, he stands above ordinary mortals, a fact that is usually symbolized in spatial terms, by his penchant for high places, the mountain top especially. The hero's superiority lies in his keen sensibility, his enlarged capacity for feeling, and in his total sincerity rather than in the traditional virtues. He considers himself beyond what others call good and evil. As Reed says: "The definition of the hero as one who 'represents . . . a socially approved norm' . . . does not apply at all to the romantic hero." [8]   He does not inspire "epic awe" but rather a mixture of fascination and repulsion; he is the victim of other men's incomprehension and jealousy. He makes others feel uneasy. If one compares him to Aristotle's idea of the tragic hero, he exhibits two or three essential differences. Aristotle's hero is above average but recognizably human. Romantic heroes tend to see themselves as a superior breed. The misfortune of Aristotle's hero is brought on in part by his hamartia or tragic flaw and is accompanied by some measure of tragic guilt; the misfortune of the romantic hero, on the other hand, is usually attributed to the fault of other men or to a flawed universe. The epic hero's tragic flaw is usually related to hubris, but the inordinate and overweening pride of the romantic hero is simply the result of a total (and often embarrassing) sincerity that does not allow of false modesty. If _hubris_ is invoked, as at the end of _René_, it is rather unconvincing, that is, it does not come off as a dominant theme.

The romantic hero, says Ridge, is also a seeker, a man of fate, a pathological hero, a poet-prophet and a rebel. As a seeker, he is usually in search of one of three things: new and exotic sensations or emotions; new values; and finally what he calls _un bien inconnu_, a spiritual dimension or ground of being that underlies--or lies beyond--the quotidian. René was in search of all three. The romantic _hantise de l'absolu_ is usually a tacit form of metaphysical anguish and is the forerunner of our own century's _hantise de l'absurde_.

As seeker, the romantic hero can be considered as continuing in some measure the medieval romance tradition: "The romantic knight is mostly anguished and roams in an apparently purposeless universe in search of an object which usually seems increasingly vague even to him."[9] But the knight-errant usually finds that object whereas the romantic hero, like most modern heroes, is doomed to a never-ending quest. If the knight-errant was uneasy about worldly and otherworldly values, he found consolation in his own values (e.g., valor) and in his undying love for his lady. This is also true, on the whole, of romantic heroes, who often find further consolation, or at least good company, in Nature.

Like the hero of classical tragedy, the romantic hero is a fatal hero, but unlike the former, he is profoundly conscious of himself in this role. While the classical hero is not aware of the catastrophe that fate and a tragic flaw will bring upon him until the anagnorisis at the end of the play, the romantic hero "watches himself struggle in the mesh of fate"[10] from beginning to end. He is doomed to misfortune and tragedy because life cannot fulfil his extraordinary and insatiable desires, live up to his superior values, or satisfy his "romantic" imagination. His fate is tied, then, to his exceptional nature and to the fact that his genius is envied by both men and gods who conspire to hurt him and seal his doom. Of all this he is tragically aware from the very beginning of his story; there will be no dramatic or Sophoclean irony in the romantic drama. If others do not actively conspire to harm him, they are bound to misunderstand and ostracize him. He becomes an outcast, a pariah. Harm inevitably comes also to those close to him, those who love him or follow him into exile. His embrace, like Manfred's, is fatal; his voeux, like René's, are malédictions.

The romantic hero usually begins his career with a short and uncomfortable stay in ordinary society, which strikes him immediately as artificial, hypocritical and vain. Society, he feels, is more interested in symbols of status than in true worth. If he is not cast out from society for being different, he has three options: retreat (e.g., René's self-imposed exile into the wilderness), open rebellion (e.g., Dumas's Antony) or concealed rebellion in the interests of both self-realization and self-preservation (e.g., Julien Sorel).

As everyone knows, the romantic hero, like his famous progenitor, Werther, is a melancholy hero. His reaction to ordinary life is either disgust, ennui or both. His estimate of his fellow man is low. His prospects for the future seem dim. The ensuing taedium vitae leads almost always to the famous "romantic" or Wertherian death wish, which represents for people like René, Lamartine and Nerval not only a rejection of this life but a mystic quest for another, "truer" life. For others, like Obermann, Nodier's Charles Munster (in Le Peintre de Salzburg, 1803, a pallid imitation of Werther) and Vigny's Moses, death is not the entrance into some Platonic or religious paradise but simply a surcease from turmoil. For still others (e.g., Antony and René of Les Natchez) a truly "romantic" (here, in the sense of extreme) passion is so beyond the ordinary that only death can consummate it.

Actually, there are at least four different forms of romantic melancholy, and I should like to urge at once that the following terms not be used interchangeably since they represent four rather distinct states of mind: (1) le mal de

René;   (2) le vague des passions;   (3) le mal du siècle;
(4) Weltschmerz.

(1) Le mal de René. First, let's go to the source:

> La solitude absolue, le spectacle de la nature, me plongèrent
> bientôt dans un état presque impossible à décrire. Sans parents,
> sans amis, pour ainsi dire seul sur la terre, n'ayant point encore
> aimé, j'étais accablé d'une surabondance de vie. Quelquefois
> je rougissais subitement, et je sentais couler dans mon coeur
> comme des ruisseaux d'une lave ardente; quelquefois je poussais
> des cris involontaires, et la nuit était également troublée
> de mes songes et de mes veilles. Il me manquait quelque chose
> pour remplir l'abîme de mon existence . . . .
>
> Toutefois cet état de calme et de trouble, d'indigence
> et de richesse, n'était pas sans quelques charmes.[11]

This is not pure melancholy but ambivalence; there is an
important admixture of expectancy and even exuberance. What
we really have here is adolescent anguish concerning one's
identity and one's future. Our young hero seeks a precise
object for his burning passions (or, more precisely, his
libidinal impulses) and for his unspent energy. He needs
a role to play in life, and even more urgently right now,
a woman to love. He wants to realize his great potential. Will
his life--will he--be worthy of his gifts? Will life satisfy
these intense (but basically normal) longings? "Does what
I love really exist?" he wonders. This state of mind is
not only one of intense anxiety but of guarded, cautious
hope. There is no feeling yet that these aspirations are
impossible of attainment. There is no ennui here, no taedium
vitae, no lassitude.

(2) Le vague des passions. Again, let us go back to
the source, which is not the above passage but the Génie
du christianisme proper.

> Il reste à parler d'un état de l'âme qui, ce nous semble, n'a
> pas encore été bien observé: c'est celui qui précède le
> développment des passions, lorsque toutes les facultés jeunes,
> actives, entières, mais renfermées, ne se sont exercées que
> sur elles-mêmes, sans but et sans objet. Plus les peuples

> avancent en civilisation, plus cet état du vague des passions augmente; car il arrive alors une chose fort triste: le grand nombre d'exemples qu'on a sous les yeux, la multitude de livres qui traitent de l'homme et de ses sentiments, rendent habile sans expérience. On est détrompé sans avoir joui; il reste encore des désirs, et l'on n'a plus d'illusions. L'imagination est riche, abondante et merveilleuse, l'existence pauvre, sèche et désenchantée. On habite, avec un coeur plein, un monde vide, et sans avoir usé de rien, on est désabusé de tout. (II, iii, 9)

Here the victim is a bit older. He is not much more experienced in life but has read and reflected more. His books (in _René_ his travels) have shown him most of life's typical experiences and sentiments; he becomes jaded and blasé through vicarious satiety; he concludes that there is no reasonable hope for happiness. "Spleen" sets in and he becomes bitter ("L'amertume que cet état de l'âme répand sur la vie est incroyable.") This surely is a new note. The _mal de René_ passage speaks of _richesse_ and of a _surabondance de vie_; this one speaks of _une existence pauvre_ and of a _monde vide_. The first passage is one of both anxious and eager expectancy; the second of disillusionment. The world, it is now concluded, will not live up to one's rich, romantic imagination. (In the interests of his general argument Chateaubriand adds that this feeling is encouraged by the _contemptus mundi_ of Christianity.)

René will experience this phase too, but _later_. The time lapse is rapid (among other things, the romantic hero is precocious), but there _is_ a time lapse and there is a _new_ state of mind. The indications of time lapse between the two states are fleeting and vague and have gone unnoticed.

> Cette vie qui m'avait _d'abord_ enchanté [!], ne _tarda pas_ à me devenir insupportable. (p. 128; our emphasis)

> Je luttais _quelque temps_ contre mon mal . . . _Enfin_, ne pouvant trouver de remède à cette étrange blessure de mon coeur . . . (p. 130).

Finding no remedy, he passes into another state, more morbid than "normal".

(3) _Le mal du siècle_. As this term suggests, or ought

to, we are dealing with a more precise form of melancholy. It is linked with history and not just adolescent psychology (which is still present, however). It derives in part from that legacy of skepticism concerning all traditional values bequeathed by the Enlightenment and in part from the confusion of values brought on by political instability, social anarchy and the acceleration of history ("Les événements couraient plus vite que ma plume," writes Chateaubriand in his memoirs). During the very brief period between 1789 and 1815 France experienced absolute monarchy, revolution, a Directorate, a Consulate, an Empire and a restored but constitutionalized or "charterized" monarchy criticized by the ultras as being too liberal--from extreme absolutism to extreme revolution to extreme reaction. Political and religious opinions were so diverse that France was becoming, nay, had already become a centrifugal civilization. By 1820 young men did not know where to turn for faith, hope or ideals. The glorious Emperor was gone and was already the victim of revisionism. The Restoration offered its youth no lofty goals and produced no inspiring leaders.

Henri Peyre thinks that the mal du siècle was radically new only by virtue of its ruthless self-analysis and in purely quantitative terms: the fact that it reached epidemic proportions.[12] But it was radically new in qualitative terms as well. It was not just an expression of the insecurities of adolescence, it was a new sensitivity to History. Before the Revolution, the Terror, the Empire and the Fall, artists did not react so violently to contemporary history. From the reign of Louis XIV to the early years of Louis XVI the political régime and the social order seemed stable if imperfect. But the Terror, to take just the greatest trauma, not only weakened belief in divine Providence, it destroyed the Enlightenment's law of irreversible secular progress. When writers after 1815 spoke of the "void," they were not simply speaking of a vague discontent but of a vacuum that was specifically political, religious and social. The fact of Terror showed

many that History was being written not by God, as Ballanche
and Lamennais still endeavored to believe, but by the shaky
hands of men. The guillotine, says Manuel de Dieguez, seemed
to function solely by men's will and not by God's long-range
plans for humanity.[13]

The best description of the mal du siècle is not in
René, where it is tactfully and tactically kept hidden (there
are, for instance, no specific references to the Revolution
or to emigration, only hints, "displacements") but in Quinet's
Histoire de mes idées and Musset's Confession d'un enfant
du siècle. Quinet himself makes a distinction between the
mal of his generation and the earlier generation's vague
des passions.

> Je ne voyais autour de moi ni un guide auquel je pusse
> me fier, ni même un compagnon dans la route où je tremblais
> et brûlais à la fois de m'engager. J'avais le pressentiment
> qu'il s'agissait d'un renouvellement presque entier des choses
> de l'esprit . . . Quoique cette souffrance allât souvent
> jusqu'au désespoir, il n'y avait là pourtant rien qui ressemblât
> au spleen, à l'ennui de la vie, à tout ce que l'on a appelé
> le vague des passions, vers la fin du dernier siècle. C'était,
> il me semble, à bien des égards, le contraire de la lassitude
> et de la satiété. C'était plutôt une aveugle impatience de
> vivre, une attente fiévreuse, une ambition prématurée d'avenir,
> une soif effrénée de l'âme après le désert de l'Empire. Tout
> cela joint à un désir consumant de produire, ce créer, de
> faire quelque chose, au milieu d'un monde vide encore. Ceux
> que j'ai interrogés plus tard sur ces années m'ont dit avoir
> éprouvé quelque chose de pareil. Chacun se croyait seul comme
> moi: chacun pensait, rêvait comme dans une île déserte.[14]

The important differences are two in number: although le
mal du siècle can and usually does include the late-adolescent
"impatience de vivre" of le mal de René and the vague des
passions, it contains none (or need not contain any) of the
latter's lassitude, spleen or ennui, and more importantly,
it is explicitly informed by a sense of history: a healthy
if anxious ambition (Balzac called it impatience d'avenir)
is struggling among "the ruins of the Empire." The young
man's whole life is ahead of him, but where is it leading?
The old régimes are dead; a new order is certainly in the

making, but as yet it has taken no definite shape nor even a specific direction. One is adrift in History without a guide. There is no consecrated authority. One feels utterly alone. Quinet sums it up well: "un désir consumant de produire, de créer, de faire quelque chose, au milieu d'un monde vide encore."

Quinet takes up this image of the void in another significant passage:

> Les grandes invasions de 1814 et de 1815 avaient laissé un fond d'impressions, d'images, à travers lesquelles j'entrevoyais toutes choses. L'écroulement d'un monde avait été ma première éducation. De quelque côté que je voulusse tourner mes yeux, je trouvais à l'horizon un grand vide; je sentais ce vide dans la poésie, dans l'histoire, dans la philosophie, dans toute chose; j'en souffrais parce que j'étais incapable de le combler, et je ne savais pas que d'autres esprits souffraient du même mal.[15]

Quinet adds that at the root of his _mal_ was not just his tender age nor his peculiar psychological makeup but the precise historical situation of France. The similarity between Quinet's _mal_ and René's is the mixture of energy, expectation and hope with a very deep anxiety about an uncertain future. The major difference is the historization, or what Pierre Barbéris calls "the politization of the _mal du siècle_"--a difference that separates, according to Barbéris, pre-romanticism from romanticism proper.[16] I should like to modify Barbéris's formula by proposing that the _mal du siècle_ is a historization of the _vague des passions_ that is, it involves, by definition, not only one's self-assessment but also, and even more, an assessment of History.

Alfred de Musset's assessment of History is more pointedly negative and his particular _mal_ is more poignantly disillusioned. "Toute la maladie du siècle présent vient de deux causes: le peuple qui a passé par '93 et par 1814 porte au coeur deux blessures. Tout ce qui était n'était plus; tout ce qui sera n'est pas encore. Ne cherchez pas ailleurs le secret de nos maux."[17] The romantic sense of alienation is here a _historical_ awareness. Seventeen ninety-three was the year the Revolution aborted or at least turned sour; it was the year the Revolution failed to keep its promises: Freedom became Tyranny; Fraternity turned into Terror; Equality existed but it was now obvious that some were more equal than others. Eighteen fourteen was the end of another dream; an era of excitement and glory was followed by an era of ennui, of reaction and revisionism; a mercantile-industrial society was founding a new order and a new moral code built upon Money.

(4) _Weltschmerz_. This has been defined in terms of two contradictory drives within the romantic hero: "one toward egoistic and skeptical self-assertion, a passionate holding fast to the feeling of self as a separate and individual identity; the other an equally passionate longing for commitment to absolutes outside the self."[18] I would define it rather as a nihilistic denial of absolutes, a premonition of the Absurd. It is more than personal sorrow, and it is more than metaphysical anguish; it is cosmic despair. The hero has come to a philosophical conclusion: This world is essentially evil and the "other world" is either unknowable, unattainable or non-existent.

René Jasinski has distinguished three generations of the _mal du siècle_: that of René, that of Musset, and that of Gautier, Flaubert and Baudelaire.[19] A more useful distinction, however, is the one I am trying to make here, a distinction between four or five distinct "maladies." The first can be characterized, briefly, as _impatience et inquiétude du désir_ (René); the second heavily stresses the _inquiétude_ (René again, but later); the third is _impatience et inquiétude d'avenir_ (Quinet); the fourth heavily stresses the _inquiétude_ (Musset); the fifth is _avenir bloqué_ (Flaubert).

The trouble with "generations" is (1) they tend to overlap and (2) they are not monopolized by a single malady. Vigny, while more contemporary to Musset and Quinet than to Chateaubriand, harks back to the latter's aristocratic, "passéiste" melancholy, that of a nobleman ostracized by a revolution.

Senancour, while more contemporary to Chateaubriand, exhibits
a Weltschmerz more typical of later generations, of Flaubert's--
and ours.

It is tempting, but it would be impractical to assemble
here all the definitions and descriptions of romantic melancholy
from all the many histories of romanticism in order to show
that these four terms have been taken by and large as synonymous.
For the moment, let two examples suffice:

> It is significant that the mal de René is synonymous
> with the mal du siècle, for no other hero epitomized the romantic
> type so well as René.[20]

> [In René, Chateaubriand] presented the first authentic
> portrayal of that new state of spiritual frustration and moral
> isolation which is called le mal du siècle. Yearning for
> a vague but indefinite ideal impossible of attainment, obsessed
> by haunting dreams of a bliss that can neither be found nor
> formulated, the victim of this malady suffers from langour
> and paralysis of the will, broods self-indulgently on his
> melancholy and anguish of soul, and, fleeing from the bitter
> realities of life which he is unable to face, sinks into thoughts
> of death and suicide.[21]

One problem here is that several different states of mind
are presented as equivalent or as existing simultaneously.
In the case of René, this is simply not true, as we will
show in more detail in the next chapter. In the case of
other romantic heroes, only one or two states may be applicable.
Another problem is that the mal du siècle is being divorced
from History and thus deprived of its main ingredient.

Another recurrent feature I have found in the romantic
hero is that although very young he is "old before his time."
The puer senex topos, as has been shown by Ernst Robert Curtius,
is as old as Latin antiquity. Says Curtius: "All early
and high periods of a culture extol the young and at the
same time honor age. But only late periods develop a human
ideal in which the polarity youth-age works toward a balance."[22]
Thus Virgil praises the virile mind that is found in Iulus'
youthful body:

Ante annos animumque gerens curamque virelem.
(Having manhood's spirit and forethought before man's years)

And Ovid will extol such a combination of youth and maturity as a heaven-sent gift granted to emperors and demigods. Similarly, the ancient Armenian poets frequently used the following formula to laud their young hero:

Other children grow by years,
But David grew by days.[23]

The topos becomes a cliché of hagiographic literature and survives into the Latin Middle Ages and beyond. Curtius has traced it, in both sacred and secular texts the world over, up to (i.e., as late as) the seventeenth and eighteenth centuries. He believes that the topos is explained less by delight in antithesis or oxymoron than as the expression of a human ideal and that its persistence over such a long period of time and over such a large area of the world is evidence of the presence of an archetypal image, an expression of the collective unconscious.

What is significant for our purposes is the radical change the topos undergoes in romantic literature. The romantic hero describes himself as a _puer_ _senex_ ("jeune et pourtant vieux"; "un vieillard né d'hier," etc.), but the stress is on the negative implications: "J'ai le malheur de ne pouvoir être jeune," says Obermann. It is cynical old age that we find in our young romantic hero. This old-young romantic is disillusioned with life before fully tasting it; he is jaded and blasé either because he passes through the normal range of human experiences with lightening speed or because his hypersensitivity or heightened imaginativeness rejects in advance the homely pleasures of terrestrial life. He is "old" too because his future is blocked by his fate.

So, rather than a sense of classical "balance" that the topos seems to work toward in late periods of a culture, we have a sense of imbalance, of a world out of joint. The negative connotations will become exacerbated in the decadent hero of the end of the century who finds himself in a culture that is not just late but overripe and decaying. The topos will continue in even more radicalized form with some of the anti-heroes of twentieth century literature. What we may have here is nothing less than a change in Western man's collective unconscious, in any case a radical change in sensibility.

The romantic hero is an enigmatic hero. He has the mysterious birth and orphanhood of many ancient heroes, whom he resembles in a surprisingly large number of ways. Otto Rank, in The Myth of the Birth of a Hero, notes that the normal relations of the ancient hero toward his father and mother regularly appear impaired, the hero being, or feeling himself to be, an orphan, a foundling or a step child.[24] The romantic hero has the same feeling; in fact he usually is an orphan. Rank sees in the orphan motive a manifestation of an Oedipal hostility toward the Father that makes of the youthful hero a rebel: "The hero himself, as shown by his detachment from his parents, begins his career in opposition to the older generation; he is at once a rebel, a renovator, and a revolutionary. However, every revolutionary is originally a disobedient son, a rebel against the father."[25] (The incest motive, intimately connected with the Oedipal situation, is also frequently found among romantic heroes, but, through displacement perhaps, usually involves a sister rather than a mother.) For the romantic hero, the Father is presented either directly or--through displacement again--indirectly in the form of established authority, organized society or traditional morality. There is also, I am convinced, a metaphysical dimension, the feeling of being abandoned by God (the heavenly Father). This is clear for instance in Vigny's Jesus (Le Mont des Oliviers).

The many obstacles that are put in the way of the hero's birth and childhood lend themselves, according to Rank, to both a positive and a negative interpretation. The positive interpretation underscores the youthful hero's triumph over adversity. But it is the negative interpretation that is especially germane to the romantic hero's situation: "Another interpretation may be admitted, according to which the youthful hero, foreseeing his destiny to taste more than his share of the bitterness of life, deplores in pessimistic mood the inimical act which has called him to earth. He accuses his parents, as it were, for having exposed him to the struggle of life, for having allowed him to be born."[26]   Rank, by the way, traces the comparison of birth to a shipwreck from Lucretius to Schiller's Robbers.

The romantic hero, like Tristan, is born in sorrow, and, like most traditional heroes, is early exposed to envy, bitter jealousy and calumny. In this connection Rank has uncovered (pp. 90-91) what he thinks to be the paranoid structure of the hero-myths: they are equivalent in many essential features to the delusional ideas of certain psychotics, especially delusions of persecution and grandeur. The paranoid is apt to claim that the people whose name he bears are not his real parents, but that he is actually the son of a princely personage. Julien Sorel, we recall, was apt to do the same. Furthermore, the egotistical and passive nature of the typical paranoid is found in many romantic heroes.

I am not urging here a psychoanalytical interpretation of the romantic hero's unconscious motives but am merely suggesting a few leads to those who might want to explore this potentially fruitful topic. I am more interested in our hero's conscious motives and feelings, his sensibility, his own appraisal of his relation to society, to history and to the future.

The romantic hero does not know whence he comes nor, except for his premonition of disaster, whither he goes. He is an enigmatic, inscrutable "force qui va." His heroic otherness is underscored not only by his mysterious origin and catastrophic end but also by the remote settings to which he is attached or into which he is exiled: the American wilderness for René, the moors and crags of Yorkshire for Heathcliff, the forbidding sea for Melville's Ahab, the uninhabited mountains for Lermontov's Pechorin, Byron's Manfred, Hugo's Hernani. Even Vigny's Christ "knows the rocks better than the smooth paths." When the romantic hero tells his own story in the first person, it is often framed by an authorial, editorial or other narrative point of view underlining the "hermeneutic distance" between the enigmatic hero and his audience. In Werther for instance the "Editor" warns the reader that it is difficult to discover the true and innermost motives of men "who are not of the common run."

Although a man of noble impulses, the romantic hero's intense individualism and hypersensitivity often result in morbid or pathological tendencies. His acute awareness of being persecuted or misunderstood borders at times on paranoia; his melancholy often degenerates into involutional melancholia, masochism, or even mere petulance; his egocentrism verges dangerously at times on egomania, narcissism and solipsism. His frequent willingness to be caught in the enemy's trap is another symptom of masochism, while his frequent association of love and death is a sure sign of sadism.

According to Mario Praz, the romantic movement produced a new and perverse sensibility in which pleasure and pain, love and hate, tenderness and cruelty are intimately linked. Praz claims the romantics to be the first in the history of art to see beauty in the grotesque and to delight in the revolting. The Romantic Agony, despite the author's protestations to the contrary, tends to reduce romanticism to this perverse sensibility--a savage reduction indeed. But it is undeniable that there is in the romantic hero, alongside his good qualities, a penchant for the perverse.

Unlike ancient and medieval heroes with their highly unified personality, the modern hero tends to be a divided, quasi-schizoid self. As Goethe's Faust laments:

> Two souls abide, alas, within my breast,
> And each one seeks for riddance from the other.
> The one clings with a dogged love and lust
> With clutching parts unto this present world,
> The other surges fiercely from the dust
> Unto sublime ancestral fields.

The dialectical tensions in which the romantic hero is involved do not produce a satisfactory synthesis but at best a tenuous equilibrium which breaks down eventually and leads either to the hero's self-destruction or to a paralysis of the will or heroic resolve.

An interesting sub-type of the romantic hero is the mad genius. Curiously enough, pathology is the least important link between the two. Like the romantic hero, the romantic madman is a pariah condemned to solitude; he cannot accept everyday reality nor commonplace rationality ("Il faut déraisonner," Musset advised his peers). His madness can be interpreted as a form of romantic escapism--but in a positive sense. The romantic madman is not at all a stock comic character. He is the hero of a genre that Nodier called le fantastique sérieux. He is an exceptional being, a seer (related then to the poet-prophet) who has clear visions of the Absolute, which the romantic hero can see only dimly if at all. The most interesting examples of this type of hero are Nodier's Michel le Charpentier and Jean-François-les-bas-bleus, Balzac's Louis Lambert and the narrator of Nerval's Sylvie and Aurélia.[27]

Two types that are discussed at length by Ridge will not be discussed here: the dandy and the poet as prophet. While they are genuine heroes of French romantic literature, they are not exemplars of what we call the romantic hero. The dandy is disqualified because he does not possess the latter's extreme and overt melancholy. While he may possess a certain form of melancholy--his aggressive artificiality can be viewed as a desperate attempt to provide himself with a simulacrum of order within a disorderly world--it is a melancholy that is more repressed than expressed. The dandy's studied impassiveness, his frigid self-control, are the very antithesis of the impassioned romantic hero. Furthermore, the dandy is a poseur who does not take himself with the total seriousness of the René-Hernani prototypes. The only dandies treated by a major writer of the romantic period are those of Musset (e.g., Mardoche, Rafaël of Les Marrons du feu and the Hassan of Namouna), and they are treated with a blend of seriousness and irony rather than solemnity. Musset's heroes are significantly different from the typical romantic hero; they will be discussed in a separate chapter.

The triumphant certainties of the poet-prophet run counter to the romantic hero's free-floating anxiety, his vague discontent and search for a vague absolute, the bien inconnu. The romantic hero is an anguished seeker whereas the poet vates has already found--and now loudly proclaims--his truth. The latter is further disqualified because he is not unique to romantic literature.

While Ridge considers the romantic hero to be basically the Self-conscious Hero, I would say, rather, that he is the Alienated Hero. After all, the honnête homme of the seventeenth century was a highly self-conscious individual too. He was keenly aware of himself as a perfectly integrated part of the social fabric and of the role he must play in it; for example, he must be conversant on all topics of polite conversation without becoming ostentatious, immodest or pedantic. What the romantic hero is basically conscious of is a sense of alienation. First, his "alienation and severance from man" as Coleridge said of Byron, then his avowed or concealed alienation from God, and finally--beginning in Musset's work especially--from himself.

* * *

The romantic hero is intimately related to the six other great myths of the romantic age: Prometheus, Satan, Faust, Don Juan, the Byronic Hero and the Napoleonic legend. In fact he is, I think, something of a composite of all of them.

The first four figures are variants of the same type: the noble outlaw, who made his first appearance in pre-romantic literature with the <u>Sturm</u> <u>und</u> <u>Drang</u> figures of Goethe's Götz von Berlichingen, Höderlin's Hyperion and Schiller's Karl Moor. Prometheus steals fire for the benefit of "heaven-oppressed mortality," he is a figure of heroic defiance struggling against a superior force and enduring perpetual persecution or torture. Satan for the romantics exemplifies the spirit of freedom and individualism, the spirit of revolt: better to reign in hell than serve in heaven. They were also impressed by his solitary grandeur, his sense of injured merit and his valiant struggle against overwhelming odds. They were more affected by Satan's suffering than his sinning and found in him a sublime figure of unhappiness, which, according to romantic dogma, from Mme de Staël to Baudelaire, is literature's greatest theme. It was Christopher Marlowe who raised the figure of Faust from an eccentric, avaricious magician to the status of a tragic hero, but it was Goethe's Faust who solely impressed the French romantics. Faust is the seeker, the symbol of man's desire to transcend his physical and intellectual limitations, the thirst not only for knowledge but for sheer power. His tragic flaw might be called epistemological <u>hubris</u>, the aspiration to divine omniscience. The Faustian spirit, like the romantic spirit, is never content, never at rest; it is emblematic not of romantic lassitude but of romantic energy and striving, an Icarus-like overreaching. The Don Juan legend, as David Winter has noted,[28] is usually interpreted along one of two general lines of analysis: Either he is driven by some cosmic force, such as longing for the ideal or the infinite, as in E.T.A. Hoffmann's version and and the second canto of Musset's <u>Namouna</u>, or he is the bored narcissist incapable of forming permanent ties to others, such as Stendhal's Don Juan and the Hassan of <u>Namouna</u>, cantos one and three. Like Satan and Prometheus, he is a <u>géant</u> <u>révolté</u>, as Banville called him, and, as Otto Rank points out, he preserves his heroic stature by the fact that he stands <u>alone</u> against a

world of opponents and alone against an underworld fraught with
danger. A second heroic stance is his courage: Baudelaire will
call him--with understatement--a calme héros.

The basic prototype of the romantic hero is undoubtedly
René-Childe Harold. The hyphen is meant to suggest that René
and the Childe Harold of the first two cantos are almost indis-
tinguishable (but more in retrospect than upon very close examination) and that their influence upon later romantic heroes was
combined and simultaneous. (Chateaubriand complained bitterly
that Byron never acknowledged his literary debt.) Both René and
Childe Harold are cynical young men, or better, late adolescents,
filled with melancholy but also haughty pride; both are "the
most unfit/Of men to herd with Man" since both deem no mortal
wight their peer. Both wander over Europe in search of "self-
restoration" but find only vanity and evanescent glory and must
turn to Nature for companionship and consolation. Harold
possesses both Cain's "unresting doom" and the Wandering Jew's
"ceaseless gloom" and, both René-like and Keats-like, is half in
love with easeful Death. He will not look beyond the tomb, he
says, "But cannot hope for rest before." René does look beyond
the tomb, but he sees nothing precise. Another difference is
that unlike René, who is much less bitter and who is rather
complacent about his shortcomings, Childe Harold harbors an intense bitterness born of a deep sense of guilt and is filled
with remorse for secret sins. A sense of guilt is not typical of
French romantic heroes, save those of Musset. Another important
resemblance between Musset's heroes and Childe Harold is the
early satiety, the premature drying up of the sensibilities in a
dissipated young man for whom, however, the great object of life
is sensation: "to feel that we exist, though in pain."

The three other Byronic heroes who most impressed the French
were Conrad-Lara, Manfred and Cain. Conrad, according to Peter
Thorslev, is the first of Byron's fully misanthropic heroes--
although there is much misanthropy in the latter cantos of Childe
Harold's Pilgrimage. He is both a Noble Outlaw and a noble

Satan, driven "to war with Man and forfeit Heaven." Manfred is
the solitary stranger filled with "a fierce thirst of death . . .
still unslaked" and is remorse-ridden, presumably because of
incest, another theme that may have been borrowed from René as
well as from the Gothic villain. His embrace is fatal, destroying the woman he once loved. As a puer senex, Manfred combines
classical precociousness with romantic cynicism.

> From my youth upwards
> My spirit walked not with the souls of men,
> Nor looked upon the earth with human eyes;
> The thirst of their ambitions was not mine,
> The aim of their existence was not mine;
> My joys, my griefs, my passions, and my powers
> Made me a stranger. Although I wore the form
> I had no sympathy with breathing flesh.

In Cain both the protagonist and Lucifer show the Byronic Hero
"in the last stage of his development . . . a metaphysical rebellion in the cause of Romantic self-assertion."[29] Cain rebels
against an unjust God who has instituted vicarious punishment,
making the innocent suffer because of the guilty. Lucifer is the
epitome of Titanic defiance of the gods:

> I have a Victor--true, but no superior . . .
> I battle it against Heaven--through all Eternity,
> And the unfathomable gulfs of Hades,
> And the interminable realms of space,
> And the infinity of endless ages,
> All, all, will I dispute!

Edmond Estève's definition of byronism is a good description of
the early phase of French romanticism and especially of the
French romantic hero: "Le fond du Byronisme peut se définir d'un
mot: c'est l'individualisme, hautain, irréductible, absolu.
Etendre son moi au-delà de toutes limites, l'affranchir de
toutes lois, ne donner à son activité d'autre but que lui-même,
ne voir dans tout ce qui existe que le reflet de son être ou le
moyen de son développement, faire de lui le centre du monde."[30]

Byron himself was another myth of the romantic age, and the
public willingly saw in him the hero of his poems. His dark,
brooding eyes, his moody and mysterious nature, contributed to

the <u>beau</u> <u>ténébreux</u> type: "the man of loneliness and mys-
tery . . . that dazzles, leads, yet chills the vulgar heart."
Lady Caroline Lamb called him "dangerous to know," and Southey
asserted that he had founded a "satanic School of Poetry."   Even
as late as 1977 critics and biographers could ask: "Was Byron
in league with the Devil?"[31]

Less significant for French romanticism than the Byronic
hero but still a leading influence on at least two important
French writers, Lamartine and Chateaubriand, was Macpherson's
Ossian.   The influence upon Chateaubriand was particularly
crucial for the development of the French romantic hero.   "Je
ne sors plus sans mon Homère de Westein dans une poche et mon
Ossian de Glasgow dans l'autre,"[32]   writes Chateaubriand in
1801, precisely when he was polishing up <u>René</u> for inclusion in
<u>Le</u> <u>Génie</u> <u>du</u> <u>christianisme</u>.   The vague melancholy set in a roman-
tic (i.e., late) Autumn of falling leaves and dismal winds, the
disenchantment with the vanity, instability and transience   of
human life, the unfulfilled aspirations, the death wish, and
perhaps most importantly, the modern, romantic intuition of "the
joy of grief"--all this will reappear in René.[33]   <u>Levez-vous</u>,
<u>orages</u> <u>désirés</u> . . .

For hero worship to become part of the romantic sensibility
a genuine historical figure was needed to supplement the many
literary models available, and it was furnished by Napoleon.
To those who worshipped him, to those who were ambivalent about
him and even to those who despised him Napoleon epitomized the
triumph of energy and will, the self-made man seeking and ob-
taining power by his own bootstraps.   Napoleon is one of Hegel's
heroes, those world-historical individuals, who through genius
(and ruthlessness) transcend their time and environment and
serve as instruments of the Idea in the gradual self-realization
of Absolute Spirit.   Several of Hegel's remarks on the world-
historical individual bear upon our discussion of the romantic
hero.   (1) The vague dissatisfaction with contemporary history:
"The spirit's inward development has outgrown the world it

inhabits, and is about to progress beyond it. Its self-consciousness no longer finds satisfaction in the present, but its dissatisfaction has not yet enabled it to discover what it wants, for the latter is not yet positively present; its status is accordingly negative."[34]   (2) The misunderstood and maligned hero: "But such great men are fastened upon by a whole crowd of envious spirits, who hold up their passions as weaknesses" (p. 86).   (3) The raising of passion from a defect to a virtue: "Passion is the prerequisite of all human excellence, and there is accordingly nothing immoral about it" (p. 86).   (4) Egoism and the rebellion against conventional ideas and morals: "They are . . . censured for having flaunted their opinions.   It is perfectly true that they rose to honour by treating accepted values with contempt. Since the innovation they brought into the world was their own personal goal, they drew their conception of it from within themselves, and it was their own end that they realized.   It was this which gave them their satisfaction in the process.   The aim of great men was to obtain satisfaction for themselves, and not for the well-meaning intentions of others" (p. 88-89).   Hegel's view of the inexorable progress of the World-Spirit may be in error, but his remarks on the world-historical individual suggest a good number of reasons why romantic individualists could identify with and strive to emulate Napoleon. Like Hegel's heroes, romantic heroes refuse to be judged by ordinary standards.   The moral freedom of the superior individual is one of the basic tenets of the romantic ethic.[35]

Not only did Napoleon provide the young romantics with a stirring example of individualism and genius, he also contributed indirectly to their historico-political malaise, the mal du siècle.   Comparing the brilliance and excitement of the Napoleonic era with the insipidity of the Restoration, budding romantics felt cheated by History. We have listened briefly to Quinet and Musset; listen now to Gérard de Nerval writing in 1827: "Cet homme-là a tant grandi de sa comparaison avec ceux d'aujourd'hui que c'est vers son règne que le poète est obligé de remonter, s'il veut trouver de belles pensées et des inspirations généreuses; hors de là, tout est dégoût et désenchantement."[36] This passage offers still further evidence that the mal du siècle is quite distinct from both the mal de René and the vague des passions. The disenchantment here has a historical specificity missing in other forms of romantic melancholy.

* * *

Rousseau was the grandfather of the romantic hero and indeed of the entire romantic movement. The two Discours show natural man, the noble savage, alienated from his true self as a result of the development of social institutions and civilization, which can totally overwhelm a passive hero like Saint-Preux with the tremendous pressures and weight of artificial conventions, prejudices and "rules of conscience"--what Freud will call the cultural super-ego. To exist is to feel, we are told by the Savoyard Vicar and later by Bernardin de Saint Pierre, but society carefully educates the child to repress his natural feelings and punishes or ostracizes the adult who gives in to them. Solitude, we learn in the seventh Promenade, is preferable to the society of the wicked, but there is no escape from misfortune when a good man is tracked down by fatality, as we learn in the first and sixth Promenades.

The best preview of the romantic hero is found not in the pallid figure of Saint-Preux but in the Rousseau of the Confessions. The enthronement of the ego, especially the nostalgic ego, is the work of both Rousseau and Chateaubriand. The latter says somewhere in Le Génie that the only subject one can really treat is one's own heart and that the greatest part of genius lies in memories.

Well before René, the Confessions portrayed the vague anxieties of adolescence:

J'atteignis ainsi ma seizième année, inquiet, mécontent de tout et de moi, sans goûts de mon état, sans plaisirs de mon âge, dévoré de désirs dont j'ignorais l'objet, pleurant sans sujets de larmes, soupirant sans savoir quoi; enfin carressant tendrement mes chimères, faute de rien voir autour de moi qui les valût.[37]

J'étais inquiet, distrait, rêveur; je pleurais, je soupirais, je désirais un bonheur dont je n'avais pas d'idée, et dont je sentais pourtant la privation. Cet état ne peut se décrire, et peu d'hommes même le peuvent imaginer, parce que la plupart ont prévenu cette plénitude de vie, à la fois tourmentante et délicieuse, qui, dans l'ivresse du désir, donne un avant-goût de la jouissance. (p. 96)

The second passage is especially significant because of the basically positive note that it strikes, and I submit it as further evidence of the need to distinguish carefully between the various forms and stages of romantic melancholy. The "privation" here is merely the other side of the "plenitude." This is adolescent impatience and eagerness to actualize one's potential--in the realm of feeling rather than action (it is mostly a woman he needs). René too will experience this plénitude de vie and will call it une surabondance de vie. This state should not be confused with le mal du siècle and certainly not with Weltschmerz. It is an ambivalent state, "tourmentante et délicieuse," with the emphasis on the positive side of the ambivalence.

The romantic hero's career will parallel rather closely the curve of Rousseau's: the difficulties of his birth, the hypersensitive youth, the contrary moods, the reveries, the mauvaise étoile that sours his life, the sense of being betrayed by enemies and friends alike. But it was Rousseau's ungrateful son, Chateaubriand, who provided the first fictional hero to serve as the basic model for the romantic age: René. We shall examine him closely in the next chapter.

To trace the romantic hero's eighteenth-century filiations more fully we must go past Rousseau and back to Prévost. The latter's heroes have been rightly called "the ultimate ancestors" [38] of the romantic hero. They are indeed the first in a long line of fated and fatal sufferers, melancholy dreamers haunted by vague desires, somber young men who believe in the divine right of passion but who, unwillingly and unwittingly, bring destruction upon those they love. Prévost's protagonists feel themselves persecuted by a "malign destiny," they have the romantic hero's suicidal tendencies and the conviction that their psychological nature and their desperate situation are seules de leur espèce. The typical hero of Prévost, like Sand's Lélia, considers himself un être à part.

Prévost is the creator of the eighteenth-century novel of sensibility. In his work, as in Télémaque (1699), sensibility is presented not only as the sign but as the very source of virtue. Both Des Grieux and Cleveland tell us that their heart is the tenderest that Nature has ever produced--thus providing us also with pre-romantic hyperbole. Prévost is also the inventor of lachrymose prose: "J'entre dans la mer immense de mes infortunes. Je commence une narration que je vais accompagner de mes larmes et qui en fera couler des yeux de mes lecteurs. Cette pensée me cause quelque satisfaction . . . j'obtiendrai la pitié des coeurs tendres." [39] The narrator of the Mémoires d'un homme de qualité (1728) had already indicated his intention to make both his protagonists and his readers swoon with tristesse and attendrissement. To Prévost must also be imputed two of the romantic hero's less attractive tendencies (not, mind you, constant traits): sentimentalism and self-pity. Prévost's hero of sensibility will have many eighteenth century brothers and sons, notably in the works of Marivaux, Nivelle de la Chaussée, Richardson (Pamela was translated into French in 1742, Clarissa in 1751) and Sterne (Tristam Shandy was translated in 1776 and 1785).

I cannot agree with those literary historians who, like Armand Hoog and Paul Van Tieghem, claim that the mal du siècle begins with Prévost. [40] The latter for instance asserts: "Chez la plupart des pré-romantiques, surtout les plus jeunes, nous rencontrons, à défaut de protestations, même mitigées, un état général de malaise, d'insatisfaction de leur destinée, de dégoût devant la vie . . . Parmi leurs héros, Patrice dans Le Doyen de Killerine de Prévost, le Cleveland du même auteur, Saint-Preux, Werther . . . en attendant René et Obermann, portent une âme ardente et inassouvie, pleine de désirs vagues; c'est déjà le "mal du siècle," Weltschmerz qui a été bien souvent décrit."[41] The reader has already guessed my complaint: le vague des passions, le mal du siècle and Weltschmerz are treated as exact synonyms. But an "ardent soul" is not a symptom of Weltschmerz and "vague desires" are not the core of (although they may accompany) the mal du siècle. The latter term should indicate in the first place a collective phenomenon, the "malady" of a specific age that reached epidemic proportions rather than that of a few isolated writers scattered through the last seventy years of the eighteenth century.[42] If the term is to retain its usefulness, it should apply strictly to the state of mind of those sensitive young men who reached manhood after the Revolution and especially after the fall of Napoleon, that is, it should indicate the encounter of a certain sensibility with History. Prévost did describe something akin to the mal de René and the vague des passions; he did not and could not invent le mal du siècle.

* * *

In the ensuing chapters we will encounter a few stereotypes of the romantic hero (I promise not to linger over them long), but most of the heroes of the major writers present unique configurations of the various traits depicted here. Thus far a very general portrait has been attempted, but truth always gets blurred in generalizations, and, as a distinguished scholar once said, God is in details.

chapter two

THE PROTOTYPE: RENÉ

From the very beginning, the romantic hero was closely
linked with history. He was ushered or, rather, pushed onto
the literary scene by the French Revolution. Until the Revolution, the French writer, with the notable exception of Rousseau,
had felt himself to be an integral part of the social fabric.
The abrupt closing of schools and the salons, the attack
on the once privileged classes, the attempt to destroy the
country's traditional religion, the abolition of a centuries-
old monarchy--all this made a clean sweep of the past. The
boundary lines of the old provinces were erased. The very
calendar was changed so as to abolish Sunday. Little wonder,
then, that young men felt themselves adrift. As a contemporary
historian has said, men who were from 20 to 30 years old
in 1800 could no longer be followers or disciples of their
immediate predecessors. The ground had been cut from under them.

This was especially true of young aristocrats like Chateaubriand for whom revolution meant emigration and exile. In
November 1791 the revolutionary Legislative Assembly decreed
that those émigrés who refused to return to their native
soil would be considered traitors, their property would be
confiscated, and they would be liable to the death penalty.
Although this decree was vetoed by Louis XVI, a similar proclamation was issued later by Robespierre. The émigré, then,
was an outlaw, a pariah in his own country.

The majority of these émigrés led miserable lives in
exile, reduced to practising trades for which they had never
apprenticed, often having to accept the most menial tasks.
In Illusions perdues Balzac tells the story of a nobleman
who refused to emigrate but who was forced to work in a printing
firm. He set the type, read and corrected proofs for decrees
announcing the death penalty for citizens hiding his fellow

aristocrats. Such a poignant situation was not uncommon.

Learning of the king's flight, Chateaubriand left the new world in December 1791, joined the émigré army, was wounded at the battle of Thionville and began a period of exile that was to last seven long years. In London he had to bear physical, economic and emotional distress. His health dangerously impaired, he often had to survive on bread and water. On more than one occasion he was on the verge of suicide. His bitterness toward the revolutionaires was heightened by the news that his older brother had been guillotined and his mother and sister imprisoned.

The Essai sur les révolutions, published in London in 1797, purports to be an objective treatise but is a profoundly skeptical work. The central theme is that there is nothing new in History or under the sun. Man is a frail creature who keeps repeating himself. Revolutionary innovations are both futile and disruptive. All government is evil, but the evilest of all is mob rule. Chateaubriand writes as a victim of the Revolution, which he predicts will soon die out, as will Christianity. As for the monarchy and the aristocracy, they are already dead and forever buried. The Encyclopedists are accused of having destroyed without recreating. What will fill the void?

In the chapter of the Essai entitled "Aux infortunés," Chateaubriand preaches to his fellow aristocrats the virtues of solitude and introspection in a world turned upside down by revolution. The mal du siècle started as a reaction to a very concrete political, social and economic situation -- a fact of literary history we attempted to establish in the preceding chapter. Young noblemen were the first to experience it; they found themselves disenfranchized, often impoverished and without useful work upon which to discharge their intelligence and their youthful energy. The despised émigré is the original version of the romantic étranger. The "vide intérieur" of which Chateaubriand speaks in this essay on revolutions also reflects a "vide extérieur," a historical vacuum, and the "bien inconnu" speaks obliquely of an uncertain political future.

This is Chateaubriand's frame of mind at the time he is working on Les Natchez, a portion of which will soon be published separately, as René. The author's highly biased reporting of the Revolution in the Mémoires is also revealing because of its very bias; it gives us an insight into the impact of the Revolution upon the development of the first important romantic hero of the nineteenth century, René. Although he had been intellectually sympathetic to the idea of democracy, Chateaubriand abhorred the violence and the mob rule of revolutionary France. The future bard of Brittany sees the tyranny of the ancien régime being exchanged for the more frightening tyranny of the majority. The Paris of 1792 is seen as a people "marching drunk" toward its destiny. The dominant atmosphere is one of universal distrust. The sovereignty of the people means that power is in the hands of a ubiquitous tyrant, a "universal Tiberius." The people are all the more frightening, he believes, because their leaders are monsters. Marat, looking like a "dressed hyena," is called a "Caligula de carrefour." Desmoulins, "Cicéron bègue," is a teller of cemetery jokes, a man who can say of the September massacres that "tout s'était passé avec ordre." Danton, "Hun à taille de Goth," has the face of a gendarme mixed with that of a lewd, cruel pimp.

This, then, was the historical situation in France as Chateaubriand and his most famous hero saw it in the 1790's. René's sense of injured superiority and his scornful view of the people at large are informed by an aristocratic sense of history. His malaise concerning the future is informed by a negative appraisal of the immediate past. In the final section of the Mémoires, written in the early 1840's, Chateaubriand, although somewhat mellowed, sums up the world of his youth--it is René's youth as well--as "a world without consecrated authority." This is the historical background to the vague à l'âme and the search for an "unknown good." The vague à l'âme, like acne, is a fairly common disease of adolescence and can usually be dismissed as an ephemeral nuisance; it has its basic etiology in normal or developmental psychology; but the prognosis worsens when History offers the patient no concrete hope, no useful work, no lofty goals and no idols to emulate. It doesn't take the wistful vague à l'âme very long, in a hypersensitive soul, to harden into the mal du siècle and in certain difficult cases into terminal Weltschmerz.

In Book XIII, chapter 2 of the Mémoires Chateaubriand states with considerable justification that the literary changes of which the nineteenth century was so proud were the result of the Emigration. This view is confirmed by Fernand Baldensperger in his important 2-volume treatise on Le Mouvement des idées dans l'émigration française (1789-1815), a work that, among other things, studies the impact of the Revolution and Emigration upon the development of French romanticism and the romantic hero. As Baldensperger notes, the essential fact of the Emigration was the abrupt end of social life and the "douceur de vivre" for some 180,000 émigrés, who came from France's most cultured classes. Their traditional sociability was replaced by a "forced individualism," as is attested by the abundant production of memoirs character-ized by a "moi dominateur." In fact, because of the uncertain-ties of History and the abolition of Society as they once knew it, there developed among the émigrés a mystique du moi. In this connection Chateaubriand will assert in his notice to the Essai sur les révolutions: "Le moi se fait remarquer chez tous les auteurs qui, persécutés par les hommes, ont passé leur vie loin d'eux."[1] The citified émigrés, even Mme de Staël, had to learn the benefits of solitude, the charms of nature and the virtues of primitive men. One of the characters in Senac de Meilhan's novel L'Emigré (1797), says: "On voit souvent, dans l'Emigration, l'homme rendu en quelque sorte à son état primitif."[2] Rousseau will come more and more into favor among the exiled aristocrats, who had been generally unfavorable toward his ideas before the Revolution (a certain number of them were already grateful to him for having learned, at his suggestion, a useful trade.) Senancour will write a Rousseauesque Rêveries sur la nature primitive, and Chateaubriand, as we have seen, will advise his fellow "infortunés" to commune with and seek solace in nature, to take advantage of their enforced solitude in order to develop their sensibility and realize that unhappiness builds character.

These new feelings toward nature, solitude, unhappiness and the Self were experienced by the émigrés before they were expressed in the new literature.[3]

* * *

Historically, it was Atala, published in 1801, that was the first work published in the nineteenth century to present a romantic hero. Chactas is presented as a half-civilized American Indian, a cross between two opposite types, both of which were popularized by Rousseau: the Noble Savage and the Man of Sensibility. Chactas speaks accordingly in a style mêlé, combining Indian epithets and periphrases with learned allusions. He is as brave as the South American Indians described by Montaigne in "Des Cannibales" and, like them, defies and insults his captors. He chafes in the civilized city of Saint Augustine saying "mon âme était tout entière à la solitude," thus furnishing later romantic heroes with their natural habitat. On the other hand, he weeps on every emotional occasion, and there are many (fifteen by my count)--which is quite a feat in light of the cherished American myth of the Indian-who-never-cries. These already numerous occasions are prolonged by the hyperbole of certain passages and the iterative past tense (the imparfait) of a number of verbs. Chateaubriand did not invent lachrymose prose; he was rather following a well established tradition in eighteenth century fiction. With Chactas, Chateaubriand presented, before René, not only the hypersensitive hero, but also the homeless wanderer and friendless stranger ("Mon père avait aussi une belle hutte . . . mais j'erre maintenant sans patrie"--a condition not so surprisingly analogous to René's and to that of François-René de Chateaubriand). And before René this little novel will hint of the piquancy that incest can add to passion.

As an Indian Chactas is a child of nature and he is an important figure in establishing the romantic association of nature with the affairs of men, especially the emotional mood of the protagonist. One source of this association is the melodramatic imagination; for example whan Atala in a moment of distress considers throwing herself to the crocodiles, the latter seem to understand: "Dans ce moment même, les crocodiles aux approches du coucher du soleil, commençaient à faire entendre leurs rugissements."[4] In another passage melodramatic coincidence is combined with le merveilleux chrétien:

> Atala n'offrait plus qu'une faible résistance; je touchais au moment du bonheur, quand tout à coup un impétueux éclair, suivi d'un éclat de la foudre, sillonne l'épaisseur des ombres, remplit la forêt de soufre et de lumière, et brise un arbre à nos pieds. Nous fuyons. O surprise! . . . dans le silence qui succède, nous entendons le son d'une cloche! Tous deux interdits, nous prêtons l'oreille à ce bruit, si étrange dans un désert. (p. 63)

In other passages, nature's storms will rise or fall with the passions of the hero: "A mesure que le Solitaire parlait, je sentais les passions s'apaiser dans mon sein, et l'orage même du ciel semblait s'éloigner à sa voix" (p. 65). In a famous passage a sympathetic moon will lend its melancholy to the funeral scene.

> La lune prêta son pale flambeau à cette veillée funèbre. Elle se leva au milieu de la nuit, comme une blanche vestale qui vient pleurer sur le cercueil d'une compagne. Bientôt elle répandit dans les bois ce grand secret de mélancolie, qu'elle aime à raconter aux vieux chênes et aux rivages antiques des mers. (p. 89)

From such poetic sympathy and empathy it is but a step to the pathetic fallacy: at the end of the novel a river will flow "sadly" past the bones of René and Chactas.

Just as Atala offers a foretaste of certain aspects of René's sensibility, the Essai sur les révolutions, published five years before Le Génie du christianisme, describes one of René's several maux: "le vague des passions."

> Est-ce un instinct indéterminé, un vide intérieur que nous ne saurions remplir, qui nous tourmente? Je l'ai aussi sentie, cette soif vague de quelque chose. Elle m'a traîné dans les solitudes muettes de l'Amérique et dans les villes bruyantes de l'Europe; je me suis enfoncé pour la satisfaire dans l'épaisseur des forêts du Canada, et dans la foule qui inonde nos jardins et nos temples. Que de fois elle m'a contraint de sortir des spectacles de nos cités, pour aller voir le soleil se coucher au loin sur quelque site sauvage! que de fois, échappé à la société des hommes, je me suis tenu immobile, sur une grève solitaire, à contempler durant des heures, avec cette même inquiétude, le tableau philosophique de la mer! Elle m'a fait suivre autour de leurs palais, dans leurs chasses pompeuses, ces rois qui laissent après eux une longue renommée, et j'ai aimé, avec elle encore, à m'asseoir en silence à la porte de la hutte hospitalière près du Sauvage qui passe inconnu dans la vie, comme les fleuves sans nom de ses déserts. Homme, si c'est là ta destinée de porter un coeur mené d'un désir inconnu; si c'est là ta maladie . . . (II, 75-76).

Chactas, as a fictional hero, was appealing but somewhat bland, especially beside the passionate Atala. In René Chateaubriand delves deeper into the psychology of his hero and offers one of the most intriguing figures in fiction. René is presented as a young man surrounded and hounded by misfortune from the very beginning of his life. His mother dies in giving him birth--a theme borrowed from Rousseau and one that will be borrowed in turn by many of René's heirs since it lends itself both to melodrama and to a facile life-death antithesis. Another melodramatic touch is that René has to be delivered by Caesarean section. His father, who neglects him in favor of his older brother, makes of him a virtual orphan: "livré de bonne heure à des mains étrangères, je fus élevé loin du toit paternel" (p. 119). Later, his father dies, leaving him a real orphan--another condition that will be shared by most of René's successors, even into the twentieth century.

Even before reaching manhood, René is the victim of a tormenting anxiety. A sensitive soul, the young René, like his sister Amélie, has "just a touch of sadness" in him and is subject to rapidly changing moods. Nothing seems to hold his interest for long. His travels, which reveal to him the glory that was Greece and the grandeur that was Rome, also teach him the vanity and evanescence of human fame, prosperity and power. The splendor of great modern cities quickly bores him. Chateaubriand summarizes René's emotional situation at this point in visual terms, as his hero sits atop Mount Aetna: "Un jeune homme plein de passions, assis sur la bouche d'un volcan . . . ce tableau vous offre l'image de son caractère et de son existence: c'est ainsi que toute ma vie j'ai eu devant les yeux une création à la fois immense et imperceptible, et un abîme ouvert à mes côtés" (pp. 124-25). The passage is rich in implications. First we see René's ardent nature and (unused) energy, both of which are symbolized hyperbolically by the volcano. Second, the hero's superiority and concomitant solitude, both of which are symbolized by the majestic height of the mountain and the distance it places between René and ordinary men "below." From this high vantage point, his whole life seems spread before him. He sees a creation that is at once "immense and imperceptible": he yearns for a <u>bien inconnu</u>, the infinite or the absolute of which he is reminded by the vastness (and vague contours) of the panorama spread before him and by the upward-striving verticality of the mountain. Finally the "abyss" below: the fatality that governs and that will ruin his life. When this thought of the abyss overwhelms him, he is consoled by Chactas, who expounds romantic dogma: "Une grande âme doit contenir plus de douleur qu'une petite" (p. 125).

Upon returning to France he feels even more isolated than he did when abroad. His social encounters make him conscious mainly of the difference between himself and other men, that is, their pettiness and his superiority. He is imediately aware of the lonely crowd: "la foule, vaste désert d'hommes."

This "désert d'hommes" is also, as Pierre Barbéris has demonstrated through intertextual analysis, the modern wasteland. Chateaubriand is treating not only a psychological "case" but--obliquely--a historical situation. René's real secret, says Barbéris, is a political secret.[5] I agree that in reading René one must be aware of the deliberate displacements. René the émigré of 1715 must be read as René the émigré of 1792. The allusion to the execution of Charles the First of England must be read as an oblique allusion to the execution of Louis XVI. René's "incertitude" reflects that of the author weighing his decision to return to Napoleon's France ("le mois des tempêtes"=18 Brumaire, according to Barbéris's historical grid). The new continent in which René wanders aimlessly can be read as the new century (Gaëton Picon) stripped of all the reassuring norms of the past. René's malady, then, is that not only of a unique individual but of a social class: the aristocracy rendered obsolete and useless by the Revolution. "Banni des lieux où se fait l'Histoire, René, condamné à lui-même, se consume en une stérile médita-tion."[6] Manuel de Dieguez expresses this important idea thus: "René s'indigne que l'Histoire le laisse s'ennuyer."[7] René's anti-social nature and sense of estrangement, even his sexual frustrations, can be read as "figures" that speak obliquely of a politico-historical alienation and as a critique of modern, bourgeois, money-dominated society. Such a reading of René is indispensable; it restores to the novel its full resonance. René's misfortune is discreetly linked to his noble lineage. He is "well born"; the family house is a château; he wonders at one point if his sister has fallen in love with a man of "inferior rank"--this last allusion was considered too explicit and was suppressed in the 1805 edition. Chateaubriand is discreet because in 1802 he cannot bewail a Revolution that Napoleon considers himself--at least publicly--to be continuing and consolidating. But, while Barbéris wants to talk politics, René and his creator want mainly to talk "psychology." So let us continue with the psychology while keeping in mind the historical and political overtones.

A crucial difference between René and other men is his distaste for the homely monotony of everyday life. Knowing full well (he says so explicitly) that normal human happiness is found in the daily round, in habits and routine, in integration into a human community, he also knows that such happiness is not for him: "Je me fatiguai de la répétition des mêmes idées" (p. 128). His growing misanthropy and sense of alienation push him to withdraw from the city and to live in near total solitude. He is soon aware of a peculiar state of mind that he describes for us in a famous passage that bears repeating:

> La solitude absolue, le spectacle de la nature, me plongèrent bientôt dans un état presque impossible à décrire. Sans parents, sans amis, pour ainsi dire seul sur la terre, n'ayant point encore aimé, j'étais accablé d'une surabondance de vie. Quelquefois je rougissais subitement, et je sentais couler dans mon coeur comme des ruisseaux d'une lave ardente; quelquefois je poussais des cris involontaires, et la nuit était également troublée de mes songes et de mes veilles. Il me manquait quelque chose pour remplir l'abîme de mon existence: je descendais dans la vallée, je m'élevais sur la montagne, appelant de toute la force de mes désirs l'idéal objet d'une flamme future; je l'embrassais dans les vents, je croyais l'entendre dans les gémissements du fleuve; tout était ce fantôme imaginaire, et les astres dans les cieux, et le principe même de vie dans l'univers. (p. 128)

This passage is often quoted as a summary of the mal de René; it is actually only one of several maux. Since our contemporary view of René and other romantic heroes is blurred by infrequently examined assumptions, a close reading of the text is necessary at this point. In what follows I am going to show the component parts of each distinct mal de René.

Les Maux de René

page	René I		Mal I
119	16 years old	a)	Delightful walks with Amélie.
	dominant note:	b)	The dead leaves of Autumn inspire a wistful and rather abstract "sadness"; premonition, probably, that this happy life cannot last forever.
	joy, accompanied by a "touch" of sadness, but not enough to create ambivalence		
		c)	This happy René writes verse: "Il n'y a rien de plus poétique, dans la fraîcheur des passions, qu'un coeur de seize années. Le matin de la vie est comme le matin du jour, plein de pureté et d'harmonie."
		d)	The sound of church bells evoke delightful sensations: the "calm" of solitude, the "charm" of religion and the "delectable" melancholy of nostalgia.
		e)	The sadness of this period is "sacred" and, again, rather abstract. "Amélie et moi, nous avions tous les deux un peu de tristesse au fond du coeur: nous tenions cela de Dieu ou de notre mère."
		f)	The first dramatic event: the death of his father. René's sole recorded reaction: thoughts of immortality and a sacred sorrow: "et dans une sainte douleur qui approchait de la joie, j'espérai me rejoindre un jour à l'esprit de mon père." This is not the mournful, "romantic" death-wish but a hope for immortality, for life eternal.
	passé simple: a sudden impulse, not a prolonged state. "un jour": for the moment René is content with his present life.		

page	René II	Mal II
122	17 years old at most	a) Anxiety about his future career. Considers the monastery (to gain time, like Chateaubriand?).
	dominant note: ambivalence and growing anxiety	b) Decides instead to travel.
		c) First anxiety concerning Amélie: her joy at seeing him leave hurts his feelings. The inconstancy of her <u>amitié</u> (?).
		d) Leaves on his trip "full of ardor" however; an ardor not yet dampened by the disillusionments of Experience: "Je m'élançai seul sur cet orageux océan du monde, dont je ne connaissais ni les ports ni les écueils." This is not a <u>voyage</u>-<u>fuite</u> but one of self-exploration. He wants to see the world, to know it, to find his place in it.
123		e) First disillusionment: the vanity and evanescence of human glory (Greece and Rome). The monuments of the past have turned to dust, often "criminal dust."
	(displacement)	f) In England: second disillusionment: the evanescence and instability of modern political régimes; allusion to the execution of an English king.
124		g) Visual summary of René's emotional situation: atop Mount Aetna. Consciousness of his great potential, his lofty goals, but also of the "abyss." See <u>supra</u>, p. 36.
125		h) His melancholy moments engendered by the very excess of his happiness. His sadness is not chronic but fleeting ("passagère").

126

the year: 1715
(displacement)

subitement=
révolution=Révolution
   the nascent
   mal du siècle

present tense=
   the narrator (René IV)
   has not lost all of his
   earlier ardor.

metaphysical ennui

i) Political and social trauma;   the end of
an era. When René returns to France; he
is shocked by the   changes   he witnesses.
"Jamais un changement plus étonnant et
plus soudain ne s'est opére chez un
peuple. De la hauteur du génie,   du respect pour la religion, de la gravité des
moeurs, tout était subitement descendu à
la souplesse de l'esprit, à l'impiété, à
la corruption." Displacement: this description applies to the France of the
Revolution as well as to the Regency.

j) René's constant ambivalence: "cette inquiétude, cette ardeur qui me suit partout."

k) René's mal   increasingly informed by a
sense of history (ancient Greece and Rome,
modern England and France). "L'étude du
monde ne m'avait rien appris, et pourtant
je n'avais plus la douceur de l'ignorance."
The famous "vagueness" of his anxiety concerns the future only. He has very definite and concrete reasons for being anxious about mankind's past accomplishments.
Will mankind's dismal history keep repeating itself in the future?   This question
is asked and answered negatively in the
Essai sur les révolutions.

l) Ennui is mentioned now for the first time.
The word in context takes on broader implications than simply boredom.

m) Amélie's attitude causes further alarm.
She is avoiding him (like a woman guilty
of an illicit passion? Suspense.)   And
why is René so upset? Two secrets.

127

political and psycho-
logical implications:
the misunderstood Hero,
but also the ci-devant
the traitor, the pariah

first stage of solitude:
the faubourg

n) Feeling now of total isolation.   Tries
"for a while" to   participate "dans   un
monde qui ne me disait rien et qui ne
m'entendait pas."   Disgusted with men
singly and in "society,"   he retreats to
the suburb in hopes of being left   totally
alone.

o) "Sometimes" wishes God would relieve him
of the burden of existence OR that the
vieil homme in him might be rejuvenated
and regenerated. The sinful old Adam but
also the cynical puer senex. Ambivalence
then: sorrow mingled with hope.   René
does not see his situation as "romantic"
yet, as unusual, as seule de son espèce:

Qui ne=René as Everyman

quelquefois=intermittence
and ambivalence

"Qui ne se trouve quelquefois accablé du
fardeau de sa propre corruption,   et incapable de rien faire de grand, de noble,
de juste?"

p) This life in the suburbs which "at first"

time lapse and change
of mood

dégoût du fini/hantise
d l'Absolu

delighted him, soon(ne tarda pas à)becomes
"unbearable." Boredom with the monotony
of everyday life and   commonplace ideas.
René is not sure what he wants of Life
but describes it as a bien inconnu, something beyond the "finite."

q) Decides that an even more profound soli-

2nd stage of solitude:
les bois . . .

tude would be beneficial (even "delight-
ful"): les bois; une chaumière; un exil
champêtre.

128-129

a disease that is
usually quickly
cured: adolescence

r) Ambivalence: "La solitude absolue . . ."
The language is definitely weighted   on
the positive side of the ambivalence:
    --"surabondance de vie"
    --"lave ardente"
    --"songes et veilles"
    --"l'idéal objet d'une flamme future"
    --"charmes"

The basic mood is one of anxious but also
eager expectation (see supra,   p. 7) .
Suprisingly few critics   have   really
caught the mood.   One who has is J.-P.
Richard: "Il a évoqué ce moment magique
de l'adolescence où l'espace de la vie
semble se creuser en tout sens devant la
conscience désirante, et où le futur se
fait appel chantant, tentation, promesse."[8]

18 Brumaire??

s) Ambivalence: sad Autumn is entered with
"delight." The season is in harmony not
only with his own état d'âme, but Every-

notre=René as Everyman

man's: "Notre coeur est un instrument in-
complet . . ."

130

t) A philosophico-religious death-wish (secret instinct; orages désirés).   This is
not a desire to end it all, but to find a
new beginning, a new and better life.   In

autobiographical impli-
cations: a
literary career

fact at times René feels within himself,
even now, "the power to create worlds."

normalcy

u) Yearning for a woman to love.

v) His disgust with ordinary life, which he
has felt ever since he can remember, comes

ne . . . que=no am-
bivalence now

back now with "a new force":   "je ne
m'apercevais de mon existence que par un

taedet me ergo sum

profond sentiment d'ennui."

131

w) Thoughts now of death by his own hand.

132-33

x) Amélie reads suicide between the lines of
René's letters and visits him. For "more
than a month," happiness regained.

happiness=Amélie

134-35

y) But as Winter ends, Amélie's health de-
clines, she is losing weight.   Anxiety
about her secret. Three more months pass
thus. Then, the letter in which Amélie
tells her brother that she is entering a
nunnery.

René III	Mal III

139

René III

dominant note:
profound and constant
grief; but not totally
"unbearable" as first
claimed.
involontaire=grief but
   not guilt (cf.
   Manfred and Childe
   Harold)

gone now is the vague
   des passions

Mal III

a) René visits Amélie at the convent while she takes her vows. The secret revealed. Grief: "On peut trouver des forces dans son âme contre un malheur personnel; mais devenir la cause involontaire du malheur d'un autre, c'est tout à fait insupportable."

b) Mal III explicitly distinguished from Mal II: "O mes amis, je sus donc ce que c'était que de verser des larmes pour un mal qui n'était point imaginaire! Mes passions, si longtemps indéterminées, se précipitèrent sur cette première proie avec fureur."

c) Another distinction: the strange joy that accompanies mal III: "Je trouvai même une sorte de satisfaction inattendue dans la plénitude de mon chagrin, et, je m'aperçus, avec un secret mouvement de joie, que la douleur n'est pas une affection qu'on épuise comme le plaisir."

d) Still further proof that this new state of mind is to be distinguished from Mal II: the sudden disappearance of the death wish. "D'ailleurs, je n'avais plus envie de mourir depuis que j'étais réellement malheureux. Mon chagrin était une occupation qui remplissait tous mes moments."

e) Another component of Mal III that distinguishes it from Mal II: pride. "Mon chagrin, par sa nature extraordinaire, portait avec lui quelque remède: on jouit de ce qui n'est pas commun, même quand cette chose est un malheur." This is a penetrating analysis of what has

been called a "new vice": the thirst for
strong emotions whatever their source,
whatever their nature and whatever their
issue; the secret pride in the "uncommon"
nature of the emotion; the tendency for
sorrow, in a hypersensitive and solitary
soul, to become masochistic, a source of
preverse and perverted pleasure. René III
not only indulges in melancholy, he savors
it and cultivates it for its own sake. He
observes it admiringly and caresses it.
He is proud of it: it is both the spice
of his life and the emblem of his superiority.

	René IV	Mal IV
141	3rd stage of solitude: the wilderness	a) Decision to leave for America (not the exciting New World but the désert): voyage-fuite.
	silva salvaticus: "man of the forest"	b) Our hero becomes a tight-lipped "savage" and a reluctant narrator. Far from in- dulging in his sorrow, he prefers not to think or talk about it. René is older now, more bitter. He will become the rugged hero of Les Natchez.

There is more to René than a passive protagonist whose
will has been paralyzed by acute melancholia and a morbid
sensibility. This is the impression that is unfortunately
given by many critics who expatiate on René's supposed abulia.
Such an interpretation simply cannot be substantiated by
close scrutiny or either René or Les Natchez. At the beginning
of René, for example, the hero, dissatisfied with his present
situation decides to do something about it: he travels.
This is not romantic escapism but romantic energy. It is
a search for the self--an ontological quest. René travels,
as Henri Michaux will do more than a century later, "pour
me parcourir." Manuel de Dieguez is one of the few critics
to emphasize this important point: "l'exploration géographique,
c'est d'abord, pour lui, un espace intérieur, une recherche
de sa distance secrète, de sa perspective."[9] And in Les
Natchez, despite his now incurable melancholy, René has still
not lost his energy, his ardor or his initiative. He can
hunt by himself for six months at a time and can build his
own cabin. When the jealous Ondouré tries to kill him, René
acquits himself well in hand-to-hand combat. He is ready
to start an insurrection among the Indians against their
French oppressors, and he fights courageously against an
enemy tribe. He offers his own life to the French authorities
in exchange for Adario's. He is as energetic, brave and
altruistic, then, as the hero of any other "western."

Impressed by René's hypersensitivity, critics have been
somewhat blind to his manliness. Although this is not a
specific theme of either René or Les Natchez, it is one of
the "givens"; it is there. René is capable of great physical
energy and courage, as we have just seen. And far from being
an effeminate who wears his heart on his sleeve or constantly
bares his soul to others, René becomes, in America, the "savage",
tight-lipped René IV. In the very first paragraph of René
we read of his taciturnity.

En arrivant chez les Natchez, René avait été obligé de prendre une épouse, pour se conformer aux moeurs des Indiens; mais il ne vivait point avec elle. Un penchant mélancolique l'entraînait au fond des bois; il y passait seul des journées entières, et semblait sauvage parmi les sauvages. Hors Chactas, son père adoptif, et le P. Souël, missionnaire au fort Rosalie, il avait renoncé au commerce des hommes . . . . Depuis la chasse du castor, où le Sachem aveugle raconta ses aventures à René, celui-ci n'avait jamais voulu parler des siennes. (p. 177)

In the next paragraph the author tells us that several years passed "thus," that is, without Chactas or Father Souël being able to get René to talk about himself. He prefers to suffer in silence. Finally, when the letter relating the death of his beloved sister increases René's obvious depression to the point that the old men fear for his sanity, they insist that he unburden himself. René relents only with reluctance and only because the wise old men "used so much discretion, gentleness and authority that he was finally obliged to satisfy them." And then, even then, he puts off his story for another day: "Il prit donc jour avec eux." This reticent hero who tells his story with such extreme reluctance is an older René whose grief no longer contains any masochistic joy or aristocratic pride. If it did, he would have told his story sooner.

This brings up another point that needs clarification: René and "romantic sentimentality." In Romanticism and the Modern Ego, a book that is required reading for those interested in clearing up some of the semantic confusion surrounding the slippery word "romanticism" and certain supposed romantic attributes, Jacques Barzun has this to say on the subject:

Sentimentality is not the mere display of feeling, nor the possession of excessive feeling--who shall say what amount is right?--but the cultivation of the feelings without ensuing action. Habitually to enjoy feelings without acting on them is to be a sentimentalist. If this is so, I have no hesitation in ascribing sentimentality to the late classical period, the eighteenth century, and in viewing the presence of sentimentality among the Romantics as either a hangover from the past or an isolated individual characteristic.[10]

We have shown that when René II takes full cognizance of his anxiety he reacts. He travels throughout Europe, not to lose himself but to find himself. It is a voyage de recherche et d'exploration, as Pierre Barbéris has called it. It is only René III who indulges in feelings for their own sake. René IV is beyond sentimentality. In short, it is accurate to say that there is sentimentality in certain moments of René's emotional career; it is inaccurate to reduce his entire career to it.

The unwholesome side of René's character is more fully developed in Les Natchez than in René. His main weaknesses are self-pity, ingratitude, paranoia, and a still more pronounced tendency toward sado-mascochism. On several occasions he will complain: "aucun hôte n'a voulu recevoir l'étranger; les portes ont été fermées contre moi" (p. 408). This complaint is deconstructed utterly by the plot: Chactas has adopted him, Outagamiz has given him his undying friendship and Céluta her love. Masochism is seen in René's eagerness to be executed and especially in the "cruel joy" he experiences in the idea of being condemned although innocent of the charges. René's sadistic side is seen especially in his cruel letter to Céluta telling her gratuitously that he does not love her and--turning the knife in the wound--painting for her his vision of the ideal woman (Amélie). He even imagines, like the Marquis de Sade, the joy of passion mingled with death: "Je croyais voir une femme qui se jetait dans mes bras: elle me disait: Viens échanger des feux avec moi, et perdre la vie! mêlons des voluptés à la mort! que la voûte du ciel nous cache en tombant sur nous" (p. 500). These pathological tendencies will be seen in many, in fact most, of René's immediate heirs and especially in what might be called his grandchild: the decadent hero of the fin de siècle.

A significant contribution of Les Natchez to the development of the archetypal romantic hero is the presentation of René as the fatal hero. In René, the protagonist's misfortunes are described more in terms of his own peculiar nature, an inner fatality ("Une grande âme doit contenir plus de douleur qu'une petite") or in terms of the inadequacy of the immediate world around him. His social maladjustment is largely blamed on society. In Les Natchez René is shown more often as the victim of an external fatality, usually cosmic in scope and supernatural in its mechanics ("atteint d'un arrêt du Ciel"). Actually, the source of this "fatalité"--a leitmotif in Les Natchez but not in René--is presented with a bewilderingly jumbled point of view. At times it is linked to the jealousy and pettiness of lesser men; at times Satan himself is behind it in order to pursue his dark ends; sometimes it is presented as an exacerbated form of that sadness Chateaubriand finds at the core of human nature and the human condition; on one brief occasion it is the Revolution that is blamed; and at the very end of the novel, Chateaubriand, hastily turning Christian author, as he did at the end of René, suggests that the real culprit is the hero's personal Sin.

This lack of focus is typical of the entire work. The first part of the novel is written in the style of an epic prose poem, and the author cranks up all the epic machinery. There are invocations to the Muse asking for divine afflatus, epic catalogs of ancestors, battalions and battle commanders, supernatural beings such as angels and demons, allegorical figures such as Fear, Death, Calumny (here called la Renommée), Homeric epithets and similes, hackneyed neo-classical kennings like "la plaine humide" and long ornamental periphrases starting with "c'était l'heure où . . ." The second part of the novel is written in the style of another genre altogether: the gothic tale or roman noir. And as he did for his epic manner, Chateaubriand pulls out all the stops: sex, violence, melo-dramatic peripeteia and coincidences, recognition scenes, frenetically sadistic cruelty. "Tout ceci est dans le goût du temps," says the author in his preface, "où l'on ne veut que des scènes qui remuent et qui ébranlent fortement les âmes" (p. 150). There is a lack of stylistic and structural unity even within each of the two parts. In the roman noir Chateaubriand still clings to certain epic motifs, and in the epic part there is a jumble, as the author himself admits, of le merveilleux chrétien, le merveilleux mythologique and le merveilleux indien. All this amounts to a work that is much less satisfying esthetically than René, but Les Natchez completes the picture of the prototypical romantic hero.

* * *

It is time now to describe the tremendous impact of René on French romantic literature; I shall also try to account for it. The success of René was first linked with that of Atala, which was offered to the public as a ballon d'essai publicitaire for Le Génie. The success of Atala was one of the most remarkable in the history of French literature--or any literature. There were no less than twelve editions just between 1801 and 1805. During the same short period there were translations into Greek, Russian, Danish and Hungarian; there were two translations into Spanish and German, three into English and four into Italian. There were poetic imitations by Millevoye, J.-B. de Saint-Victor and by the aging Delille. Musical adaptations of the novel continued to the very end of the nineteenth century in the form of romances, ballets and operas. One operatic version was produced shortly after the original edition of Atala, another as late as 1892. Berlioz wrote a libretto for it that was never performed. The novel inspired paintings, including the famous Funérailles of Girodet, plays, including a lyrical drama by Dumas fils in 1848; it inspired vaudevilles, melodramas, pantomines and parodies. It inspired decorations on clocks and plates. Country inns were adorned with colored engravings representing Chactas, Atala and Father Aubry. In Paris their wax figures filled the boxes of the bouquinistes. Little girls were baptized with the name of the heroine. Balzac used it as his nickname for Mme Hanska as well as for one of the characters in La Cousine Bette. There was even a "coiffure Atala." And to crown its success it even had its literary bataille. In short, the novel's success touched every artistic medium, both sophisticated and popular, and every social class.[11]

Most of the reasons for its success are obvious: the novelty of the exotic setting, the poignant charm (and lack of complexity) of the protagonists, the sumptuous style. A less obvious but important reason was the dominant mood of the finale.

> Ainsi passe sur la terre tout ce qui fut bon, vertueux, sensible! Homme, tu n'es qu'un songe rapide, un rêve douloureux; tu n'existe que par le malheur; tu n'es quelque chose que par la tristesse de ton âme et l'éternelle mélancolie de ta pensée! (p. 99)

Mme de Staël admired the novel for one reason: it made her "cry a lot." For her, we recall, melancholy literature is the most philosophical: sadness penetrates deeper into man's character than any other disposition of the soul. She particularly admired those souls who are dissatisfied with common life and with "anything that can be measured." This is an almost prophetic announcement of the arrival of René, who is so easily fatigued by the finite.

The success of René, although less immediate and spectacular than that of Atala was impressive and ultimately had a deeper impact on French and European literature. As early as 1805 Chateaubriand could speak of the "preference" over Atala that a good number of people had accorded René. The reasons for its success are many. Two have already been mentioned: it was a sequel to Atala, and it presented a study in melancholy. Another had to do with the story itself and the charm of the hero--the public was more impressed with the "immoral" hero than with the moral tacked on to the end. Another is the ever-enchanting style of the Enchanter. Still another had to do with lucky timing (or was it clever opportunism?): the Génie appeared on 14 April 1802, just four days before the proclamation of Napoleon's Concordate with the Papacy. Since the final years of the eighteenth century, persecution of the Church had been on the wane, and a conservative backlash had been forming which was warmly receptive to the re-introduction of Christianity into French life. As every literary historian has noted, René, with its Christian "point of view" and conveniently wrapped as it was in the orthodoxy of Le Génie, came "à son heure" and fell "à pic."

In 1803, the year after the initial publication of the novel, Chateaubriand received a fan letter from a young English boy by the name of G. Gordon, Lord Byron. In 1809 Lamartine wrote a friend that he could not read René without weeping. In 1818 Hugo declared: "Je veux être Chateaubriand ou rien." In 1820 Sainte-Beuve read René and was overwhelmed by the shock of recognition: it seemed to be an exact portrait of his own soul. This admiring public was an adolescent public: Byron was 15, Hugo and Sainte-Beuve were 16, Lamartine was 19. Vigny, George Sand and Flaubert were about the same age when they were first overwhelmed by René. French fiction had finally given the anxious adolescent a protagonist with whom he could fully identify.

* * *

A politico-religious malaise was experienced by Chateaubriand as early as the Essai sur les révolutions of 1797 in which he refuted the Enlightenment idea of perpetual secular progress and human perfectibility and predicted the demise of both Christianity and the Revolution. Ironically, that very year and the following one were to witness religious conversions by two of romanticism's most illustrious unbelievers, Novalis and Chateaubriand. Even more ironical is the fact that the two conversions had identical causes. Novalis, within a period of twenty-six days lost his fiancé and his favorite brother. Chateaubriand experienced a similar double tragedy: the death of his mother and his beloved sister, Lucile.

Both conversions were emotional rather than intellectual affairs, and it was the emotional side of religion that had the greatest appeal for both writers. Chateaubriand was never more than a demi-croyant. René's yearning for the absolute and his bien inconnu are vague because for him, as for Musset's Rolla, the heavens have been depopulated. As Sainte-Beuve said: "René est le fils d'un siècle qui a tout examiné, tout mis en question."[12] It is significant that he considers but then rejects the monastic life and especially that he does not take Father Souël's Christian advice. He dies unregenerate. His vague spiritual yearnings seem to rise from a diluted religion naturelle, and discreetly reflect, in my view, an anguish rather than a faith. Pierre Reboul can with some justification speak of René as "la Nausée de l'An IX" and of the hero's metaphysical ennui.

Pierre Barbéris believes that René's secret is a political one and that the novel is a modern text in that it offers a critique of the individual's relation to society, in this case the society of the revolutionary period and the beginning of the Napoleonic era, which go unnamed. Barbéris accepts Lukács and Goldmann's socio-critical view that the novel is an epic genre characterized essentially by its presentation of an insurmountable break between the hero and the socio-political-economic situation in which he finds himself. Such a reading of René, says Barbéris, is one of the possibles du texte. This is true to a certain degree, and the Essai and the Mémoires offer adequate intertextual evidence, but I believe that there is also a metaphysical dimension to René's "secret." There is a definite break, despite all the sanitized and christianized packaging, between the hero and the cosmos. It is ironic that Chateaubriand who contributed so greatly to the Christian revival in the early nineteenth century, managed to reflect--ever so discreetly--a malaise that was in large part religious. During the romantic period there will be a cross-current of belief-disbelief, and an

anguished agnosticism will become prevalent among young intellectuals. More than any other single writer it is Chateaubriand
 who was responsible for this widespread ambivalence, largely
because with René he created a hero who sent out conflicting
signals.

"Les romantiques--mes fils."
Chateaubriand

"Le mal du solitaire René . . .
est assez endémique en ce siècle; la
famille est nombreuse, je le crois,
qui l'invoque tout bas comme l'aîné
des siens."
Sainte-Beuve

chapter three

THE IMMEDIATE HEIRS

As a progenitor of literary heroes, René was nothing
if not prolific. Chateaubriand will complain in the Mémoires
d'outre-tombe about all the Renés "pullulating" in the new
romantic literature. Even a family list limited to the most
illustrious of René's immediate heirs is long: Obermann,
Adolphe, Antony, Joseph Delorme, Amaury; Childe Harold, Manfred
and other Byronic heroes; Raphaël, Félix, Louis Lambert and
other heroes of Balzac; Hernani, Didier, Ruy Blas and other
heroes of Hugo; Chatterton, Cinq Mars and other heroes of
Vigny; Lorenzaccio, Octave and other enfants du siècle.
Most of them are original creations, some mere stereotypes,
but by their sheer number they show that the concept of a
"romantic hero" was to solidify into a myth and become the
first emblem of our modern discontent. To survey them all
would require a very large (and very repetitious) book.
Since the prototypical romantic hero has just been analyzed
in some detail and in some depth, this chapter will be limited
to filling in the general portrait sketched in the initial
chapter by providing some concrete examples of the romantic
hero's most salient traits, especially as they are found
in four of the more interesting of René's heirs, Obermann,
Antony, Didier and Vigny's Jesus. The first three were chosen

because they have been rather neglected; the third one deserves the neglect but is interesting as evidence that the romantic hero had indeed developed into a widespread mythic pattern that could be stereotyped. The fourth one, to our knowledge, has not been discussed before in terms of the prototypical romantic hero.

* * *

Ennui, Melancholy and Despair

The difficult circumstances of the romantic hero's birth or early childhood and adolescence serve as metonymies of his moral isolation, the feeling that, largely because of his uniqueness and innate superiority, he will never find a kindred spirit. Ordinary life and ordinary men seem brutish and mean, a better life does not seem within his grasp--this is the chief reason the romantic hero gives for his ennui, melancholy and despair. It would not be practical to describe or even to list all the melancholics among romantic heroes since there are a few, if any, exceptions. We shall therefore focus on one interesting exemplar, Senancour's Obermann, whose despair and even whose ennui have implications that go deeper than his sociological and psychological situation and come closer than with most other protagonists of the period to those of contemporary heroes.

Obermann is less a novel in the traditional sense than a philosophical or intellectual diary. It is a fictional autobiography, with more emphasis on the autobiography than on the fiction. There is no plot, no forward movement at all, no suspense, no interaction of characters and no dénouement. The hero himself says of certain novels: "Quant à l'argent, beaucoup de personnages de roman n'en ont pas besoin; ils vont toujours leur train, ils font leurs affaires, ils vivent partout sans qu'on sache comment ils en ont." (Letter

LII).[1]   This is also true of Obermann.   All we know of his
état civil is an inheritance of unspecified amount and of
obscure origin.   The only significant episode that might
have developed into a plot is an incipient love affair that
fizzles out before it has a chance to get started.   Obermann
is a young idler, a solitary intellectual without family,
without a country and without a profession.   His letters
do not constitute an epistolary novel in any real sense,
they do not relate the adventures of his life, quite simply
because there are no adventures in his life.   As he tells
his anonymous friend: "Un solitaire ne vous parlera point
des hommes que vous fréquentez plus que lui,   Il n'aura pas
d'aventures, il ne vous fera pas le roman de sa vie.   Mais
nous sommes convenus que je continuerai à vous dire ce que
j'éprouve."   (LX).   The letters relate the hero's feelings
and ideas, each new letter introducing not a new episode
but a new theme.   Obermann confides to his friend his ideas
on just about everything: life, death, immortality, suicide,
love, marriage, friendship, faith, doubt, free will, determinism,
the use of stimulants, money, travel, books,   He himself
admits: "mes lettres ressemblent beaucoup trop à des traités"(L).

    If one were to try to pin a precise generic label on
this work, perhaps essais romancés would be as accurate as
any.   The affinity between Obermann and the Essais of Montaigne
is everywhere apparent: in the attempt to paint oneself
in order to find universal man (the "romantic" impulse here is
used in the service of a "classical" goal); in the solitary
and sedentary life of the author; in the frequent gleanings
from writers of antiquity; in many of the central ideas:
Obermann shares Montaigne's que sais-je skepticism, his love
of order and horror of disorder, the belief that nothing
natural can be dangerous or evil, and especially the view
of man as ondoyant et divers.   Like Montaigne, Obermann possesses
a paresse naturelle, preferring a quiet study in an ivory
tower to the hustle and bustle of work and travel: "Nos

livres peuvent suffire à l'homme impartial, toute l'expérience
du globe est dans nos cabinets" (LXVIII). (Senancour's admiration for Montaigne is made explicit in Letter XXXVIII.)

Senancour and Montaigne are kindred spirits; Senancour
and Chateaubriand are rivals. Obermann, first published
in 1804, is in part a réplique to Le Génie du christianisme,
published two years earlier. But the influence of René is
apparent and, combined with that of Montaigne and of Senancour's
peculiar psyche, produces a highly individualized romantic
hero.

Like René before him and Adolphe after him, Obermann
finds it impossible to live a normal, routine life, especially
to assume a profession. Like René--the later René--he is
consumed with ennui and lassitude. Everything surrounding
him inspires only a profound indifference. Finding the social
structure une hiérarchie de mépris he decides to live
"absolutely alone and isolated." Like René, he laments:

> Dès long-temps la vie me fatigue, et elle me
> fatigue tous les jours davantage. (LXI)

> L'ennui m'accable, le dégoût m'atterre. (LXII)

> Etranger à ce qui m'environnait, je n'avais
> d'autre caractère décidé que d'être inquiet et
> malheureux. (XI)

> Que mettre à la place de cet infini qu'exige
> ma pensée? (XLI)

Hardly twenty-one years of age at the beginning of the book,
he is, like René, the puer senex: "J'ai le malheur de ne
pouvoir être jeune" (I). Like René, he is afflicted with
le vague à l'âme: "Je ne sais ce que je suis, ce que j'aime,
ce que je veux; je gémis sans cause, je désire sans objet,
et je ne vois rien, sinon que je ne suis pas à ma place"
(LXII). His darkest moments inspire a death wish, which
he calls l'instinct du soir and le besoin de ténèbres (XLI).

Obermann is a romantic hero for another reason: he
likes "romantic" things. Romantique is his favorite adjective,

and his insistent use of it is significant in the history of the meaning and popularity of the word. It is a little known fact that no author except Mme de Staël used the word in a single work with such frequency and such relish. Most often the adjective is used to describe a natural scene (usually untamed and uninhabited nature) that is out of the ordinary and that inspires in the observer a sense of wonder. For Obermann, it takes something "romantic" to stir his jaded sensibility. The "romantic," in truly sensitive souls, not only awakens a renascence of wonder but even intimations of a mysterious, ideal, transcendent realm.

A major difference between René and Obermann is that the former's ennui begins in late adolescence, the latter's with birth: "les longs ennuis de mes premiers ans" (I). Even before experiencing life, Obermann is jaded and blasé: "mes yeux demi-fermés ne sont jamais éblouis; trop fixes, ils ne sont point surpris" (ibid). While René possesses a "surabondance de vie," which means, among other things, great potential energy, youthful impatience and expectancy, Obermann is constitutionally ("naturellement") lethargic. A key word in Obermann is the verb attendre.

> J'attendrai . . . Il faut bien différer, et
> long-temps peut-être: ainsi je passe ma vie. (IV)

> . . . il faut que j'attende. (ibid.)

> Je suis condamné à toujours attendre. (XII)
> Vous savez employer la vie; moi, je l'attends. (LXXIV)

> Ma destinée, enfin, semble me retenir, elle
> me laisse dans l'attente, et ne me permet pas
> d'en sortir: elle ne dispose pas de moi, mais elle
> m'empêche d'en disposer moi-même. (LXV)

René, like the Byronic and Hugolian Hero, is a volcano; Obermann admits: "je suis éteint" (LXXXIX). He is basically a passive individual. He sees himself as a sensitive, intelligent and articulate observer of human life, not as an active participant. He is an "absent" among the living, his life is an abdication.

> Pour moi, qui ne prétends pas vivre, mais
> seulement regarder la vie . . . (LXXXIX)

> Je voudrais connaître la terre entière. Je
> voudrais non pas la voir, mais l'avoir vue. (LXVIII)

The past infinitive is revealing: he is not interested in direct experience but in what he calls la vie intérieure, the contemplative life. As with many other romantic souls, the memory of an experience is more vivid and more meaningful to him than the original experience itself. Obermann is an intellectual hero--a fact which distinguishes him from the Hernani or force qui va type.

Obermann does not possess the energy to perform the desperate deeds of other romantic heroes, nor does he strike haughty, brooding poses. He presents a mask of outward calm beneath which lies a profound anguish: "Vous avez su que mon calme ressemblait au sourire du désespoir" (LXXXIX). His life is characterized, as he himself tells us, by an apathie inquiète, a condition not far removed from Thoreau's "quiet desperation."

Another important difference between René and Obermann is that while the former was a dreamer of vague dreams, the latter is a thinker of precise thoughts. Some thoughts express traditional wisdom, others anticipate very modern ideas such as Baudelaire's correspondences, Sartre's Absurd and Camus's revolt against the Absurd. Here are his thoughts on correspondences, inspired, as so often with Baudelaire, by colors and perfumes: "Soit que j'aie cherché ces émanations invisibles (the scent of flowers), soit surtout qu'elles s'offrent, qu'elles surprennent, je les reçois comme une expression forte, mais précaire, d'une pensée dont le monde matériel renferme et voile le secret. Les couleurs aussi doivent avoir leur éloquence: tout peut être un symbole" (XCI). Here are his thoughts on the Absurd, which he calls the burlesque:

> Nous ne sommes autre chose dans l'univers
> que des figures burlesques qu'un charlatan agite,

oppose, promène en tous sens; fait rire, battre,
pleurer, sauter, pour amuser . . . qui? Je ne le
sais pas. (XLIII)

    La vie m'ennuie et m'amuse. Venir, s'élever,
faire grand bruit, s'inquiéter de tout, mesurer
l'orbite des comètes, et, après quelques jours,
se coucher sous l'herbe d'un cimetière, cela
me semble assez burlesque pour être vu jusqu'au
bout. (LXXVIII)

A more sardonic answer to the question as to whether life
is worth living is hard to find anywhere in French literature.
Here are his thoughts on the just man's revolt against an
unjust human condition: "L'homme est périssable. Il se
peut; mais périssons en résistant, et, si le néant nous est
réservé, ne faisons pas que ce soit une justice" (XC).

    What is perhaps even more modern than the despair in
Obermann's thinking is its inconclusiveness. It is typical
of him to ponder with equal seriousness the diametrically
opposed notions of correspondences and the Absurd, of both
the possibility and the impossibility of transcendence.
The problem of free will versus determinism is treated in
exactly the same equivocal fashion. Obermann asks more questions
than he answers. His agnosticism is not merely religious
and metaphysical, but epistemological. Like Montaigne he
keeps wondering: what can we really know? After considering
the arguments on both sides of a question, he will characteris-
tically conclude: "Pour moi, je ne sais que douter" (LXXXI).
Like Camus's, his ambition is to become a lay saint without
God and to determine whether he can live with just what he
knows and only that. In Obermann, the Cartesian _cogito_,
confident, rational and "classical," is replaced by the
first--and for many the last--premise of romanticism: _je
sens donc je suis_.

    Je sens est le seul mot de l'homme qui ne veut
que des vérités. Et ce qui fait la certitude
de mon être en est aussi le supplice. Je sens,
j'existe pour me consumer en désirs indomptables. (LXIII)

The intellectual climate of the early years of the nineteenth century ranges between two poles: those described
in Le Génie du christianisme and in Obermann. The Christian
optimism of the former is subtly deconstructed by the René
episode. However, metaphysical anguish, of which there are
but discretely vague intimations in René, is the very stuff
of Obermann. In Senancour's rather slighted work we find
some of the deepest roots not only of romanticism, but of
romanticism's twentieth-century offspring: the literature
of despair.

* * *

The Rebel

The French romantic hero appears not only in the guise
of the Noble Rebel or Generous Outlaw, the most famous example
being Hernani, but also as a somewhat less than noble rebel,
such as Julien Sorel, and even as an ignoble rebel: I am
thinking here of Dumas' Antony and shall use him as my exemplary
figure of the romantic rebel since Hernani is already better
known than he deserves, and since I shall discuss the complex
Julien Sorel in considerable detail in a subsequent chapter.

Even before his initial entrance on stage, Antony is
presented to us as a beau ténébreux in the dialogue between
Clara and Adèle. One sister sees in him "his anxious nature,"
the other "his proud heart"; both are fascinated by his intense,
"somber" eyes. He is clearly of the lineage of René and
the Byronic Hero. "Oh! si tu l'avais suivi comme moi, au
milieu du monde, où il semblait étranger, parce qu'il lui
était supérieur, si tu l'avais vu triste et sévère au milieu
de ces jeunes fous, élégants et nuls."[2] Here, the "loner's"
solitude is explicitly linked with his superiority. In a
burst of melodramatic coincidence and magnification, Antony
happens to arrive in front of Adèle's house just as runaway

horses are threatening her life. The horses, of course, are no match for him. The first act ends with a bang: Antony, in order not to be removed from Adèle's house, where he is being treated for an injury incurred in his brush with the horses, tears the bandage from his bleeding wound. This is his first dramatic, or better, melodramatic, rebellion against normal patterns of behavior.

Being of illegitimate birth, Antony is ostracized by polite society--at least this is his complaint. Since the action takes place during the Restoration and is first performed in 1831, the theme is already a bit dated because French mores and attitudes had become rather liberalized by then. In any event, Antony sees himself as a rebel against society's hypocritical "morality." The play's essential theme, as Henri Clouard points out, is "la passion amoureuse qui empoigne et tue."[3] That is, the moral rebellion is more significant than the social one. Antony resembles Julien Sorel: social convention and bourgeois morality are not going to stand in the way of the rights of love. Compared to Antony, however, Julien is an angel. Since Adèle makes a sincere and conscientious effort to be faithful to her husband, Antony pursues her, rapes her, keeps her and in the end kills her--and not just for the honorable motives that many critics have ascribed to him. Henri Clouard for example: "Antony prend sur lui toute l'infamie . . . Adèle ne sera plus qu'une victime à plaindre: en quoi il s'affirme homme de sacrifice et d'honneur."[4] In actual fact, the final gesture is an ambivalent mixture of sacrifice and sadism--and the emphasis is really on the latter. Earlier in the play Adèle had said of Antony: "Je le reconnais bien à ces idées d'amour et de mort constamment mêlés" (p. 133). And at the very end of the play, the hero's sadistic association of love and death is made explicit: "Et moi aussi, je veux mourir! . . . mais avec toi; je veux que les derniers battements de nos coeurs se répondent.

Que nos derniers soupirs se confondent" (p. 213). And finally
there is something diabolical in Antony's questions during
the famous dénouement.

                              ANTONY
                  Tu disais tout à l'heure que tu ne craignais pas
            la mort?

                              ADÈLE
                  Non, non . . . Oh! tue-moi, par pitié.

                              ANTONY
            Une mort qui sauverait ta réputation, celle de ta fille?

                                        (p. 215)

He is not asking her, he is brow-beating her. The movement
of the passage suggests that he is not really thinking of
her reputation (especially since her husband and society
already know the truth), but of his own selfish motives.
This is an act of violence provoked by jealousy and revenge:
he had admitted earlier that he would kill her if he could
not have her.

The play's extreme violence is a landmark of sorts in
the history of the theater, and its enormous initial success
forces one to ponder the historical implications of violence
so warmly applauded.

* * *

The Misunderstood and Fatal Hero

The romantic hero's least attractive trait is a certain tendency toward self-pity. Antony complains rather illogically that he is the most friendless and homeless of men. Didier will sigh: "Tout me déchire." One of the romantic hero's most frequent complaints is that he is so different from the common run of men that he is destined to be misunderstood and maligned.

The romantic hero even tends to feel that there is a conspiracy of cosmic proportions against him and his quest for happiness. It is Hugo's heroes who complain the loudest on this point, so let us listen to one of them, but just briefly. We must treat Hugo's heroes in rather cavalier and cursory fashion here since the author himself did so. The least of his dramatic aims was to create what the French call caractères. His heroes do not move by any kind of inner necessity, nor are they really governed by a true Fate or exterior Necessity: they are moved by the puppet strings held so firmly and so obviously in the author's hands. This, basically, is all that the fate of his fated heroes amounts to. His characters are not individuals, they are ideas on legs. In Hugo's theater character does not determine incident; the protagonists are dominated by the obstacles that the author is pleased to put in their way. Reversing the classical formula, Hugo brings the coup de théâtre to stage center and leaves psychology in the wings.

Didier describes himself as "fatal et méchant," a formula that is no doubt meant to express a cause and effect relationship inspiring pity rather than disdain. It is the "fate" of the romantic hero to bring harm not only to himself but also to those close to him, especially the woman he loves.

Vous m'avez voulu suivre! Hélas! ma destinée
Marche, et brise la vôtre à sa roue enchaînée.
. . . .
Mais je dois t'avertir, oui, mon astre est mauvais.
J'ignore d'où viens, et j'ignore où je vais.
Mon ciel est noir.--Marie, écoute une prière.
Il en est temps encore, toi, retourne en arrière.
Laisse-moi suivre seul ma sombre route; hélas![5]

(III, vi)

Hernani will warn Doña Sol in almost the very same terms:
Oh! fuis! détourne-toi de mon chemin fatal,
Helas! sans le vouloir, je te ferais du mal!

(III, iv)

Fatalism, in Hugo's hands, becomes melodrama. If Hernani
lets himself and his lovely bride die at the hands of a senile
man-of-honor-turned-villain, it is because the author, not
the Fates, has so decreed. However, romantic fatalism is
expressive of a very real problem: the impossibility or
near-impossibility, for sensitive souls, of ever finding
a satisfying life in this world or the next. One of Jean
Anouilh's characters will express this romantic complaint
thus: "God hates happiness."

* * *

Solitude

Like him, René's immediate heirs are solitary creatures,
usually from their earliest childhood. More often than not
they are orphans like Sainte-Beuve's Amaury and Hugo's Didier,
or of illegitimate birth like Dumas's Antony. They are young
men without family, friends or country. Antony's lament--

Les autres hommes, du moins, lorsqu'un événement brise
leurs espérances, ils ont un père, une mère! . . . des bras
qui s'ouvrent pour qu'ils viennent y gémir. Moi! Moi! je
n'ai pas même la pierre d'un tombeau où je puisse lire un
nom et pleurer . . . .

> Les autres hommes ont une patrie; moi seul, je n'en ai
> pas! . . . car qu'est-ce que la patrie? Le lieu où l'on
> est né, la famille qu'on y laisse, les amis qu'on y regrette
> . . . Moi, je ne sais pas même où j'ai ouvert les yeux . . . Je
> n'ai point de famille, je n'ai point de patrie. (p. 140)

is typical and is echoed for instance by Joseph Delorme

> J'ai toujours été seul à souffrir;
> Sans un coeur près du mien j'ai passé sur la terre.[6]

and at some length by Didier

> J'ai pour tout nom Didier. Je n'ai jamais connu
> Mon père ni ma mère. On me déposa nu,
> Tout enfant, sur le seuil d'une église. Une femme,
> Vieille, et du peuple, ayant quelque pitié dans l'âme,
> Me prit, fut ma nourrice et ma mère, en chrétien
> M'éleva, puis mourut, me laissant tout son bien,
> Neuf cents livres de rente, à peu près, dont j'existe.
> Seul à vingt ans, la vie était amère et triste.
> Je voyageais. Je vis les hommes, et j'en pris
> En haine quelques-uns, et le reste en mépris.
> Car je ne vois qu'orgueil, que misère et que peine
> Sur ce miroir terni qu'on nomme face humaine.
> Si bien que me voici, jeune encore et pourtant
> Vieux, et du monde las comme on l'est en sortant;
> Ne me heurtant à rien où je ne me déchire;
> Trouvant le monde mal, mais trouvant l'homme pire.
> Or je vivais ainsi, pauvre, sombre, isolé. (pp. 973-74)

Thus, just a few moments after the curtain goes up,
does Didier give us a complete resumé of his romantic credentials, punctuating them with romantic versification. Marion
de Lorme was written in June 1829, three months before Hernani,
but it was not performed until two years later, after the
censorship of the Restoration had been abolished. Charles
X was afraid that the public would see an analogy between
the weak Louis XIII and his own tottering régime. If it
had not been for the censor, the battle of Hernani would
have been fought over Marion Delorme. The censor did Hugo
a favor. It is quite obvious that as early as 1829 the romantic
hero had become a stereotype, and that, not Didier himself,
is interesting. The age had found its hero: the pariah
without friends, family, country or even social standing,
whose exile is partly self-imposed since he scorns the society

that shuns him; the _puer_ _senex_: young but already old and
bitter; the misanthropic and fatalistic hero rushing headlong
toward misfortune and death.

We are not done with the theme of solitude; variations
on it will be seen immediately and throughout the entire
course of this book. The romantic hero's solitary condition
is emblematic of an estrangement that is more than social:
it represents his relationship to his entire universe.

* * *

A Surprising and Interesting Composite:
Vigny's Jesus

Almost the entire opus of Alfred de Vigny is devoted
to the romantic hero. His fictional and dramatic work was
intended to be an "épopée en prose de la désillusion" devoted
to the pariahs of modern society: the nobility in _Cinq_ _Mars_
(1826); the poet in _Stello_ (1832) and _Chatterton_ (1835);
the soldier in _Servitude_ _et_ _Grandeur_ _Militaires_ (1835).
It is the Poet especially who is modeled on the prototype
of the romantic hero; he is pitted against the Politician
and the Businessman with the inevitable conflict between
"ceux qui planent" and those who love "la médiocrité qui
se vend bon marché." Poetry strives toward the truth, society
rests on the acceptance of half-truths and, often, downright
lies. _Chatterton_ portrays vividly the solitude and maladjustment
of the Poet in a materialistic society which persues and
rewards only utilitarian functions. Since the proud hero
refuses to compromise, suicide is the only way out. But
even in a less materialistic society, the Poet--like all
romantic heroes--would be unhappy since nothing can replace
for him what he sees while dreaming.

The myth of the romantic hero pervades not only Vigny's
fictional and dramatic work, but the poetry as well--and

in some rather unexpected places such as his Biblical figures. His Satan (in _Eloa_, 1824) is a romantic rebel and pariah, his Moses symbolizes the solitude of the superior individual: he, too, is a melancholy stranger:

> Sitôt que votre souffle a rempli le berger
> Les hommes se sont dit: il nous est étranger.

The poem's refrain reveals the romantic hero's _taedium vitae_ and the inevitable death wish:

> Laissez-moi m'endormir du sommeil de la terre.

I am convinced that even the Jesus of _Le Mont des Oliviers_ is a romantic hero. A close and rather detailed reading will be necessary to prove my point. The discussion that follows should prove more fruitful than a detailed analysis of an obvious romantic hero like Chatterton.

Perhaps there is no more convincing evidence of the ubiquity of the romantic hero in the first half of the nineteenth century than the fact that he informs not only the romantic conception of the Devil but of Christ himself.

Vigny's Jesus is not just vaguely related to the romantic hero, he is clearly a composite of nearly all the traits we have just discussed, and, providing us with a final example of each, will serve as a summary figure to round out the discussion.

Even before examining the poem, when one considers the Jesus of the New Testament, one can already see that he might well serve as an illustrious exemplar of the Solitary Hero, the Misunderstood Hero, the Melancholy Hero (of Gethsemane and the Cross), the Fatal Hero and even the Nobel Rebel struggling against a society of pharisees. Otto Rank has already shown that Jesus shares the enigmatic birth of many literary heroes. And the boy Jesus is seen as a _puer senex_ when questioned in the temple by the amazed elders. Both Joseph Campbell (_The Hero with a Thousand Faces_) and Allan Dundes (_The Hero Pattern and the Life of Jesus_) have shown that the Jesus

of the New Testament is a special version of a widespread
mythic and heroic pattern. The Mountain of the Temptation,
the Mountain of the Transfiguration, the Mount of Olives
and the Cross at Calvary provide the elevated sites associated
with the superior individual. If the historical Jesus shows
none of the symptoms of the Pathological Hero (although unbelievers see him as a man who thought he was God), he does
share in a mutual deviation from the normal. The very least
one can say here is that for the creation of a prototypical
romantic hero "the Jesus material" is a priori as interesting
as the "Hernani material." Hernani is not a particulary
good example of the Solitary Hero even though _he_ thinks he
is. He has a beautiful fiancée and a whole band of fellow
outlaws to keep him company. He is not, as we have suggested,
a particularly convincing example of the Fatal Hero. And
his contradictory attitudes toward his enemy, Don Carlos,
seem contrived by the author (the reader and spectator smile
knowingly when Hernani asks his fellow conspirators, who
have just had a sudden and rather inexplicable change of
heart: "Qui donc nous change tous ainsi?"). Thus, it is
not perversity or l'esprit de contradiction but a sense of
logic that impells me to choose Vigny's Jesus and not Hernani
as René's prototypical heir.

In the opening thirty-four lines of Le Mont des Oliviers
Vigny is careful to stress Jesus' human side, his frail,
"mortal" nature. He is shown walking hurriedly and nervously
while his disciples sleep. In the chill of the night he
is "frissonnant comme eux."[7] He calls to his Father, but
there is no answer. He is dumbfounded ("étonné") by this
inexplicable silence. A "bloody sweat" breaks out on his
face. He is "frightened." This emphasis on Jesus' human
nature not only reflects the poet's traumatic reaction to Dr.
Strauss's book on the life of Jesus, but it is essential
for the thematic structure of the poem: it conditions the
reader to accept and identify with Jesus as a purely human
hero (one does not identify with a god).

At the end of the first section Jesus, remembering all he has suffered for thirty-three years and shocked ("étonné") by his Father's apparent indifference, "becomes man," that is, fully human. For the space of this brief, bitter moment Jesus is disowning his Father and renouncing his own divine nature. Pierre-George Castex mentions a fragment of a projected poem in which Vigny depicts Jesus proclaiming his purely human nature and ancestry: "Je ne suis pas le Fils de Dieu!"$^{\varepsilon}$ Castex adds: "Le Mont des Oliviers ne va pas aussi loin" (ibid.). But the poem does go that far. The suggestion of rebellion, of a conversion in reverse, is implicit in the force of the <u>passé</u> <u>simple</u>: "Jésus . . . devint homme" (i, 26-27) and "Eut sur le monde et l'homme une pensée humaine" (i, 32). The structural unity of the poem hinges on these lines. Jesus is going to identify with Man, he is going to see the problems of the human condition with human eyes. The importance of the epithet "humaine," coming at the rhyme, must not be overlooked; it introduces the second movement of the poem. The unorthodox monologue in section two is not a departure from but a development of what has preceded, it is what the poem is all about. Jesus is presented as a Promethean figure, rebelling against divine authority.

The central theme of section two is Jesus' complaint that he is being relieved of his mission before its completion:

> Avant le dernier mot ne ferme pas mon livre.
> (ii, 2)
> ....
> N'ayant que soulevé ce manteau de misère.
> (ii, 50)

It is true that Jesus' attitude toward his mission is ambiguous, or rather, ambivalent:

> Si j'ai coupé les temps en deux parts, l'une esclave
> Et l'autre libre;--au nom du Passé que je lave
> Par le Sang de mon corps qui souffre et va frémir
> Versons-en la moitié pour laver l'avenir!
> (ii, 21-24)

In the first two lines Jesus claims to have already successfully divided time into two parts having absolved the Past and freed the future. Why then is the future (which is not dignified by a capital letter as is the Past) characterized in the final line as an unfinished task? If there is a real semantic distinction between "freeing" the future and "washing it clean," it must be this: thanks to the crucifixion mankind will be redeemed from original sin, it will be given a fresh start, but will remain vulnerable: it retains free will and hence will continue to sin. Christ anticipates these future, unabsolved sins still to come. Thus he seems to have doubts about the total efficacy of his Crucifixion. Its value seems to be solely retroactive. The Sacrifice seems premature. Despite the tactful tone, this amounts to nothing less than a lack of confidence in divine judgment: the Father has poorly timed the Crucifixion.

An even bolder passage follows:

> Mal et Doute! En un mot je puis les mettre en poudre,
> Vous les aviez prévus, laissez-moi vous absoudre
> De les avoir permis.—C'est l'accusation
> Qui pèse de partout sur la Création!—
> (ii, 53-56)

Here Jesus sees his role not as Redeemer of mankind but as God's advocate. He suggests that God himself is on trial and is asked to give an accounting to mankind, an explanation of the many enigmas of his Creation. This reversal of God's role from judge to accused is expressed even more boldly in an outline of a projected poem that Vigny planned to call "Jugement dernier": "Ce sera ce jour-là que Dieu viendra se justifier devant toutes les âmes et tout ce qui est vie. Il paraîtra et parlera, il dira clairement pourquoi la création et pourquoi la souffrance et la mort de l'innocence, etc. En ce moment, ce sera le genre humain ressuscité qui sera le juge, et l'Eternel, le Créateur, sera jugé par les génerations rendues à la vie."[9] Here we see the full implications of "Jésus . . . devint homme" and "pensée humaine." In this tacit quarrel between God and Man, Jesus is siding with the latter. If God will not speak in his own defense, let Jesus speak for Him, or let others, like Lazarus, who have seen the secrets of the other world.

The aggressiveness of the plea is startling in its boldness, but it is not inconsistent with the section that precedes nor the one that follows. Christ's yielding to his Father's will is presented in section three. The formal division itself suffices to indicate that the rebellious mood is over. The transition is further signaled by a change of epithet: "humaine," which closed the first section and introduced the second, now yields to "divin":

> Ainsi le divin Fils parlait au divin Père.
> (iii, 1)

The resumption of the Father-Son relationship is underscored by the repetition of the epithet. However, Jesus' submission does not diminish his anguish, it "redoubles" it. Vigny nicely manages to effect the transition in accordance with the Biblical account without a drastic change in characterization. While submitting to his Father's will, Jesus does not relinquish his anguished quest for light:

> Il se prosterne encore, il attend, il espère . . .
> Mais il renonce et dit: "Que votre volonté
> Soit faite et non la mienne, et pour l'Eternité!"
> Une terreur profonde, une angoisse infinie
> Redoublent sa torture et sa lente agonie.
> Il regarde longtemps, longtemps cherche sans voir.
> Comme un marbre de deuil tout le ciel était noir.
> (iii, 2-8)

The basic problem, underlined by the final antithetical rhyme, remains unresolved.

The exposition makes it clear that we are dealing with Jesus not as God-Man but as a purely human figure, in fact an archetypal romantic hero in revolt against the rules (in this case, silence) imposed upon him. In addition to the rebelliousness implicit at the end of section one and explicit in section two, Vigny's Jesus exhibits nearly all the other traits one associates with the romantic hero. He endures, for example, the solitude of the superior individual: "Jésus marchait seul" (i, 1). As in Moïse, the poet is careful to put symbolic distance between the hero and his disciples. Jesus also possesses the brooding melancholy of the beau ténébreux: "Triste jusqu'à la mort, l'oeil sombre et ténébreux" (i, 6). He is also presented as a Fatal Hero thanks to the poem's first simile foreshadowing the Crucifixion: "Vêtu de blanc ainsi qu'un mort de son linceul" (i, 2). An even bolder simile shows Jesus with bowed head "croisant les deux bras sur sa robe / Comme un voleur de nuit cachant ce qu'il dérobe; / Connaissant les rochers mieux qu'un sentier uni" (i, 7-9). Here we see the romantic hero as pariah and outlaw. As we have seen, the romantic hero, more often than not, is not just an outcast but an orphan, a bastard son, disowned or dispossessed. The parallel here is poignant: Jesus' fitful cries to his Father fall on deaf ears: "Le vent seul répondit à sa voix" (i, 20).

In his Journal Vigny has expressed his admiration for those heroes who dare defy the gods: "Quand un contempteur des dieux paraît, comme Ajax, fils d'Oïlée, le monde l'adopte et l'aime; tel est Satan; tels sont Oreste et Don Juan. Tous ceux qui luttèrent contre le ciel injuste ont eu l'admira-tion et l'amour secret des hommes."[10] The poet was furnished with more recent romantic models in Byron's Manfred and Cain. This "caïnisme" or "prométhéisme" was of course an important romantic theme on both sides of the Channel.

Vigny's wavering religious stance was representative of the cross-current of belief-disbelief among many Christian intellectuals of the romantic period that helps explain why "negative theology" surfaced so frequently during the nineteenth century. As Sartre says, in L'Idiot de la famille: "L'inspira-tion, originellement, relevait de Dieu; en France, après la déchristianisation de la bourgeoisie jacobine, la question se complique: Hugo, poète vates, prétend encore écrire sous

la dictée d'en haut, mais beaucoup de romantiques--en particulier
Musset--incertains, victimes d'un agnosticisme auquel ils
ne se résignent pas, remplacent l'Être suprême, à la source
de leurs poèmes, par la douleur de l'avoir perdu."[11] The
conflicting demands of faith and reason, perhaps best exemplified
in Kierkegaard's brave but intellectually anguished "leap"
of faith, are already adumbrated in the religious anguish
of many a romantic hero. Whether he leans toward theism
or atheism, the romantic hero's _feelings_ at least tend to
be ambivalent. When he believes, he asks, like Vigny's Christ,
who will help his unbelief. When he doubts, he asks, like
Musset's Rolla, who will give him faith:

> Jésus, ce que tu fis, qui jamais le fera?
> Nous, vieillards nés d'hier, qui nous rajeunira?

And when Rolla laments:

> Je ne crois pas ô Christ, à ta parole sainte.

the epithet is not sarcastic but nostalgic. Sarcasm, in
fact, is reserved, just as earnestly as Blake's "Mock on,
mock on, Voltaire, Rousseau," for the _philosophes_ of the
Enlightenment:

> Dors-tu content, Voltaire, et ton hideux sourire
> Voltige-t-il encore sur tes os décharnés?
> Ton siècle était, dit-on, trop jeune pour te lire;
> Le nôtre doit te plaire, et tes hommes sont nés.

Voltaire's men had indeed been born, but the loss of faith
left a vacuum, which, being abhorrent to nature, triggered
a wistful nostalgic reaction and provided the romantics with
a new lyrical theme--metaphysical anguish--which has come
to dominate the literature of the twentieth century with
the successive failures of Science, Marxism, and Eastern
Philosophy to fill the void or provide a rejuvenating faith.
Latter-day romantics--"hippies," "yippies," "Jesus-freaks,"
and what have you--have continued the tradition not only
by shocking the bourgeois but by resurrecting a purely human
and anguished Jesus as "Superstar," an ambivalent term wavering

between sarcastic and nostalgic irony, that is, suggesting both adulation and deflation. Jesus' descent from God to Hero to Superstar (surely a stylistic notch below Hero) must be taken as one of the parameters of faith in the western world.

Sartre's characterization of Flaubert as an "agnostique-malgré-lui" (L'Idiot de la famille, p. 2077) would fit many a romantic hero before and since, and Flaubert's determination to "souffrir en présence du Dieu absent" (ibid., p. 2073; Sartre's italics) has an exact analogue in Le Mont des Oliviers, an important poetic device of which is an ironic apostrophe to a God whose main attribute seems to be absenteeism. It is this ironic tension, as much as anything else, that holds the poem together.

Vigny's poetic license to make of his Christ a romantic hero, heir to the doubts of the Enlightenment and witness to the new critical exegesis of the Bible, should go without saying. But even judging the poem on its historicity, one need not see in it a violent departure from either the letter or the spirit of the Gospels. The poem deals not with an entire career but with one of the darkest moments in it. The somberness, although not developed at length, is already present in the Gospel accounts.[12] And Mark's Gospel tells us that Christ will have an even more somber, bitter moment on the Cross when he cries out at the ninth hour: "Eli, Eli, lama sabacthani?"

* * *

As stated at the outset, the goal of this chapter has been limited to providing a number of concrete examples for the generalizations of the first chapter. Examples, of course, could be multiplied endlessly. The portrait sketched in the initial chapter is not yet complete, but I conclude here because numerous additional examples and nearly a dozen more romantic heroes will be discussed, from different angles, in the two chapters that follow.

We have not yet seen any heroes of Alfred de Musset. While they conform to the basic model in many respects, they also exhibit features that represent a significant departure from the norm. They shall have to be treated separately.

chapter four

THE BLACK SHEEP OF THE FAMILY: MUSSET'S HEROES

The preceding chapter described René's direct descendents. Musset's heroes are also in that direct line of descent, and the family resemblance is still very noticeable; but they also have an alien strain that makes them unique. Musset was by temperament the most romantic of the romantics, but his attitude toward romanticism as a movement or school, that is, as it became institutionalized and conventionalized, was sarcastic to the extreme. He deflated its clichés, harpooned its idealisms (there were many), ignored its taste for local color, ridiculed its worship of nature, and satirized its many attempts to define itself. He was "the spoiled brat of romanticism," at once its chief exemplar and its chief detractor. One result of this ambivalence was the creation of a distinctive type of romantic hero.

Actually, Musset created two basic types of hero. One is tender, devoted, selfless and idealistic; the other is cynical, selfish and perverse. The two types were in fact two sides of Musset himself. By a process of dédoublement, he often presents both sides in a single play through contrasting characters: Fortunio and Clavaroche, André del Sarto and Cordiani; Stéfani and Steinberg'; and in the famous Caprices de Marianne, Coelio and Octave. The first type is a tender version of the romantic hero; the second closely resembles the Byronic hero--not so much through imitation but because Musset himself resembled Byron and the Byronic hero. Like Childe Harold, this type of hero is very young but already knows all the baseness of life. Like Childe Harold, he attempts to drown despair in pleasure and debauchery. The author delights in exaggerating the sins of his wayward heroes. Razette, of La Nuit vénitienne, for example, is the first in a long line of gambler-heroes (a deliberate deflation

of the Noble Outlaw) and is depicted as "le premier mauvais
sujet de la ville" just as Rolla is "le plus grand débauché
de Paris" and Lorenzaccio "le modèle titré de la débauche
florentine."

Rolla does not deviate significantly from the prototypical
romantic hero, and I want to use him principally as foil
to three heroes that do: Frank of La Coupe et les lèvres,
Octave of La Confession d'un enfant du siècle and Lorenzaccio.
Rolla has all the requisite qualifications to be certified
as a genuine heir of René.   He is even explicitly linked
to no fewer than four of the great myths of the romantic
age: Faust, Satan, Prometheus and Don Juan.   He is the disillusioned puer senex ("un vieillard né d'hier"), a man of
passion rather than reason--

> Ce n'était pas Rolla qui gouvernait sa vie,
> C'était les passions.[1]

--a young man without a profession, without a family, a man
whose only "friends" are his gambling, drinking and whoring
companions.   His misanthropic scorn and Byronic cynicism
are applied to common people and to kings alike.   The word
"love" has no meaning to him.   He is a solitary hero who
walks alone and "naked in this mascarade called life."   The
only thing he believes in is the romantic watch-word: freedom.
Since life has no meaning, he will spend his last penny on
a prostitute and then kill himself.

But this hardened débauché is presented as an exceptional
being, fearless, fair-minded and proud of being different
from the crowd:

> Jacque était grand, loyal, intrépide et superbe.
> L'habitude, qui fait de la vie un proverbe,
> Lui donnait la nausée.
>   (II, 52-55)

He is basically good-hearted and sincere:

> C'était un noble coeur, naïf comme l'enfance.
> Bon comme la pitié, grand comme l'espérance.
>   (II, 73-74)

His vices are not the result of an inherently corrupt nature, they are the product of his times. This _enfant_ _du_ _siècle_ is presented as a _victim_ of the _siècle_. He has had the misfortune to be born in an age of total unbelief. The real culprit is "Voltaire" and the other "démolisseurs stupides": the _philosophes_ of the Enlightenment.

> Je ne crois pas ô Christ! à ta parole sainte:
> Je suis venu trop tard dans un monde trop vieux.
> D'un siècle sans espoir naît un siècle sans crainte;
> Les comètes du nôtre ont dépeuplé les cieux.
> (I, 54-57)

> Dors-tu content, Voltaire, et ton hideux sourire
> Voltige-t-il encor sur tes os décharnés?
> ....
> Il est tombé sur nous, cet édifice immense
> Que de tes larges mains tu sapais nuit et jour.
> (IV, 1 6)

> Vois tu, vieil Arouet? cet homme plein de vie,
> Qui de baisers ardents couvre ce sein si beau,
> Sera couché demain dans un étroit tombeau.
> Jetterais-tu sur lui quelques regards d'envie?
> Sois tranquille, il t'a lu.
> (IV, 76-80)

* * *

_La_ _Coupe_ _et_ _les_ _lèvres_ (1832) is a "dramatic poem," a genre that Musset here introduces into French literature and that is modeled on Goethe's _Faust_ and Byron's _Manfred_. The hero, Charles Frank, is a young man of twenty filled with both a deep appetite for and an even deeper hatred of life. His bitter toast at the beginning of the poem is couched in terms of a Faustian curse.

>   Malheur aux nouveau-nés!
> Maudit soit le travail! maudite l'espérance!
> ....
> Maudits soient les liens du sang et de la vie!
> Maudite la famille et la société!
> Malheur à la maison, malheur à la cité,
> Et malédiction sur la mère patrie![2]
> (I, i)

The curse is soon translated into action: Frank rejects
the society of his fellow hunters and in a rage burns his
father's house, thus severing symbolically all ties with
humanity.

While seeking his fortune, in the second act, he encounters
and kills a great lord and takes the lord's beautiful mistress,
Belcolore, as his own. Lucky not only in love but in gambling
and war, he tastes wealth and glory but remains the "somber-
eyed" hero.

Much, but not all, of his bitter nihilism is explained
in the soliloquy that ends act IV. Frank, like Rolla, describes
himself as a child of an impious age that believes in nothing.
Musset alludes to the pernicious legacy of the materialist
philosophy of the previous century

> Je renierai l'amour, la fortune et la gloire;
> Mais je crois au néant, comme je crois en moi.
> Le soleil le sait bien, qu'il n'est sous la lumière
> Qu'une immortalité, celle de la matière,
> (IV, i)

and to the nefarious "analyseurs" of the Enlightenment.
The result of this intellectual legacy is disaster:

> L'amour n'existe plus; la vie est devastée.
> Et l'homme, resté seul, ne croit plus qu'à la mort.
> (Ibid.)

This statement anticipates one of Malraux's: the death of
God will bring on the death of man since the latter will
be able to define himself "vertically" only in terms of the
one remaining absolute: death itself. Like Malraux's heroes,
Frank defines man as the only animal who knows he is going
to die and who knows that death leads nowhere. Henceforth,
he says, women will be giving birth to old men. He adds
that the last bitter fruit of the tree of knowledge is doubt,
and he rhymes science with silence.

The desperate cry at the end of the soliloquy

> Oh! si tu vas mourir, ange de l'espérance,
> Sur mon coeur, en partant, viens encor te poser.
> (Ibid.)

will be acted out symbolically at the end of the poem. Frank
returns to his native village and to the childhood sweetheart,
Déidamia, he had left behind. Déidamia is a symbol not only
of hope for the future but of the lost purity and innocence
of Frank's youth. Just moments before the nuptials are to
be performed, just before the cup touches the lips, Déidamia
is murdered by Belcolore, symbol of Frank's--and modern
man's--incurable doubt.

Frank's bitterness is informed not only by metaphysical
despair but also by something we have not yet seen in other
romantic heroes: self-hatred. Frank sees himself as a withered
flower, as a young man "bent over by scorn...and shame,"
drained by debauchery of all human feeling. Self-hatred
informs also the famous scene in which Frank simulates his
death and, disguised, attends his own funeral. The scene
is richer than the interpretations it usually receives suggest.
Frank is not simply exploring human ingratitude and confirming
his misanthropy; this is also an exercise in masochistic
self-hatred. He interrupts the eulogies to present himself
in the worst possible light. We have here, then, a significant
new note: the romantic hero's rage turns inward, against
himself. The chorus, who represents Frank's fellow huntsmen,
explains this at the very beginning of the poem.

> Tu te hais, vagabond, dans ton orgueil de roi,
> Et tu hais ton voisin d'être semblable à toi.
> (I, i)

* * *

Octave, another enfant du siècle, at first believes in and cares for nothing but love: "Je n'avais connu de la vie que l'amour, du monde que ma maîtresse, et n'en voulais savoir autre chose." [3] When he learns of his mistress's infidelity, his one last illusion is shattered. Under the tutelage of the libertine Desgenais, he becomes a débauché and delights in painting himself even worse than he is. But debauchery does not cure his despair; he has a better heart than his wicked friend. The death of his father brings about a moral revolution, or rather, it brings out Octave's better side. He imitates the virtuous and regular life of his beloved father and admits that he is now truly happy for the first time in his life. He meets and falls in love with Brigitte, a widow, for months being content to be her friend. He finally declares himself, but Brigitte, who secretly returns his love, insists upon a platonic relationship. Finally, after more than half a year, this charming friendship becomes a charming love affair. The novel could have ended here. Sainte-Beuve wished it had.

But the novel does not end here, and this beautiful romance turns sour. Immediately upon becoming Brigitte's lover, Octave has inexplicable attacks of ill humor and meanness. The two sides of his nature are at war: "Je me montrais alternativement dur et railleur, tendre et dévoué, sec et orgueilleux, repentant et soumis" (p. 203). His gratuitous jealousy and cruelty finally push the loving Brigitte into the arms of another man.

There are resemblances between this novel and Adolphe. Both heroes are young idlers whose will power is paralyzed by their inner contradictions; in both novels love sours as soon as it is consummated; the woman in each case is ten years older than the man; Ellénore dies from the wrenching experience, Brigitte almost does. But Adolphe is the story of a young man who is probably incapable of true love; La

Confession is the story of a young man who cannot love well
or long.

Octave's strange behavior could be explained in Tainian
terms: la race, le milieu, le moment. Deep within Octave,
encoded in his romantic genes, is a sado-masochistic need
to suffer and to inflict pain. At the beginning of the novel,
for example, he had attached the portrait of his first mistress
to a discipline: "...au bout de laquelle était une plaque
hérisée de pointes. J'avais fait attacher le médaillon sur
la plaque et le portais ainsi. Ces clous, qui m'entraient
dans la poitrine à chaque mouvement, me causaient une volupté
si étrange que j'appuyais quelquefois ma main pour les sentir
plus profondément" (p. 90). And toward the end of the novel
he asks: "Comment se fait-il qu'il y ait ainsi en nous je
ne sais quoi qui aime le malheur?" (p. 245). A second factor
is his early training in debauchery. Vice clings to the
skin, as Lorenzaccio will learn, and as Octave himself says:
"La curiosité du mal est une maladie infame qui naît de tout
contact impur" (p. 248). A third factor is the historical
moment: "Je suis né dans un siècle impie, et j'ai beaucoup
à expier" (p. 283). It is this last factor that Musset
emphasizes--especially in the famous second chapter. The
age's skepticism, which for Musset is the chief ingredient
of romantic melancholy, has spread even to the relations
between the sexes. Octave consequently feels the need to
test Brigitte's love and to toy with it: "Tu jouais avec
le bonheur comme un enfant avec un hochet" (p. 277). The
novel's theme is on ne badine pas avec l'amour, but the problem
is presented within the context of a precise historical situation, which, as the novel's title also indicates, enlarges
the scope of the subject treated so that we are dealing not
simply with one young man's "malady" but with that of an
entire generation, le mal du siècle.

The title also indicates that this novel is a confession,
that the hero, as he himself admits, "has much to expiate."

Like the romantic hero Octave sees himself as l'homme fatal
but with an important difference. He realizes that he is
the source even more than the victim of the evil that besets
him and that torments the woman he loves.

> Faire le mal! tel était donc le rôle que la Providence
> m'avait imposé! Moi, faire le mal! moi à qui ma conscience,
> au milieu de mes fureurs mêmes, disait pourtant que j'étais
> bon! moi qu'une destinée impitoyable entraînait sans cesse
> plus avant dans un abîme et à qui en même temps une horreur
> secrète montrait sans cesse la profondeur de cet abîme où
> je tombais! moi qui partout, malgré tout, eussé-je commis
> un crime et versé le sang de ces mains que voilà, me serais
> encore répété que mon coeur n'était pas coupable, que je me
> trompais, que ce mauvais génie, je ne sais quel être qui habitait
> le mien, mais qui n'y était pas né! moi, faire le mal! Dupuis
> six mois j'avais accompli cette tâche: pas une journée ne
> s'était passée que je n'eusse travaillé à cette oeuvre impie,
> et j'en avais en ce moment même la preuve devant les yeux.
> L'homme qui avait aimé Brigitte, qui l'avait offensée, puis
> insultée, puis délaissée, quittée pour la reprendre, remplie
> de craintes, assiégée de soupçons, jetée enfin sur ce lit
> de douleur où je la voyais étendue, c'était moi! (pp. 273-
> 74)

The passage is significant. It begins not only with one
of the major themes but also with the style, the tone, the
very vocabulary (la Providence; une destinée impitoyable;
un abîme) of René and Les Natchez but then shifts to the
really dominant theme, which is Octave's personal guilt.
Guilt is not one of the attributes of the typical French
romantic hero, although it is one of the important traits
of the Byronic hero. It is in Musset's work especially that
the theme of guilt becomes attached to the romantic hero.

* * *

Lorenzo de Médicis, the protagonist of Musset's Lorenzaccio and the greatest dramatic hero of the nineteenth century theater in France, was once an innocent and bookish adolescent, steeped in the great lives of Plutarch and dreaming of glory--which he planned to achieve by becoming a tyrannicide. He wants to accomplish a dazzling deed that will assure him earthly immortality in the manner of the ancients. The choice of victim is dictated simply by the latter's power and prestige: the first one that occurs to Lorenzo is the Pope himself! He finally settles on his profligate cousin, Alexandre de Médicis, the Duke of Florence. The choice appeals to his sincere sense of political justice as well as to his pride. To ingratiate himself with Alexandre he feigns to share the latter's taste for debauchery; Lorenzo becomes the despised Lorenzaccio. To camouflage his conspiracy he feigns cowardice; the apparent "femmelette" is also knicknamed "Lorenzetta." He even plays the double agent, revealing the names of many republican conspirators, thus doing more harm than he will prevent by killing the wicked tyrant.

But Lorenzaccio is caught in his own trap. Vice, which he had first worn as an outer garment, has stuck to his skin. His taste for debauchery is no longer feigned but real, and it has changed his view of humanity. Most women now seem impure, most men selfish and cowardly. For whom, he asks, am I working? He is convinced that the assassination will be in vain since the zeal of the republicans is purely verbal. Nevertheless he will accomplish his act, not out of love for humanity but because it is the only thread that links him to the purity of his past; it is all that is left of his virtue. Having accomplished the act, which is his sole raison d'être, he lets himself be assassinated.

Lorenzaccio bears a good number of resemblances to Hamlet.[4] Like Hamlet he plays a role to deceive his victim. He even feigns near madness at times. Like Hamlet, he lashes with sardonic irony the fawning courtisans that infest the city of Florence (and by displacement the Paris of the July Monarchy). His only moral joy is the unmasking of hypocrites. Like Hamlet, he is a melancholy prince and, like him, constantly defers the assassination he has assigned himself. But Hamlet procrastinates because of his sensitive nature, his scruples; Lorenzaccio procrastinates because he is enjoying his Machiavellian machinations and his debauchery. And, since the act is ultimately useless and meaningless in any event, time is not of the essence. Hamlet hesitates, but never does he doubt the efficacy of his act nor the righteousness of his cause. His act is authenticated by the otherworldly voice of his dead father. (Lorenzaccio, in a Shakespearean reminiscence, wonders if it is his father's specter that inspires him to commit the assassination.) Musset's hero, on the other hand, has no assurance that his act is justified. He experiences what Sartre and Kierkegaard call "the anguish of Abraham." He is painfully aware of the ambiguousness of his moral "situation" and knows that his act will never be validated on this of the other side of the grave.

Lorenzaccio also resembles Julien Sorel in many respects. Like Julien, he dreams of glory and conceives of duty strictly in terms of what he owes himself. Like Julien he abhors injustice and treats with bitter sarcasm the moral mediocrities that surround him (Julien, being a plebeian, must keep his sarcasm to himself). Like Julien he wears the mask of hypocrisy to accomplish his goal and conceives of his actions in terms of military strategy. Like Julien's, his life is cut short because of a crime of violence. But experience matures Julien: he learns to love and dies wisely. Lorenzo, on the other hand, regresses: he learns only to scorn.

The poignant contrast between the innocent Lorenzo and the corrupt Lorenzaccio is brought out by his mother. Here is Lorenzo:

> Tant de facilité, un si doux amour de la solitude! Ce
> ne sera jamais un guerrier que mon Renzo, disais-je en le
> voyant rentrer de son collège, avec ses gros livres sous le
> bras; mais un saint amour de la vérité brillait sur ses lèvres
> et dans ses yeux noirs; il lui fallait s'inquiéter de tout,
> dire sans cesse: "Celui-là est pauvre, celui-là est ruiné;
> comment faire?" Et cette admiration pour les grands hommes
> de son Plutarque![5]

but now...

> Il n'est même plus beau; comme une fumée malfaisante,
> la souillure de son coeur lui est montée au visage. Le sourire,
> ce doux épanouissement qui rend la jeunesse semblable aux
> fleurs, s'est enfui de ses joues couleur de soufre, pour y
> laisser grommeler une ironie ignoble et le mépris de tout. (p. 81)

Thus, our **beau** _ténébreux_ is no longer **beau**, as his own
mother testifies, and his ironic scorn is not presented as
righteous indignation but as "ignoble." Lorenzaccio has
the romantic hero's melancholy, solitude, misanthropy and
presentiment of disaster, but he is taken off his lofty pedestal.
Compare for instance René watching fallen leaves flowing
gently down a river to this: "Cracher dans un puits pour
faire des ronds est mon plus grand bonheur. Après boire
et dormir, je n'ai pas d'autre occupation" (p. 116). His
despair has a distinctly modern ring: his bitter, biting
sarcasm is directed at himself as much as it is at others.

> Je suis devenu vicieux, lâche, un objet de honte et
> d'opprobre. (p. 135)

> De quel tigre a rêvé ma mère enceinte de moi?... De
> quelles entrailles fauves, de quels velus embrassements, suis-
> je donc sorti? (p. 160)

Lorenzaccio tells us that he is a hollow man, emptier than
a tin statue (p. 200), he wonders why children don't throw
mud at him as he passes by. Like the romantic hero he complains
of being a **puer** **senex**, but he deflates the pathos of his
predicament: "Je suis plus vieux que le bisaïeul de Satan"
(p. 200). His sense of humor is informed by a tragic sense
of life, by what Senancour called the "burlesque" and by
what more recent authors have called the "Absurd": "S'il

y a quelqu'un là-haut, il doit bien rire de nous tous; cela est très comique, très comique, vraiment" (p. 175). An attenuated form of this tragic laughter will appear in romantic irony, an exacerbated form in the humour noir that permeates so much of the literature of the twentieth century.

I have treated Musset's heroes separately (and have more to say about them anon) not only because they differ markedly from most of René's immediate heirs but also because I want to emphasize a major thesis of this book: there is a direct line of descent--in both senses of the word--from René to the contemporary anti-hero, and Musset is an important link in the chain. Schematically, it proceeds thus:

1. René et al--melancholy but proud hero. Despite certain pathological tendencies, presented as, or sees himself as, almost superhuman.

2. Musset's Frank, Octave and Lorenzaccio-- melancholy but guilty hero. Tragic guilt. "Tragic" because the hero still possesses a modicum of tragic dignity: his anguished lucidity for one thing; his sincerity for another; his sense of and yearning for a lost purity for still another.

3. Romantic irony (Musset's Hassan, Stendhal's Julien, Gautier's d'Albert and Albertus). The hero, while still admired, is the object of authorial or narrative ambivalence. His dignity (there is still more, much more, than a shred of it) is constantly deflated. The hero as fool, clown, but still hero. In the case of Musset's Fantasio and Hugo's Triboulet, one can speak of the "clown as hero"

or, like Jean Starobinski, of the héroïsation romantique du bouffon.[6]

4. The decadent hero of the _fin_ _de_ _siècle_-- no ambivalence now; emphasis definitely on the "hero's" perversity. The decadent hero is superior intellectually to the herdman--naturally--but René's overwrought sensibility has by now become overripe, gamey.

5. The anti-hero of the 20th century--not only decadent but often sub-human; usually identified allegorically with a single "romantic" vice: passivity; nihilism; crime; sadism; masochism; satanism; don juanism; narcissism; solipsism, etc. There is hardly a single trait that makes anti-heroes "anti" that is not adumbrated in René. But it is in Musset's work that one sees a crucial shift, a modern emphasis upon non- and anti-heroism, self-deprecation, authorial alienation from the hero and the very work in progress, an instability of narrative point of view. In a word: irony.

* * *

It is time now to examine in quite close detail (because we will be exploring some largely unexplored territory) the third link in this five-link chain.

chapter five

ROMANTIC IRONY FROM MUSSET TO LAFORGUE

Since romantic irony, as Henri Peyre has pointed out, has been studied chiefly by German scholars, and since the German scholars themselves have been in rather radical disagreement as to the precise nature of this form of irony, a working definition may be in order at the outset.[1] In a Dictionary of Literary Terms we are told that "The romantic ironist detaches himself from his own artistic creation, treating it playfully or objectively, thus presumably showing his complete freedom."[2] Henri Peyre stresses the crucial point that this ironic detachment comes not after but during the creative performance itself: "Through that irony, the creator stressed his independence of is own creation precisely as he was accomplishing it."[3] It should also be stressed that the ironic detachment, playfulness, self-parody and so forth, are imposed upon a material that is fundamentally or at least in large measure, serious--hence the irony. We are dealing, then, with a rather complex and highly paradoxical form of irony. The author presents us with a theme or a hero that he takes seriously to a significant degree, but he nonetheless cannot take his work as a whole with total seriousness nor can he relate to his hero with total sympathy.

There may very well be as many reasons for an author to use (or to admire) romantic irony as there are authors. For Germans like Schlegel, romantic irony is an intangible spirit hovering over the whole work and reflects a metaphysical stance: "The universe as experienced by man is for Schlegel an infinitude which cannot be reduced to rational order, a chaos, a complex of contradiction and incongruity, for our limited intellects cannot fathom the order of the absolute. We may at times catch a glimpse of this order, but once we try to realize it for ourselves or express it to others we

are involved in contradiction or paradox."[4]   For English
and French writers, especially Byron, Musset, Stendhal and
Gautier, romantic irony is a less transcendental and more
tangible phenomenon and is readily identifiable by the specific
stylistic devices and literary strategies employed.   One
impetus to romantic irony was the desire to avoid the embarrassing sentimentality, bathos and hyperbole that marred so
much preromantic and early romantic literature.   A frequent
antidote administered by the romantic ironist is the sudden
passage from one mood to another, for example having hot
baths of sentiment followed by cold douches of irony, as
Jean-Paul Richter put it.   Another antidote is to break
the spell of poetic enthusiasm or exalted sentiment by a
cumbersome intrusion of the author's presence (subjective
irony).   Or the hero can be placed in an embarrassing or
demeaning situation (objective irony).   Or the author can
apologize to the reader for the weakness of the poem or novel
in progress (naive irony).   A well known example of romantic
irony is the passage in Byron's Don Juan in which the hero
indulges in blatant hyperbole and sentimentality when taking
leave of his mistress and Spain then suddenly, and anticlimac-
tically, becomes sea-sick.

> And oh! if e'er I should forget, I swear--
>   But that's impossible, and cannot be--
> Sooner shall this blue Ocean melt to air,
>   Sooner shall Earth resolve itself to sea,
> Than I resign thine image, oh, my fair!
>   Or think of anything, excepting thee;
> A mind diseased no remedy can physic--
> (Here the ship gave a lurch, and he grew sea-sick.)
>
> Sooner shall Heaven kiss earth--(here he fell sicker)
>   Oh, Julia! What is every other woe?
> (For God's sake let me have a glass of liquor,
>   Pedro, Battista, help me down below.)
> Julia, my love--(you rascal, Pedro, quicker)--
>   Oh, Julia--(this curst vessel pitches so)--
> Belovèd Julia, hear me still beseeching!"
> (Here he grew inarticulate with retching.)

A similar example of playfulness interrupting a serious mood is found in one of Pétrus Borel's Contes immoraux ("Passerau l'écolier") in which the hero says to his executioner:" Je désirerais ardemment que vous me guillotinassiez." The blade of the guillotine is dulled by the pedantic verb tense. Sometimes the playfulness is seen as early as the work's title (e.g., Charles Lassailly's "anti-book": Les Roueries de Trialph, notre contemporain, avant son suicide). Similarly the title of Jules Janin's L'Ane mort is the first hint we have that the author is going to turn parody (of the Gothic novel) into autoparody. Sometimes the unexpected playfulness comes at the very end of a work, as in Mérimée's Chroniques du règne de Charles IX, a serious historical novel, in fact one of the best produced during the romantic period: "Mergy se consola-t-il? Diane prit-elle un autre amant? Je le laisse au lecteur, qui, de la sorte, terminera le roman à son gré."

A second impetus to romantic irony was the tendency of the romantic imagination to view History as a mixture of grandeur and farce or, as Edmund Burke expressed it, a "monstrous tragi-comic scene."[5] This view of History precludes on the author's part an attitude of total seriousness toward what he is trying to accomplish. A third source of romantic irony was the tension between the romantic hero's search for the Ideal and the simultaneous awareness of the search's futility; a fourth source was the tendency to institute a critical self-analysis at the very moment an emotion reached its peak of intensity. A fifth impetus was the modern tendency to see man not as the classical homme absolu but as a paradoxical animal who can be depicted accurately only in terms of paradox. Man, according to this view, is a complex network of contradictory impulses, wavering between idealism and cynicism, between altruism and solipsism, between reason and emotion and, for the orthodox, between good and evil.

Historically, it was Victor Hugo who first asked his fellow Romantics in France to ponder the esthetic implications of man's dualism. One can therefore take 1827 and the Préface de Cromwell, not as the actual starting point (for reasons that will be discussed immediately), but as the initial spring-board of or "call for" romantic irony in France. It is Alfred de Musset who is its first important practitioner in poetry and in drama.

In his influential Preface, Hugo argues for a Shakespearean mixture of the comic and tragic because such a mixture is found in the very heart and soul of man and therefore at the very center of the human experience. Robert Penn Warren, explaining the importance of the coarse humor of Mercutio in Romeo and Juliet says that "the poet wishes to indicate that his vision has been earned, that it can survive reference to the complexities and contradictions of experience."[6] But Shakespeare's vision is "earned" not simply through this rather facile structural device but chiefly through the density of his characterization and his style. Hugo, rather naively, thought that the mere juxtaposition of the comic and the tragic, the sublime and the grotesque, would guarantee that the romantic drama would achieve this earned vision and that it would capture life in its very complexity. But Hugo's mélange des genres is mere antithesis, not ambivalence or paradox. There is no romantic irony to be found in the Hugolian Hero. He may rub elbows with buffoons in comic scenes tacked on to the main business at hand, but his attitude toward himself remains essentially simple: he takes himself seriously and even tragically. So does the author.

Alfred de Musset's heroes on the other hand often give off a sense of romantic irony not just because one can feel within the same character a tension between opposite impulses, but especially because the author's attitude toward his charac-ters as well as their own attitude toward themselves seems ambivalent. Their cynical frivolousness is presented initially as the only appropriate life style in view of their Weltschmerz. But at the same time they do not take their cynicism too seriously. They tend to see themselves, rather, as sad clowns--a type of hero to which we have become accustomed in the twentieth century since it is one of the chief heroes of our literature and of our painting. Fantasio, for example, remains unemployed because, as he says, people don't hire teachers of Melancholy; and so, to excape his creditors, he gaily dons the jester's togs. Octave, in Les Caprices de Marianne, another instructor in Melancholy, carries as his sword "une batte d'Arlequin." But just as we are getting used to interpreting Octave and Fantasio as silly, flippant clowns, they turn out to be, in their role as friends, both steadfast and courageous. One effect of romantic irony is immediately obvious: it tends to keep the reader not off balance but on his toes.

As Byron had done for English Literature, Musset created a special breed of romantic hero: the cynical, playful débauché who does not take Life too seriously and who lives his own life, as Baudelaire will ironize a quarter of a century later, "under the whip of Pleasure, that merciless torturer." One is tempted to call him the Ambivalent Hero, who does not simply laugh while crying as Heine's heroes do, but who makes fun of his own distress or, when he makes fun of others, it is with a nuance of regret. In La Coupe et les Lèvres, the Chorus says to Franck: "Tu te fais le bouffon de ta propre détresse" and, a page later: "Tu railles tristement et misérablement."

This ironic tension between idealism and cynicism is found in Namouna, one of Musset's longest but least understood poems. What little attention has been given to the poem has been directed mainly at the Don Juan figure that the poet sketches in the second canto. Nowhere is there a discussion of the romantic irony that informs the poem from beginning to end and that provides the key to an understanding of the poem's total impact.

* * *

Romantic Irony in Musset's Namouna

Irony in Musset is basically a tendency to deflate, often at the expense of his fellow romantics, often at his own expense. When the irony is directed at certain tendencies of the romantic movement, this, of course, is not romantic irony since the author is not identifying in the least with what he is mocking. For example, when Musset irreverently likens the moon shining over a belfrey to a trivial dot over an i, or a Byronic hero perched on the Jungfrau to a fly on a sugar loaf, he is not deflating his own style but the clichés of his contemporaries. Similarly when Musset, in Namouna (I, xxiii-xxiv), apologizes for the lack of local color in this "oriental tale," because, as he says, he has never been to the Orient and has "never stolen anything from a library," this is not true romantic irony either since it is really directed at the superficial local color of Hugo's Orientales. In a passage such as the following, from the dédicace to La Coupe et les Lèvres:

> Vous me demanderez si j'aime ma patrie.
> Oui; --j'aime fort aussi l'Espagne et la Turquie.
> ....
> Vous me demanderez si je suis catholique.
> Oui; --j'aime aussi les dieux Lath et Nésu.
> ....
> Vous me demanderez si j'aime la sagesse.
> Oui; --j'aime fort aussi le tabac à fumer.

The last line, on first reading, may seem to be deflating the author's own ego, but the context and the parallel structure of the couplets make it clear that the irony is still being directed outward at conventional wisdom--just as it is against patriotism and catholicism--rather than the author's supposed hedonism and anti-intellectualism. It is conventional life, not the poet himself, that is not being taken seriously, just as in Byron's lines

> I say--the future is a serious matter--
> And so--for God's sake--hock and soda water![7]

However, in _Namouna_ we witness a curious mixture of irony-at-the-expense-of-romanticism and romantic irony, the latter directed against Hassan, the very hero of Musset's poem. Consider the following passage:

> Il n'avait ni parents, ni guenon, ni maîtresse.
> Rien d'ordinaire en lui,--rien qui le rattachât
> Au commun des martyrs, --pas un chien, pas un chat.
> Il faut cependant bien que je vous intéresse
> A mon pauvre héros.--Dire qu'il est pacha,
> C'est un moyen usé, c'est une maladresse.
> Dire qu'il est grognon, sombre et mystérieux,
> Ce n'est pas vrai d'abord, et c'est encor plus vieux.[8]

Musset is poking fun at the hackneyed hero of romanticism: the orphan, the outcast, the pariah, solitary both in his _état_ _civil_ and in his moral-intellectual superiority, the _beau_ _ténébreux_: somber, mysterious, misanthropic and melancholy. But at the same time he is deflating his own hero. First, he dashes the reader's hopes of encountering a more flamboyant hero and, more importantly, he abruptly halts the narrative to ponder the technical problem of enlisting the reader's sympathy. Throughout the entire poem, as here, the narration of Hassan's story is interrupted thematically by the intrusions of the author and structurally by the intrusion of the present tense upon the regular narrative tenses. The reader is constantly shuttled between the past exploits of Hassan and the present preoccupations of his creator.

The intrusion of the present tense begins as early as the poem's second stanza:

> Hassan avait d'ailleurs une très noble pose,
> Il était nu comme Ève à son premier péché.
> Quoi! tout nu! dira-t-on, n'avait-il pas de honte?
> Nu, dès le second mot!--Que sera-ce à la fin?
> Monsieur, excusez-moi,--je commence ce conte
> Juste quand mon héros vient de sortir du bain.
>   (I, i-ii)

The description of Hassan's _entrée_ _en_ _scène_--deflating in itself--is interrupted first by the anticipated exclamations

of the scandalized reader and later by the vocative and imperative of the penultimate line. Then the narrative completely
breaks down as Musset switches to the present of the narrative
act: "Je commence ce conte/Juste quand. . . ."

Musset constantly uses the present tense to express
his independence of his own hero:

> Au fait, s'il agit mal, on pourrait rêver pire.--
> Ma foi, tant pis pour lui:--je ne vois pas pourquoi
> Les sottises d'Hassan retomberaient sur moi.
>   (I, xxx)

> --Je rappelle au lecteur qu'ici comme là-bas
> C'est mon héros qui parle, et je mourrais de honte
> S'il croyait un instant que ce que je raconte
> Ici plus que jamais, ne me révolte pas.
>   (I, xxxix)

In his brillant analysis of a passage from Rousseau's
Confessions, Jean Starobinski has shown how the author achieves
subtle ironic effects by shifting from the narrative past
to the present as "qualitatively privileged tense."[9] The
present of the narrative act conveys not only a foreknowledge
of what is going to be related (and is thus invested with
Sophoclean irony) but also the superior wisdom and experience
of the writing writing now, so that the relation of author
to character (or, in Rousseau's case, of author-past vs.
author-present) is one of amused condescension. We are dealing
with romantic irony because Musset, like Rousseau, does identify
with the character he is mocking. It must be borne in mind
that romantic irony is a double irony, it works in two opposite
directions at once: the poet will declare himself alienated
from his hero, but this alienation itself is also
ironic--it masks the author's limited but genuinely sympathetic
identification. Romantic irony commits itself to what it
criticizes. Despite his many (ironic) declarations of independence and detachment, Musset offers Hassan, as we shall see,
as an important incarnation of his world view.

By stanza xxxii the romantic irony shifts from the hero
to the poet himself who despairs of being able to finish

his rambling poem; that is, there is a shift from subjective and objective irony to naive irony. In stanza lxi Musset admits having digressed so long that he has forgotten where he has left his story. Then he will apologize to the reader for a hiatus here, a barbarism there, and so forth. What we really have here is romantic irony in triplicate: first, the poet pokes fun at his hero; then at himself and his poem; and finally the reader is constantly discouraged from identifying with Hassan by being made selfconscious through the many vocatives directed at him by the poet. The hero is constantly wedged between the reader and the writer:

> Tu vois, ami lecteur, jusqu'où va ma franchise,
> Mon héros est tout nu,--moi, je suis en chemise.
> (I, lxxv)

Another source of romantic irony in Namouna is the poem's overall structure. Musset keeps promising his reader to get on with the story but keeps putting it off. The narrative proper does not begin until the third and final canto--a mere fourteen stanzas compared to the fifty-five stanzas of the second canto and the seventy-eight stanzas of the first. The poet even devotes the first four of the final fourteen stanzas to still another apology for rambling off the subject, leaving only the last sixty lines (out of a total of 882) to the actual plot of this "oriental tale." Thus the hero of the story and the story itself are treated with ironic detachment from beginning to end. The obvious fact is that we are not dealing with narrative poetry at all--even to mock the heroic would require more narrative than we are given--but with the poetry of ideas. The poem must be read not only on its comic level (brilliantly done in itself) but on a deeper one.

* * *

The second canto is devoted not to Hassan at all but to Musset's idea of the perfect Don Juan. Musset's Don Juan has none of the vulgarity, the gratuitous cruelty, the cynicism, the hatred of both God and man found in many of his illustrious predecessors:

> C'est qu'avec leurs horreurs, leur doute et leur blasphème
> Pas un d'eux ne t'aimait, Don Juan; et moi, je t'aime.
>   (II, xxxix)

He is rather the "candide corrupteur" loving and leaving three thousand women in his search for an ideal one. It is important to note that the hyperbolic figure, tripling the usual number of Don Juan's conquests, is serious rather than comic in effect. Although his thirst--which is of a moral as well as esthetic and erotic nature--is never satisfactorily quenched, Don Juan never gives up hope:

>   . . . tu mourus plein d'espoir.
> Tu perdis ta beauté, ta gloire et ton génie
> Pour un être impossible et qui n'existait pas.
>   (II, liii)

Maurice Allem misreads Musset's Don Juan: "Cet homme privilégié, que la nature avait fait inaccessible aux soucis vulgaires et qu'elle avait formé d'une essence presque divine, en arrive, dans sa marche désespérée de femme en femme, de déception en déception, à mettre son bonheur dans une cruauté sadique envers les pauvres créatures coupables de ne lui avoir point donné le bonheur qu'il attendait de l'amour."[10]   There is no sadism in Don Juan's dealings with women, only a fierce optimism urging him on in his quest.

The relationship between the idealized Don Juan and Hassan is crucial for an appreciation of the total impact of the poem. This relationship is expressed in the last two lines of the canto:

> Ce que don Juan aimait, Hassan l'aimait peut-être.
> Ce que don Juan cherchait, Hassan n'y croyait pas.

Thus Don Juan goes from woman to woman because of an impossible dream, a quixotic quest, whereas Hassan goes from woman to woman since, knowing such a quest is hopeless, one woman is as good as another.[11] Here, Hassan is misread by Philippe Van Tieghem: "La femme est pour lui simple passe-temps. . . Et, cependant, ses amours rapides le bouleversent jusqu'au coeur, jusqu'à l'âme, il se laisse conduire sans crainte 'du plaisir au bonheur'; il conserve l'illusion de pouvoir vivre sur la terre le rêve idéal qui l'habite."[12] It is Don Juan who is love's martyr, not Hassan; the latter, as we have just seen, "n'y croyait pas." Although Musset is stressing the difference between the two types of Don Juan in the lines quoted above, they are nevertheless linked not only by the parallel syntax but also by the tentative "peut-être" suggesting a latent idealism in Hassan: he would gladly remain faithful to a perfect woman if such a woman existed. Hassan's doubt links him to the author ("un être impossible. . .qui n'existait pas.") In fact there can be no doubt that Hassan, no less than Musset's other heroes, is a projection of the poet himself, a point that is important to keep in mind when judging the causes and effects of romantic irony.

On its deepest level the poem, despite its comic surface, must be read as a somber meditation on the ethical implications of the world devoid of a perfect being in heaven as well as on earth and denied self-delusion by virtue of its new-found skepticism. The only response to such a bleak situation is Hassan's quantitative ethic: since the spiritual longings of man will never be satisfied, the modern Don Juan (Hassan) must live within the confines of the senses, deriving what consolation from them he can and prolonging his pleasure as long as he can.

One of the curious effects of the second canto is that, while Hassan does not even figure in it, sympathy is indirectly built up for him. We have mentioned the latent idealism: it is only Hassan's superior lucidity (Voltaire's men have by now been born) that prevents him from being as naively idealistic as Don Juan. There is also a suggestion of a certain courage, for Hassan as well as for Don Juan, to live in the face of ugly Reality. And the absence of self-pity, automatically precluded by the romantic irony, makes Hassan more sympathetic than many another romantic hero.

But the romantic irony also prevents Hassan from being inflated into an idealized creation. The chief source of irony directed against him is the fact that he is not only obliged to compete with but is overshadowed by the Don Juan of the canto-long digression. But Don Juan, too, is a victim of romantic irony: he is treated seriously but is wedged between the Hassan of the first and final cantos which are, furthermore, written basically in a comic vein. The final irony is that neither hero is given the title role, which belongs to an inconsequential servant girl whose plight is described in less than thirty lines. The total effect of the poem--and this seems to have escaped all the critics-- is an irony directed at modern man: with our disabused cynicism and scientism, our unredeemed sensualism, Hassan is the only Don Juan figure we deserve.

* * *

There is a significant passage at the beginning of <u>Namouna</u> that throws light not only on the romantic irony of the poem itself but also on the particular kind of vision that impels the poet to use it.

> Vous souvient-il, lecteur, de cette sérénade
> Que don Juan, déguisé, chante sous un balcon?
> --Une mélancolique et piteuse chanson,
> Respirant la douleur, l'amour et la tristesse.
> Mais l'accompagnement parle d'un autre ton.
> Comme il est vif, joyeux! avec quelle prestesse
> Il sautille! -On dirait que la chanson caresse
> Et couvre de langueur le perfide instrument,
> Tandis que l'air moqueur de l'accompagnement
> Tourne en dérision la chanson elle-même,

> Et semble la railler d'aller si tristement.
> Tout cela cependant fait un plaisir extrême.--
> (I, xiii-xiv)

This "extreme" esthetic pleasure, produced by the ironic counterpoint in <u>Don Giovanni</u> is based on the spectator's recognition of a psychological and moral truth:

> C'est que tout en est vrai, --c'est qu'on trompe
>   et qu'on aime,
> C'est qu'on pleure en riant; --c'est qu'on est innocent
> Et coupable à la fois; --c'est qu'on se croit parjure
> Lorsqu'on n'est qu'abusé; c'est qu'on verse le sang
> Avec des mains sans tache, et que notre nature
> A de mal et de bien pétri sa créature:
> Tel est le monde, hélas! et tel était Hassan.
> (I, xv-xvi)

Thus, just as convincingly and much more succinctly than the <u>Préface de Cromwell</u>, this mini-manifesto urges a <u>mélange des genres</u> based on a new kind of ironic vision which, in its turn, is based on a view of man not as a smooth, uniform monolith but as a creature of ambivalence and paradox, what Laforgue will call "l'innombrable clavier humain." Musset's description of Hassan, which immediately precedes this passage, provides an ilustration:

> Il était très joyeux, et pourtant très maussade.
> Détestable voisin,--excellent camarade,
> Extrêmement futile,--et pourtant très posé,
> Indignement naïf,--et pourtant très blasé,
> Horriblement sincère,--et pourtant très rusé.
> (I, xiii)

Romantic irony is more than a stylistic device used in the service of a limited context: it is a mode of vision with psychological and philosophical implications. The author's ambivalent attitude (alienation--identification; antipathy--sympathy) toward the hero of his story stems from a moral agnosticism informed by a view of the human psyche as fundamentally unstable, contradictory and unpredictable or, as Montaigne, Senancour, Constant and Gide would put it, <u>ondoyant</u> <u>et</u> <u>divers</u>. The pseudo-scientific foresight of an earlier generation of <u>idéologues</u> and, for that matter, the more modest hindsight

or our own generation's <u>caractérologues</u>, are summarily dismissed
by a skeptical irony directed not only outward at the incompre-
hensible Other but also at the elusive, slippery Self. This
instability, this multiple ego or, if you prefer, this existential freedom, will be studied extensively in the twentieth
century by writers as different as Proust, Pirandello, Eugene
O'Neill and Nathalie Sarraute. The originality of Musset's
paradoxical vision in <u>Namouna</u>, especially within the historical
context of the romantic movement, is pointed out by Philippe
Van Tieghem: "pour la première fois, Musset, dans ce poème,
a trouvé son domaine propre: le point de jonction de la
vie sentimentale et de la vie morale, le carrefour de l'idéal
et de la corruption, du plaisir et du désespoir. Un pareil
motif d'inspiration est plus dramatique que lyrique, parce
que la position de l'auteur est éminemment instable et contradic-
toire; elle s'oppose à la position statique de l'idéalisme
de Lamartine et au dynamisme optimiste de Hugo."[13]

Thus nineteenth century French Literature is given a
new kind of comic vision, tinged with sadness and seriousness,
but not taking the seriousness too seriously. It started
with Musset in poetry and in drama and with Stendhal in the
novel and will have distinguished variations performed by
Gautier, Flaubert, Baudelaire, Charles Cros and Laforgue.
The twentieth century will take romantic irony and turn it
into <u>humour</u> <u>noir</u>: the playfulness will still be there, but
the tragic overtones will be emphasized. With romantic irony
we are still dealing with skepticism and disillusionment
leading to a comic sense of life.

* * *

Romantic Irony in <u>Le Rouge</u> <u>et</u> <u>le</u> <u>Noir</u>

In his recent treatise on romantic irony in French Literature, René Bourgeois has noted an astonishing and important
fact: "Si l'ironie de Stendhal a déjà été l'objet d'études
détaillées et exhaustives, il ne semble pas qu'on ait jamais
pu parler à ce propos d'ironie romantique."[14]   Grahame C.
Jones, for instance, examines Stendhal's ironic attitude
toward the hero of <u>Le Rouge et le Noir</u> but concludes that
it is "benign."[15]   Julien is simply the charmingly awkward
<u>ingénu</u> whose ineptitude we are to admire: "Dans l'esprit
de Stendhal l'ironie va de pair avec l'admiration: le héros
qu'il ridiculise jouit de son estime; les défauts qu'il signale
chez lui sont des qualités qu'il respecte."[16]   But M. Bourgeois
himself, in his chapter on Stendhal, does not discuss the
crucial issue of the author's attitude toward his protagonist
but simply the latter's attitude toward the world.   And in
the three pages he devotes to <u>Le Rouge</u> he simply shows us
that Julien is not an ironist in any sense of the word, correctly
concluding that "c'est le rôle de l'ironiste de se laisser
deviner, de laisser suffisamment percer à jour sa vraie pensée
pour que l'ironie ait un sens."[17]   Julien, of course, cannot
afford what H. E. Hass has called the transparency of ironic
dissimulation.   We are not concerned here with the hero's
ironic attitude, or lack of it, but with the author's attitude,
or better, since one must be constantly on one's guard against
the infamous intentional fallacy, the author's <u>presentation</u>
of his hero.

Victor Brombert has written a superb book on
Stendhal's irony, but fails, like Jones and Bourgeois,
to do justice to the author's use of romantic irony.   In
fact he does not discuss it all.   He makes only one fleeting
reference to it at the end of his book, quoting Vladimir
Jankélévitch's remark that romantic irony can be as ingenuous
as enthusiasm. [18]   Since Brombert's theme is the "oblique

way" of Stendhalian style, he must discuss mainly the affirmative value of the sarcasm directed at Julien. The "prétendue critique," we are told, is really "admiration dissimulée." When the author is condescending, patronizing, shocked, surprised or disgusted at his hero, we are constantly advised that this is an oblique invitation to admire the young man's charming naiveté. True. But it is at the very same time an invitation to laugh at the hero's expense. It must be kept in mind that Stendhalian irony, like all romantic irony, is a double one, it moves in two opposite directions at once: the sarcasm does mask genuine enthusiasm, but it is also, and simultaneously, genuine sarcasm. Brombert alludes several times to the "double sens" of nearly every stylistic device in Stendhal's repertory but concentrates, as he must for the sake of his argument, on the positive connotations. He insists that it is the author's "fear of the reader" that forces him to hide his enthusiasms under the mask of irony. He cannot quite bring himself to admit even that "often" or "occasionally" the sarcasm is really sarcastic: "Mais qui dira qu'au moment où il se pose en juge, il ait cessé de sentir? Qui affirmera qu'à l'instant même où il prétend se désolidariser de ses personnages, il ne sente envers eux une sympathie autrement plus tenace et plus subtile que celle qui lui arrache des exclamations d'enthousiasme?"[19] Epithets of blame such as sot, ridicule, sottise and faiblesse, when applied to Julien, are interpreted as "termes de louange." This has been the traditional approach to Stendhalian irony. The approach is not wrong so much as it is incomplete.

I am going to accentuate the negative here; that is, I am going to look at the sarcasm in terms of romantic irony and not merely antiphrasis in hopes of restoring the balance and of doing fuller justice to the uniqueness and richness of Stendhal's ironic style. In the first place, while it is true that the author's principal attitude toward the hero of Le Rouge is one of enthusiasm and admiration, Julien has many real faults, and the author makes no attempt to conceal them. In the second place, both Jones and Brombert have very well explained the psychological bases of Stendhal's unstable point of view with regard to his hero.[20] And in the third place, it is one of Stendhal's esthetic biases, too well established to be documented here, to abhor novels, so dear to chambermaids and the marquises who resemble them, presenting flawless heroes. As often as not until the final section of the novel, Julien, in his role as lover and thinker, is a comic figure, ridiculed, chastised, berated, belittled--and loved.

The only real discussion of romantic irony in Le Rouge up to now is found in several pages of Morton Gurewitch's solid doctoral dissertation, European Romantic Irony. He studies it from the point of view of Julien's ambivalent nature: the mingling of romantic and antiromantic traits; the Wertherian Don Juanism; and especially the internal warfare between Innocence and Experience.[21] It is a good discussion but incomplete. Gurewitch focuses on the novel's hero but neglects the novel's tone. The author's ironic attitude toward his material is presented almost parenthetically. We are told that Stendhal does cast "several" astringent glances at Julien and that he does "occasionally" reprove him.[22] These remarks over-attenuate the sarcastic texture of the novel. The war between Innocence and Experience is waged not so much between Julien and Julien as between the young and inexperienced Julien and the mature and experienced narrator. Gurewitch has painted much of the picture; the following discussion should fill in the rest.

* * *

Stendhal is pitiless in his description of Julien's youthful ignorance and awkwardness at the beginning of the novel. Uneducated, inexperienced, provincial, Julien walks and talks like the country bumpkin that he is, moving from one ridiculous extreme of behavior to the opposite. His initial interviews with Mme de Rênal are filled with awkward silences interrupted only by bombastic and often unintelligible speeches. "Si par malheur il se forçait à parler, il lui arrivait de dire les choses les plus ridicules. . . . Mme de Rênal remarqua que, seul avec elle, il n'arrivait jamais à dire quelque chose de bien que lorsque, distrait par quelque événement imprévu, il ne songeait pas à bien tourner un compliment."[23] His extreme timidity, as is often the case, leads to an equally extreme temerity. Reviled by so many nineteenth-century critics as a vile, scheming roué, Julien is in reality a comically awkward figure in his role as lover. Here, for example, is the first kiss: "Rien de moins amené, rien de moins agréable et pour lui et pour elle" (p. 294). Here is his strategy as seducer: "La journée fut ennuyeuse pour Julien, il la passa tout entière à exécuter avec gaucherie son plan de séduction" (ibid). Here he is as Don Juan: "Julien s'obstinait à jouer le rôle d'un don Juan, lui qui de la vie n'avait eu de maîtresse, il fut sot à mourir toute la journée" (p. 295). If the author speaks of Julien's cleverness, it is either an antiphrasis, "Il comprenait que, par sa conduite savante de la veille, il avait gâté toutes les belles apparences du jour précédent" (p. 296) and "Ce raisonnement était fort sage" (p. 611), or a sarcastic oxymoron, "son adresse si maladroite" (p. 298). Desperately trying to act suave, he will enter Mme de Rênal's bedchamber with trembling knees and voice and making a "frightful racket." During his first entry into Mathilde's bedroom, he fares no better. Here he is the victim not of a sarcastic authorial intrusion but of objective irony.[24] Armed to the teeth with daggers, pistols, in fact "every manner of weapon," he looks under the bed and in all corners of the room for imagined conspirators. When Mathilde tenderly touches his arm, he thinks it is an assassin and pulls out his dagger! At a loss for words, he calls upon his memory and recites several beautiful sentences from La Nouvelle Heloïse.

As thinker, as well as lover, Julien is a constant victim of romantic irony. It is his imagination especially that gets him into trouble. His greatest intellectual failing is a frequent tendency to exaggerate a danger, a triumph or a defeat. Here, for example, is what the author says of the episode in which Julien fears that M. de Rênal will discover the portrait of Napoleon hidden in his bed: "Il était pâle, anéanti, il s'exagérait l'étendue du danger qu'il venait de courir" (p. 272). Here is Julien bemoaning the loss of Mathilde's love: "Là, il put s'exagérer en liberté toute l'atrocité de son sort" (p. 548). His awkwardness is compounded by his exaggerated awareness of it: "Il fut gauche et s'exagéra sa gaucherie" (p. 293) and "Pour comble de misère, il voyait et s'exagérait son absurdité" (p. 257). Whenever he manages to be less than awkward, he exaggerates his cleverness: "Si Julien avait eu un peu de l'adresse qu'il se supposait si gratuitement, il eût pu. . ." (p. 296). If he manages not to fall off a horse, he immediately sees himself as one of Napoleon's heroic officers charging a battery of cannon. In the seminary he thinks he has molded himself by now into a consummate hypocrite; the author thinks otherwise: "Toutes les premières démarches de notre héros qui se croyait si prudent furent, comme le choix d'un confesseur, des étourderies. Egaré par toute la présomption d'un homme à imagination, il prenait ses intentions pour des faits, et se croyait un hypocrite consommé. Sa folie allait jusqu'à se reprocher ses succès dans cet art de la faiblesse"(p. 383). This reproach is repeated a few pages later: "Depuis qu'il était au séminaire, la conduite de Julien n'avait été qu'une suite de fausses démarches" (p. 386). Or, when upbraided by Mathilde, he will fall into the other extreme and exaggerate his shortcomings: "Loin de songer le moins du monde à se défendre en cet instant, il en vint à se mépriser soi-même. En s'entendant accabler de marques de mépris si cruelles, et calculées avec tant d'esprit pour détruire toute bonne opinion qu'il pouvait avoir de soi, il lui semblait que Mathilde avait raison et qu'elle n'en disait pas assez" (p. 566). In such periods of depression, Julien's judgment is so warped that he overestimates all the mediocre and spiteful people he has met: "En repensant aux adversaires, aux ennemis qu'il avait rencontrés dans sa vie, il trouvait toujours que lui, Julien, avait eu tort" (p. 589). These moments of exaggerated self-abasement and "excès de modestie ridicule" (ibid.) do not preclude delusions of grandeur. Learning that the Marquis de la Mole has just named him Monsieur Julien Sorel de la Vernaye, illegitimate son of a nobleman: "Julien ne fut plus maître de son transport, il embrassa l'abbé, il se voyait reconnu . . . . Serait-il bien possible, se disait-il, que je fusse le fils naturel de quelque grand seigneur exilé dans nos montagnes par le terrible Napoléon? A chaque instant cette idée lui semblait moins improbable" (p. 641).

When Mme de Rênal tells him: "Soyez prudent, je vous l'ordonne", the oversensitive Julien wonders whether he should take offense at the last word: "elle pourrait me dire _je l'ordonne_, s'il s'agissait de quelque chose de relatif à l'éducation des enfants, mais en répondant à mon amour, elle suppose l'égalité. On ne peut aimer sans _égalité_. . . . et tout son esprit se perdit à faire des lieux communs sur l'égalité" (p. 295). The more perceptive Fabrice del Dongo, on the other hand, does _not_ misinterpret these very same words, _je vous l'ordonne_, which Clélia addresses to him; he knows he has every reason to be delighted. Julien has a similar defensive reaction later with Mathilde. When this beautiful and brilliant girl, perhaps the most exciting young woman in all Paris, asks him not to leave town, our touchy hero is piqued by her choice of vocabulary: "mais devinerait-on à quoi fut sa seconde pensée. . . . Il fut offensé du ton impératif avec lequel elle avait dit ce mot il faut" (p. 523). His error is all the more blatant in that Mathilde says this il faut in a trembling, almost inaudible voice. And even a third time Julien is piqued by a tender imperative: "Adieu, fuis" (p. 632).

In many other passages Stendhal will mention Julien's "stupid" or "foolish" ideas; he will also tell us of his hero's frequent inattention to details (p. 286), confide that he would never make a good administrator (p. 399), suggest that his esthetic sense is neither innate nor precocious (p. 493) and that often his ideas, although original, are inappropriate to the occasion or the context (p. 451).

Julien's biggest blunder is his blindness with regard to Mme de Rênal. It is here that all his weaknesses, both as lover and thinker, converge. His touchiness and suspicious-ness lead him to underestimate a woman worthy of his love if ever there was one. He can see in her only a rich woman, that is, someone who has been brought up in the "enemy camp." He conceives of his relationship with her in terms of military strategy, of victories and defeats. He draws up battle plans. (When the "enemy" is Mathilde, he will go on a military "reconnaissance.") Mme de Rênal's very beauty is interpreted as an ambush, her beautiful clothes as the "vanguard" of Paris, as "feminine artillery" etc. This is not just an uncomfortable feeling of being in an inferior social class; this is an inferiority complex. And Julien's large arsenal of defense mechanisms is more comic than charming. It is not until the very end of the novel and of his life that Julien appreciates Mme de Rênal à sa juste valeur and understands the depth of his love for her. It is not until then that he "grows up."

His seduction of Mme de Rênal is not a case of base conniving as so many critics have complained but the desperate and usually ludicrous attempts of an awkward adolescent trying to prove himself to himself as well as to this woman he imagines saying with a sneer: "Le petit n'a pas osé." His main motivation is to reduce the distance between himself and her. Far from being a vile seducer, Julien, in sexual matters, is not even precocious: "Certaines choses que Napoléon dit des femmes, plusieurs discussions sur le mérite des romans à la mode sous son règne, lui donnèrent alors, pour _la première fois_, quelques idées que tout autre jeune homme de son âge aurait eues depuis longtemps" (p. 265; our emphasis). It is true that in _Le Rouge_ we have all the stages of an ordinary seduction:

1° I must hold her hand.

2° I must tell her I love her.

3° I must kiss her.

4° I must enter her room this very night.

But, and this is of capital importance, each stage is independent of the others; it is not part of a _plan suivi_. Stage one is motivated, as the author explicitly tells us, not by love but "duty" (i.e., what Julien owes to himself): "Julien pensa qu'il était de son devoir d'obtenir que l'on ne retirât pas cette main quand il la touchait" (p. 265). In stage two it is not his sensuality but his pride talking:

> Il avait fait _son devoir_, _et un devoir héroïque_. Rempli de bonheur par ce sentiment, il s'enferma à clef dans sa chambre, et se livra avec un plaisir tout nouveau à la lecture des exploits de son héros.
>
> Quand la cloche du déjeuner se fit entendre, il avait oublié, en lisant les bulletins de la grande armée, tous ses avantages de la veille. Il se dit, d'un ton léger, en descendant au salon: il faut dire à cette femme que je l'aime (p. 269)

In stage three it is not a question of love or seduction but of making up for a humiliation. He has just had one of his many moments of awkward silence, and as usual he overreacts:

Julien resta profondément humilié du malheur de n'avoir
su répondre à Mme de Rênal.

Un homme comme moi se doit de réparer cet échec, et saisis-
sant le moment où l'on passait d'une pièce à l'autre, il crut
de son devoir de donner un baiser à Mme de Rênal (p. 294).

Stage four sounds like the height of audacity, but when Julien
says to Mme de Rênal: "Madame, cette nuit, à deux heures,
j'irai dans votre chambre", the author is quick to add:
"Julien tremblait que sa demande ne fût accordée" (p. 296).
And a few lines later: "Rien cependant ne l'eût plus embarrassé
que le succès" (p. 297).   And finally as he enters Mme de
Rênal's bedroom, neither he not the author has any idea as
to what he will do: "Mais, grand Dieu! qu'y ferait-il?
Il n'avait aucun projet" (ibid.).

Both as lover and thinker, Julien compares unfavorably
with Fabrice del Dongo, Lucien Leuwen and even the Octave
of Armance.   Fabrice, we are constantly told, is a truly
"charming" creature, even his rival, Count Mosca, admits
that he is "irresistible."   Lucien is everything Julien wishes
to be.   He is a dashing young second lieutenant, distinguished
in appearance and manners, wealthy, educated, admired by
the ladies.   Unlike Julien he has no complexes and no ulterior
motives.   He is sincere, even frank, feeling not the slightest
need to hide under the mask of hypocrisy his scorn for the
many mediocre and despicable people he encounters.   Although
Octave, like Julien, is an imperfect lover, it is not through
any fault of his own but rather "a decree of nature."   Except
for his physical handicap, Octave outshines poor Julien in
most respects.   He is articulate whenever he wants to be,
dances with magnificent grace, is endowed with "perfect taste,"
physical beauty and courage.   The few times Stendhal directs
any criticism at him it is felt as purely cautionary (as
when the author informs his aristocratic reader that his
hero's jaundiced view of Parisian high society is exaggerated),
or it is attenuated by an adverb -

Il comptait un peu trop sur sa clairvoyance. (p. 62)

> Nous avouerons qu'il outrepassa un peu le degré
> d'impertinence toléré. (p. 130)

or with a chiasmus the author will give back with one hand
what he took away with the other: "Octave se disait à haute
voix des choses folles et de mauvais goût, dont il observait
curieusement le mauvais goût et la folie" (p. 115). The
words "observait curieusement" indicate a lucidity that belies
the folly.

When the point of view shifts to irony, and the author
wants to put some distance between the protagonist and the
reader, Julien will become "notre héros," "notre provincial,"
"notre plébéien révolté" or "notre jeune philosophe," the
latter of course when Julien's thinking is particularly
weak.[25] Calling the hero "our hero" is like calling a spade
a spade: it can be dangerous. The device is used frequently
in Lucien Leuwen and La Chartreuse but merely as a traditional
fictional license, a vestige of the "oral" style, and does
no violence to the objective representation or to the hero's
stature. But in Le Rouge it converges with an already sarcastic
or ironic context and deflates the hero's charisma and machismo.

The reader's identification with Julien is interrupted
several hundred times by subjective irony, those famous intrusions of the author who for instance will remind us that
this is just a novel (here the subjective irony combines
with naive irony and scores a triple hit: the hero, the
author and the work); or that Julien is just an adolescent;
or who will allow the present and conditional tenses to intrude
upon the regular narrative tenses. Only minor intrusions
are caused by the descriptive present, the generalizing present
and the digressive present; the latter, like the others,
is usually confined to just a few lines and does not denigrate
the hero or his story. The dramatic or historic present
is also used by Stendhal but does not constitute an ironic
intrusion since it is not an interruption but an intensification
of the narrative. But when Stendhal first introduces the

theme of Julien's hypocrisy and adds: "Ce mot vous surprend?" (p. 238), a slightly jarring note is introduced. Not only does the present tense interrupt the narrative but the reader is made self-conscious, thereby compounding the technical problem raised (the reader's anticipated surprise or shock). More damaging still is the present of the narrative act: not only does Stendhal spare the reader certain details, he informs the reader that he is doing so.

> Le lecteur voudra bien nous permettre de donner très peu de faits clairs et précis sur cette époque de la vie de Julien. Ce n'est pas qu'ils nous manquent, bien au contraire (p. 392).

> Mais il est sage de supprimer la description d'un tel degré de félicité. (p. 559)

> Le monologue que nous venons d'abréger. . . (p. 605).

The excisions and abridgments that the author informs us he is obliged to perform upon the novel do not increase the work's stature in our eyes, they deliberately lessen it. As Georges Blin says: "Il ne peut donc entrer en scène pour spécifier qu'il opère des retranchements que s'il cherche à nous persuader lourdement que les événements débordent son récit dont il dénonce de lui-même la trop lâche trame. . . Il est, en outre, périlleux de souligner que l'on pratique des omissions parce que c'est empêcher de faire abstraction de l'auteur et parce que, de ce fait, comme l'a noté J.-P. Sartre, on rejette le lecteur hors du temps des héros pour le rattacher à celui du seul narrateur."[26]

Whenever Julien waxes lyrical, Stendhal counters with subjective irony and switches to the "ethical present" or what Jean Starobinski calls the "present as qualitatively privileged tense": "J'avoue que la faiblesse dont Julien fait preuve dans ce monologue me donne une pauvre opinion de lui" (p. 438). As we have seen, Musset, another master of romantic irony, uses this ethical present to the same effect.

116

> --Je rappelle au lecteur qu'ici comme là-bas
> C'est mon héros qui parle, et je mourrais de honte
> S'il croyait un instant que ce que je raconte,
> Ici plus que jamais, ne me révolte pas.
> Namouna, I, xxxix

Similarly, in La Chartreuse, Stendhal will ironically plead artistic immunity: "Pourquoi l'histoiren qui suit fidèlement les moindres détails du récit qu'on lui a fait serait-il coupable? Est-ce sa faute si les personnages, séduits par des passions qu'il ne partage point malheureusement pour lui, tombent dans des actions profondément immorales?"[27]

The author's attention is constantly switching from his hero to his reader. Sometimes it is done indirectly:

> On voit que Julien n'avait aucune expérience de la vie.
> (p. 551)

> Il faut lui pardonner une faiblesse; il fondit en larmes.
> (p. 403)

The reader is treated to mock-lyrical apostrophe ("ô mon lecteur," p. 445), mock-heroic hyperbole ("Nous craignons de fatiguer le lecteur du récit des mille infortunes de notre héros," p. 395) and confidential asides ("De tels caractères sont heureusement fort rares," p. 530). If the author gives the hero a sincere compliment, he tones it down with the present tense and the modesty of a narrator enjoying only limited omniscience: "C'est, selon moi, l'un des plus beaux traits de son caractère; un être capable d'un tel effort sur lui-même peut aller loin" (p. 463). Occasionally the narrative is halted by a hypothetical question that the author poses the reader: "A ce coup terrible, éperdu d'amour et de malheur, Julien essaya de se justifier. Rien de plus absurde. Se justifie-t-on de déplaire?" (p. 565). Although the author does not launch into a digression here, the reader is invited to. The latter might very well lay down his book at this point and sketch a maxim or an essay on the subject.

Victor Brombert has given us an excellent discussion of the use of the conditional mood as part of Stendhal's strategy of _interventionnisme_, but the point needs to be made that this device, too, short-circuits the reader's identification with the hero. Not only does the conditional remove us from the hero's current activities (creating what B. F. Bart calls para-stories grafted upon the main one), it measures the distance between these inept activities and those of the ideal strategist: Henry Beyle alias Stendhal.

> Sans cette sottise de faire un plan, l'esprit de Julien l'eût bien servi, la surprise n'eût fait qu'ajouter à la vivacité de ses aperçus. (p. 293)

> Si Julien avait eu un peu de l'adresse qu'il se supposait si gratuitement, il eût pu . . . . (p. 296)

> En un mot, rien n'eût manqué au bonheur de notre héros, pas même une sensibilité brûlante dans la femme qu'il venait d'enlever, s'il eût su en jouir. (p. 299)

> Si au lieu de se tenir caché dans un lieu écarté, il eût erré au jardin et dans l'hôtel, de manière à se tenir à la portée des occasions, il eût peut-être en un seul instant changé en bonheur le plus vif son affreux malheur. (p. 549)

> S'il eût été un peu moins gauche et qu'il eût dit avec quelque sang-froid à cette femme. . . (p. 551)

And there are many sentences that could easily have been put into the conditional:

> Julien n'eut pas assez de génie pour se dire: Il faut oser. (p. 558)

> Il n'eut pas le génie de voir que. . . (p. 565)

These disparaging conditionals and quasi-conditionals weaken the book's positive one: what would Julien have been like if circumstances had allowed him to serve with Napoleon, to follow the Red rather than the Black? They suggest that Julien is not a tactician, military or otherwise, that he would have been an officer of daring and energy but not of genius. The reader can well imagine our intelligent but thoroughly unprecocious hero stumbling up the military ladder of success through trial and many errors.

In addition to the objective and subjective irony aimed at Julien, Le Rouge abounds in naive irony directed at itself and its author. One instance is the famous digression, "Cette page nuira de plus d'une façon au malheureux auteur", in which Stendhal, among many other interesting things, apologizes for the lack of verisimilitude in Mathilde's character. He will also apologize for an alleged structural flaw (p. 476) and, as he often does, for letting politics intrude into the narrative like a pistol shot at a concert (p. 570). The political details, our author ingenuously admits, were added at the insistence of his publisher to give more seriousness to a novel the latter considers "frivolous." Stendhal will even apologize for the dullness of an entire section of the novel: "Tout l'ennui de cette vie sans intérêt que menait Julien est sans doute partagé par le lecteur. Ce sont là les landes de notre voyage." (p. 610) Naive irony, although directed at the work rather than at the hero, affects the latter as well since it plays down the seriousness of his story and even removes us from it.

* * *

The mélange des genres, of which romantic irony can be considered a species (or, more accurately, the genus), was an attempt, on the technical side, to avoid classical "monotony" and, on the psychological side, to present modern man as a complex creature of dualism and ambivalence. Julien's particular ambivalence is not so much a question of dichotomies between reason and emotion or innocence and experience; it is rather a constant tension between what Henri Beyle called l'espagnolisme and la logique, that is, between the courage and energy required to create one's own identity, to carve out one's career, and, on the other hand, the instinctive (and intelligent) prudence that knows and observes the ground rules of the stadium in which society and history, whether we like it or not, force us to play. Julien's logique is

frequently illogical, his prudence often borders on paranoia--
which does not at all spoil the reader's pleasure: on the
comic level he can enjoy a sense of superiority over the
likeable hero, a compensation for and a catharsis of his
own weaknesses; on the tragic level he can look forward to
the hero's moral progress. What is remarkable about romantic
irony is that it allows the reader to feel all this simultaneously.

Despite his many comic moments and antics, Julien is
not properly a comic hero. And despite his many sublime
or near-sublime moments, his tragic dignity and tragic flaw,
he is not properly a tragic hero either. In Northrop Frye's
terms, Stendhal mingles both high and low mimetic with the
ironic mode. Julien is at once the alazon (someone who pretends
or tries to be something more than he is) and the ieron (the
hero who deprecates his heroism), the mixture producing a
sort of pícaro-type. Much of our sense of Stendhal's subtlety
and modernity comes from this modal counterpoint. Romantic
irony creates a hybrid genre delicately poised between comedy,
in which the protagonist is a victim-fool, and tragedy, in
which the protagonist is a hero-victim; it produces pathedy,
in which the protagonist is a hero-fool.[28] As John Nist
has said, both tragedy and comedy squint, they look at man
with one eye closed. Pathedy looks at man with both eyes
wide open. It sees his sublimity and his grotesqueness but
does not nail him to either pole. Nist says of Chaucer--
the supreme pathedist of English Literature--that he sees
man as something of immense yet limited value. Pathedy,
of which romantic irony is an important new species (an
older species is the picaresque) involves, as I see it, an
awareness both of man's potential for greatness and of his
inevitable limitations. Julien's sublimity has its limits
but so too does his silliness--he is a much more noble and
certainly more interesting specimen than the traditional
pícaro. Through romantic irony Stendhal has created a unique

form of pathedy. He has given us a protagonist who is 8 or 9 parts hero to 1 or 2 parts fool. At times we want to put Julien on a pedestal, at other times we want to wring his neck. Those who would see in Julien a higher percentage of fool (the term includes "schemer," "rogue" and "roué" as well as "ingénu") than I have suggested would do well to take the beam out of their own eye before casting the first stone; for one thing, it will improve their aim. Stendhal has simply chosen to show rather than conceal his hero's faults and limitations. Julien, then, is neither comic nor tragic, he is pathedic. He is a unique brand of romantic hero: scoured with irony and ambivalence, he is cleansed both of bathos and self-pity. He inspires admiration, sympathy and empathy--but also Hobbesian laughter.

Romantic irony involves not only the hero's ambivalence but the author's; there is never an uninterrupted flow of sympathy or antipathy but a constant rotation, often a commingling, of the two. In Le Rouge it is not so much a question of authorial alienation as of a pre-Brechtian Verfremdung. The reader is invited to examine the hero's deeds critically rather than to be lulled into an unthinking identification with an idealized hero. Julien's comic flaws, indeed, become a tragic flaw in the end. As Alvin Eustis has wisely observed: "In each of Julien's love affairs, his motives are not so much social ambition as the need to increase his importance in his own eyes. His downfall is not to be attributed, in the cant phrase of the critics, to society's narrow victory over a threat to its existence, but to a tragic flaw in his character: an acute sensitivity that takes the form of sudden, unreasoning rages." [29]

Stendhal knew he would pay a price for refusing to present a flawless hero. He knew that his book would be appreciated only by "the happy few" and that his hero was destined to be maligned. We mentioned earlier Robert Penn Warren's explanation of the coarse humor of Mercutio in Romeo and Juliet.

His remarks are also apposite here. "The poet wishes to indicate that his vision has been earned, that it can survive reference to the complexities and contradictions of experience." Stendhal, in giving us a sympathetic portrayal of a romantic hero so complex that his flaws outnumber, although they do not outweigh, his good qualities, has achieved this earned vision. And he has achieved it in large measure through romantic irony.

* * *

Gautier's Handling of Romantic Irony

The last two romantic heroes to be examined are the creations of Théophile Gautier: d'Albert and Albertus, both of whom are autobiographical figures who tell us much of the author's most intimate feelings during his early, romantic period. The entire first section (chapters 1-5) of Mademoiselle de Maupin is devoted not to the heroine but to the hero, who gives us a lyrical confession in the enfant du siècle mode, although the siècle is displaced for the sake of historical accuracy to the turn of the eighteenth century. The main components of d'Albert's psyche are the ones we have come to expect: boredom, melancholy, misanthropy, cynicism, solitude and the vague élans sans but, the latter shared by the heroine who is an alter ego of d'Albert and Gautier as well as the incarnation of their ideal.

D'Albert resembles a number of other romantic heroes we have already visited. The novel begins exactly like Obermann, with the hero writing to a friend not of the events of his life, since there aren't any, but of his ideas and feelings. The language is almost identical: "Mais, puisque tu veux absolument que je t'écrive, il faut bien que je te raconte ce que je pense et ce que je sens, et que je te fasse l'histoire de mes idées, à défaut d'événements et d'actions."[30] A passive

hero, he spends his life, like Obermann, "waiting." For
what? He does not know. He is tormented by the same vague
desires and passions as René; like René's, one of their objects
is an ideal woman; but another component is latent homosexuality.

Like Adolphe, d'Albert is supremely indifferent to every-
ting around him and, like him, enjoys a luke-warm affection
for a mistress he soon wants to be rid of. The hero's indeci-
siveness in this regard is finely analysed and is worthy
of the pen of Benjamin Constant: "Je lui en veux presque
de la sincérité de sa passion qui est un lien de plus et
qui rend une rupture plus difficile ou moins excusable"
(p. 127). Like Adolphe, d'Albert speaks to his mistress
of love for fear of speaking of its disappearance.

When he describes for us his heroic otherness, d'Albert
gives us an almost direct translation from Manfred: "Mon
coeur ne bat pour rien de ce qui fait battre le coeur de
l'homme.--Mes douleurs et mes joies ne sont pas celles de
mes semblables" (p. 242). At times he is a stranger even
to himself;" Le sens de mon existence m'échappe complètement.
Le son de ma voix me surprend à un point inimaginable, et
je serais tenté quelquefois de la prendre pour la voix d'un
autre " (p. 243)--a disconcerting sensation that will be
retold by Malraux in La Condition humaine.

As we have come to expect, d'Albert describes himself
as a puer senex.

> N'est-il pas singulier que moi, qui suis encore aux mois
> les plus blonds de l'adolescence, j'en sois venu à ce degré
> de blasement de n'être plus chatouillé que par le bizarre
> ou le difficile? . . . .
> Je suis attaqué de cette maladie qui prend aux peuples
> et aux hommes puissants dans leur vieillesse:--l'impossible."
> (pp. 140-141)

He is explicitly called by Rosette a beau ténébreux (p. 165),
and he calls himself a marked man, a fated and fatal hero:
"Chacun naît marqué d'un sceau noir ou blanc. Apparemment
le mien est noir" (p. 250).

But we are not allowed to take d'Albert's problems, which are real and grave, with tragic seriousness. The novel is frequently interrupted by allusions to the fact that this is a novel, a "glorious novel," an "illustrious novel," a "truly French novel" etc. On p. 231 the author tells us that it is boring to write a novel and even more boring to read one. In one place the author will excuse himself for an awkward simile, in another the hero will apologize for the inordinate length of a really fine and sincere burst of lyricism: "Ouf! voilà une tirade d'une longueur interminable, et qui sort un peu du style épistolaire.--Quelle tartine" (p. 67).

The story proper is framed with ironical detachment. Here is the beginning:

> En cet endroit, si le débonnaire lecteur veut bien nous le permettre, nous allons pour quelque temps abandonner à ses rêveries le digne personnage qui, jusqu'ici, a occupé la scène à lui tout seul et parlé pour son propre compte, et rentrer dans la forme ordinaire du roman, sans toutefois nous interdire de prendre par la suite la forme dramatique, s'il en est besoin, et en nous réservant le droit de puiser encore dans cette espèce de confession épistolaire que le susdit jeune homme adressait à son ami, persuadé que, si pénétrant et si plein de sagacité que nous soyons, nous devons assurément en savoir là-dessus moins long que lui-même. (p. 146)

And here is the ending, the moment when d'Albert finally receives Madeleine's nocturnal visit, which is both the climax of the "plot" and the beginning of the dénouement: "Qui fut étonné?" says the narrator to the reader, "Ce n'est ni moi ni vous, car vous et moi nous étions préparés de longue main à cette visite" (p. 360). Thus, d'Albert's great moment is deflated by Gautier more cruelly than Stendhal would ever have done to Julien. The reader is not allowed to share vicariously the hero's excitement: "Il fit un petit cri de surprise tenant le milieu entre oh! et ah! Cependant j'ai les meilleures raisons de croire qu'il tenait plus de ah! que de oh!" (p. 361). The novel's sad ending is punctured by a final intervention: "Sur la fin de la semaine, le malheureux amant désappointé reçut une lettre de Théodore

[Madeleine], que nous allons transcrire. J'ai bien peur qu'elle ne satisfasse ni mes lecteurs ni mes lectrices; mais, en vérité, la lettre était ainsi et pas autrement, et ce glorieux roman n'aura pas d'autre conclusion" (p. 369).

* * *

Not only is Gautier's Albertus still another incarnation of the romantic hero, but the author seems to go to some pains to insure that he is a typical one. A number of critics have condemned the lack of originality in the poem, but I don't believe that the presentation of a unique hero is really one of the author's or, better, the work's intentions. At any rate Albertus is indeed a stereotype of the romantic hero. He has, for instance, the regard de lion of the Hugolian hero:

> Son regard de lion et la fauve étincelle
> Qui jaillissait parfois du fond de sa prunelle
> Vous faisaient frissonner et pâlir malgré vous.[31]
> (LXI)

--a reminiscence too of the Byronic hero whose cold stare dazzles but also "chills" the vulgar heart. Albertus' lip is "severe" and forms the mocking smile of the Giaour. But his principal expression, the narrator tells us, is a "great disdain" for everything and everybody. A sad, bored, solitary misanthrope, "his door is closed to all." He is, inevitably, a puer senex:

> --S'étant toujours enquis, depuis qu'il était né,
> Du pourquoi, du comment, il était pessimiste
> Comme l'est un vieillard. . .
> (LXIX)

> --C'est un très grand fléau qu'une grande science;
> Elle change un bambin en géronte; elle fait
> Que, dès les premiers pas dans la vie, on ne trouve,
> Novice, rien de neuf dans ce que l'on éprouve.
> Lorsque la cause vient, d'avance on sait l'effet;
> L'existence vous pèse et tout vous paraît fade.

> --Le piment est sans goût pour un palais malade,
> Un odorat blasé sent à peine l'éther:
> L'amour n'est plus qu'un spasme, et la gloire un mot vide,
> Comme un citron pressé le coeur devient aride.
> --Don Juan arrive après Werther.
> (LXX)

Driven by a Faustian urge to obtain divine omniscience and omnipotence, he learns all of human knowledge that one can learn and, possessing that, promptly wants to die. Only fear deters his suicidal hand. But at 20 he is already ripe for death.

Like Musset's Hassan, Albertus does not believe in true love and settles for a quantitative ethic in which repeated superficial pleasures serve as opiate to his anguish.

> . . . Qu'importe, après tout, que la cause
> Soit triste, si l'effet qu'elle produit est doux?
> --Jouissons, faisons-nous un bonheur de surface;
> Un beau masque vaut mieux qu'une vilaine face.
> (LXXII)

Although good-hearted at bottom, he believes neither in wordly or otherwordly values and proposes for his life no lofty goals:

> Il laissait au hasard aller son existence.
> (CXXIII)

In a second Faustian impulse, he sells his soul to the devil in exchange for a brief moment of love with the beautiful witch, Véronique. Although he knows perfectly well that the love won't last, he is still greatly shocked when the beautiful maiden at midnight (the conventional hour should warn us not take with excessive gravity the conventionality of the hero) turns into the old hag once again, and the Devil, after an orgy in which all the inhabitants of Hell participate, comes to claim him for his own.

A sad career indeed, but the tale is not told of course in the lugubrious tone that my resumé suggests. We are advised in the Preface that the tale is only "semi-diabolique"; it is also "semi-fashionable"; the latter, significantly, is the most prominent adjective in the poem and tells us at once that the clichés and plagiarisms are meant to be ironically transparent and the hero something less than heroic. The poem is half-serious and half-ironic, the mixture producing romantic irony. We need not linger over the devices used to produce this irony; we have seen them in Namouna and in Le Rouge: authorial intrusions, some of which disparage the very poem in progress, digressions (i.e., structural irony), asides to the reader and especially a constant short-circuiting of the narrative in favor of allusions to the composition of the narrative. In stanza LIX, to take a single example, the poet tells us that it is "now time to get back to the subject" of this rambling and disconnected poem; then, instead of simply introducing us to the hero, he tells us that "before going further, it might be a good idea to sketch his physical portrait." The portrait itself is done with a certain playfulness and désinvolture:

> --Ses cheveux, sous ses doigts en désordre jetés,
> Tombaient autour d'un front que Gall avec extase
> Aurait palpé six mois, et qu'il eût pris pour base
> D'une douzaine de traités.

Gautier, then, uses most of the basic strategies of the romantic ironist. Rather than giving a detailed rehearsal of them, it would seem more profitable at this point to explore the serious implications of the irony in both works, especially since this is still largely unexplored territory. As late as 1975 a critic can wonder whether Albertus can be interpreted at all,[32] and another critic considers the poem unsuccessful because "the style continually distracts from the subject."[33] Similarly Maupin has been condemned by a good number of critics for its incoherent structure.[34] In my view the style of both the poem and the novel, especially their romantic irony, is both the foundation of their subject matter and the key to their interpretation. I also believe that Gautier, more than any other French writer, gives us many insights into the mainsprings of romantic irony.

Consider first the concluding stanza of Albertus.

--Ce poème homérique et sans égal au monde
Offre une allégorie admirable et profonde;
Mais, pour sucer la moëlle il faut qu'on brise l'os,
Pour savourer l'odeur il faut ouvrir le vase,
Du tableau que l'on cache il faut tirer la gaze,
Lever, le bal fini, le masque aux dominos.
--j'aurais pu clairement expliquer chaque chose,
Clouer à chaque mot une savante glose.--
Je vous crois, cher lecteur, assez spirituel
Pour me comprendre.--Ainsi, bonsoir.--Fermez la porte,
Donnez-moi la pincette, et dites qu'on m'apporte
         Un tome de Pantagruel.
                    (CXXII)

Despite the cavalier, tongue-in-cheek tonality, there is a half-serious Rabelaisian invitation to find the "sustancifique mouelle" within the bone, to find serious subject matter despite the playful treatment. The invitation is convincingly reinforced by the fact that roughly 50 percent of Albertus and 95 percent of Maupin are dead serious.

A serious theme that runs throughout the poem and that can be considered its chief one is the instability of human sentiments. In one of his digressions, the narrator tells us about his own love life which was an ecstatic but evanesecent affair.

Tout ce bonheur n'est plus. Qui l'aurait dit? nous sommes
Comme des étrangers l'un pour l'autre; les hommes
Sont ainsi;--leur toujours ne passe pas six mois.
                    (LVI)

Leur toujours ne passe pas six mois--this antithesis catches one of the moods behind romantic irony. A critic who has captured the mood well is Vladimir Jankélévitch, in his insightful treatise on L'Ironie ou la bonne conscience:

Nos sentiments sont éphémères et nos croyances instables. . .
la passion finira, malgré tous nos serments; nous jurons
nos grands dieux que la personne aimée est irremplaçable
et, quand nous l'avons remplacée, nous n'envisageons
pas sans humour cet absolu décevant qui est toujours
éternel pendant le fait et provisoire après coup. Usure
ou conversion--un sentiment n'est jamais éternel que
jusqu'à nouvel ordre! Un voeu définitif n'est définitif
que jusqu'à Pâques! Quelle créature ici-bas peut dire
Toujours?[35]

Even the witch Véronique recognizes this sad truth:

> L'homme d'un jour n'aime qu'un jour.
> (XLCVI)

The romantic ironist presents us with sudden shifts of tone or mood that are playful on the surface, but if one looks beneath this surface, one sees the dangerous undertow. In Mademoiselle de Maupin, for instance, the author shows us how the vague des passions can lead to cynicism, then to emotional aridity and finally to self-irony. For lack of the right nourishment the passions feed on each other and become internecine:

> Toutes mes passions inoccupées grondent
> sourdement dans mon coeur, et se dévorent entre elles
> faute d'autre aliment. (p. 45)

> Il s'agite en moi beaucoup de désirs vagues qui
> se confondent ensemble, et en enfantent d'autres qui
> les dévorent ensuite. (p. 160)

> Rien n'est fatigant au monde comme ces tourbillons
> sans motif et ces élans sans but. . . . Je me ris au nez
> à moi-même. (pp. 43-44)

Even when a man's heart is not filled with vague passions, it is filled with "absurdities," irreconcilable "contradictions" which prevent him from ever being more than "half-happy" or half-sad, half-moral or half-immoral, half-serious or half-ironical. Romantic irony is indeed the science of the Half rather rather than the whole. Not only do human sentiments keep changing, they change with such alarming rapidity that one's actions cannot keep up with them.

> Quand j'écris une phrase, la pensée qu'elle rend
> est déjà aussi loin de moi que si un siècle se
> fût écoulé au lieu d'une seconde, et souvent il
> m'arrive d'y mêler, malgré moi, quelque chose
> de la pensée qui l'a remplacée dans ma tête.
> Voilà pourquoi je ne saurais vivre,--ni comme
> poète ni comme amant.--Je ne puis rendre que les idées
> que je n'ai plus;--je n'ai les femmes que lorsque
> je les ai oubliées et que j'en aime d'autres; -- homme,
> comment pourrais-je produire ma volonté au jour,
> puisque, si fort que je me hâte, je n'ai plus le sent-
> iment de ce que je fais (p. 248).

How then can one measure the moral worth of others or even or oneself at any particular moment? "Il y a des moments où je ne reconnais que Dieu au-dessus de moi, et d'autres où je me juge à peine l'égal du cloporte sous sa pierre ou du mollusque sur son banc de sable" (p. 92). Romantic irony expresses a moral agnosticism ("J'ai perdu complètement la science du bien et du mal," p. 177) based partly on the fact that human sentiments are contradictory and fleeting and also on the conviction that there are no absolute standards. The heroic mode, under these conditions seems "silly" (p. 178); the mock-heroic is the best defense against disillusion, self-mockery against self-deception. All this can be read on Albertus' face:

> Un front impérial d'artiste et de poète,
> Occupant à lui seul la moitié de la tête,
> Large et plein, se courbant sous l'inspiration,
> Qui cache en chaque ride avant l'âge creusée
> Un espoir surhumain, une grande pensée,
> Et porte écrits ces mots:--Force et conviction.--
> Le reste du visage à ce front grandiose
> Répondait. --Cependant il avait quelque chose
> Qui déplaisait à voir, et, quoique sans défaut,
> On l'aurait souhaité différent. -L'ironie,
> Le sarcasme y brillait plutôt que le génie;
>   Le bas semblait railler le haut.
>   (LX)

The peculiar tension produced by romantic irony also reflects the unbridgeable gap between reality and ideality. In _Albertus_ we catch a fleeting view of the gap in the following lines:

> Bénévole lecteur, c'est toute mon histoire
> Fidèlement contée, autant que ma mémoire,
> Registre mal en ordre, a pu me rappeler
> Ces riens qui furent tout, dont l'amour se compose
> Et dont on rit ensuite.--Excusez cette pause:
> La bulle que j'avais pris plaisir à souffler,
> Et qui flottait en l'air des feux du prisme teinte,
> En une goutte d'eau tout à coup s'est éteinte;
> Elle s'était crevée au coin d'un toit pointu.
> --En heurtant le réel, ma riante chimère
> S'est brisée. . .
>   (LVII)

And in Maupin we have a very vivid image of this romantic
dilemma: "Je ne puis ni marcher ni voler; le ciel m'attire
quand je suis sur terre, la terre quand je suis au ciel;
en haut, l'aquilon m'arrache les plumes; en bas, les caillous
m'offensent les pieds. J'ai les plantes trop tendres pour
cheminer sur les tessons de verre de la réalité; l'envergure
trop étroite pour planer au-dessus des choses" (p. 240).
Romantic heroes, even those not treated with romantic irony,
all share this predicament. In each one the idealist is
restrained by the cynical realist, and the latter is restrained
by the idéaliste malgré lui. Since he has a home in neither
world, he yearns for the one while immersed in the other,
or, when presented from the viewpoint of romantic irony,
he shuttles--playfully and painfully--between the two.

In Maupin the hero describes his life in terms of this
shuttle but also as "un piétinement absurde." And when the
narrator of Albertus speaks of cette sotte histoire, both
the general and the immediate context make the epithet poly-
valent: it applies similtaneously to the poem in progress,
to the hero's career and to Life in general. It is still
another intimation of the Absurd.

* * *

Some Later Developments of Romantic Irony

Before the romantic period the narrator's attitude toward his hero or his story, or the hero's attitude toward himself in the first person narratives, was usually unequivocal: It was either positive or negative. Or, if it was ambivalent, the ambivalence was clearly stated; or, if it was ironical, the irony was transparent, since it was almost always a form of antiphrasis, the narrator obviously blaming the person or thing he pretended to praise, or vice versa. With the romantic period the narrative point of view begins to become problematical; we cannot measure the exact dosage of antipathy or sympathy, of identification versus alienation in works informed by romantic irony; we can only feel the tensions, observe the shuttlings and oscillations, admire the complexities, puzzle at the paradoxes. This type of irony did not die out with the romantic period; it reappears, in modified form, throughout the rest of the nineteenth century and becomes, in our own century, l'humour noir, the kind of laughter in which is heard the gnashing of teeth. Although this chapter is already long, I do not wish to conclude it before suggesting, as briefly as I can, some important transformations of romantic irony that occured after the romantic period and that will have significant repurcussions in twentieth century literature, especially in regard to authorial and narrative point of view and to the presentation of the literary "hero."

1857 was an annus mirabilis for romantic irony; in that year it was to receive two distinguished variations: the moral irony of Baudelaire and what we might call the realistic irony of Flaubert. Kierkegaard has noted that the ironist cannot openly take sides and René Bourgeois has said that "l'ironie ne permet jamais de conclure";[36] neither does the realistic esthetic of Flaubert. In Madame Bovary Flaubert will camouflage and transform what can still be called a form of romantic irony with realistic "objectivity" so that the author's attitude toward his heroine remains ambiguous as well as ambivalent from beginning to end. The negative edge of the irony is clearly felt, but we also feel the presence of a modicum of muted sympathy, and also a moderate measure of identification so that we are not very surprised when the author tells us, after the fact, that "Bovary, c'est moi." We see clearly the weaknesses of this silly romantic girl, but the author goes to some pains to make us aware also of the extenuating circumstances: Emma's unfortunate (i.e., romantic) education, a matter more of chance than choice, the mediocrity and callousness, in fact the downright bêtise of all the men in her life.

Flaubert's insistent use of the style indirect libre produces, in my opinion, a new and subtle form of romantic irony, an ambivalent and unstable point of view toward his heroine that is never made explicit. We are given Emma's very thoughts and words, which tend to make us sympathize and identify with them, but these words and thoughts are uttered not by her directly but by the narrator. They are filtered by another consciousness. An ironic distance or screen is thus established between the heroine and the reader. To take a single example:

> Elle se répétait: "J'ai un amant! un amant!", se délectant à cette idée comme à celle d'une autre puberté qui lui serait survenue. . . .
> D'ailleurs, Emma éprouvait une satisfaction de vengeance. N'avait-elle pas assez souffert![37]

In the last sentence we are given the privileged observer's direct view of Emma's mind: the thoughts, the very words, the very intonation. But at the same time we are aware of the ironical presence of the narrator. One feels that the latter is not in total agreement with the sentiment expressed, that Emma is exaggerating her suffering and is deceiving herself. She is not a superior woman worthy of an extraordinary husband; she has simply married a man even more mediocre than herself.

We are dealing here with romantic irony--or something very close to it--because we have that double-edged or two-directional point of view: an amalgam of identification and alienation. Emma emerges from the novel neither as a tragic heroine--she does not possess sufficient dignity for that--nor as a comic heroine--there is, after all, too much sympathy and identification established for that--but as a _pathedic_ heroine. We can both blame her and pity her; we cannot measure her.

Flaubert creates his ironic distance not through the transparent devices of rhetorical irony but through a careful and subtle handling of point of view, through an ironic network of implicit analogies and unobtrusive symbols (e.g., butterflies suggesting _une femme qui papillonne_) and through ironic counter-point. Not once does the narrator tell us explicitly that the heroine is a mediocre person, but we sense the ironic analogies between Charles' ridiculous cap and Emma's ridiculous wedding cake: they are both complicated, several-tiered structures, dominated by circular forms and possessing a grotesque mixture of styles; both are are supreme examples of bad taste--as is the Town Hall at Yonville that echoes them ironically later on. Not once does the narrator tell us directly that Emma, despite her good points (e.g., sincerity and the urge to self-realization) is morally corrupt, but in the following scene for instance--

> . . . et, tandis que M. le président citait Cincinnatus à sa charrue, Dioclétien plantant ses choux, et les empereurs de la Chine inaugurant l'année par des semailles, le jeune homme expliquait à la jeune femme que ces attractions irrésisti-bles tiraient leur cause de quelque existence antérieure.
> --Ainsi, nous, disait-il, pourquoi nous sommes-nous connus? quel hasard l'a voulu? C'est qu'à travers l'éloignement, sans doute, comme deux fleuves qui coulent pour se rejoindre, nos pentes particulières nous avaient poussés l'un vers l'autre.
> Et il saisit sa main; elle ne la retira pas.
> "Ensemble de bonnes cultures!" cria le président.
> --Tantôt, par exemple, quand je suis venu chez vous. . .
> A. M. Bizet, de Quincampoix."

> --Savais-je que je vous accompagnerais?
> "Soixante et dix francs!"
> --Cent fois même j'ai voulu partir, et je vous ai suivie,
> je suis resté.
> "Fumiers." [38]

--the 70-franc prize seems to go not only to the peasant but to Emma-the-prostitute, just as Rodolphe seems deserving of the prize for horse manure. But the subtlety of the sarcasm in _Madame Bovary_ is such that the muted sympathy is never quite destroyed. Emma's death is not read as "something she deserved, the bitch" but as something, if not tragic, sad.

* * *

All roads of modern French literature seem to lead to and from Baudelaire. In his article on romantic irony, M. Boucher has spoken of it as "la conscience de la coexistence des contraires." [39] Baudelaire's entire opus is centered on his intuition of the irreducible duality of _homo duplex_ and his two contradictory and _simultaneous_ postulations: "Il y a dans tout homme, à toute heure, deux postulations simultanées, l'une vers Dieu, l'autre vers Satan. L'invocation à Dieu, ou spiritualité, est un désir de monter en grade; celle de Satan, ou animalité, est une joie de descendre." [40] Man's painful consciousness of these contradictory impulses has been exacerbated by modern civilization, of which Baudelaire is perhaps the chief poet. Verlaine correctly saw Baudelaire's originality as that of depicting "l'homme physique moderne, tel que l'ont fait les raffinements d'une civilisation excessive, l'homme moderne avec ses sens aiguisés et vibrants, son esprit douloureusement subtil." [41] Modern man's unique illness--spiritual apathy--is countered by a desperate longing for spiritual health, but this dialectical opposition produces no wholesome synthesis or resolution, just physical and metaphysical tension, grating contradictions. The result stylistically is a sardonic form of moral irony. Baudelaire will speak of "nos aimables remords," "l'oreiller du mal," "le fouet du Plaisir," "le sein martyrisé d'une antique catin," and of "débauchés. . .brisés par leurs travaux." Baudelaire's oxymorons are more than stylistic devices; he **believes** in them. Baudelairian man, modern man, is a creature of paradox.

René Bourgeois has said that "La satire romantique a ceci de particulier qu'elle réunit dans le même mouvement 'la victime et le bourreau'et que l'écrivain se sent à la fois dans l'objet et hors de l'objet."[42] This sado-masochistic side of romantic irony and the dissonant blend of identification and detachment are essential aspects of Baudelaire's poetry: the torturer identifies with his victim, in fact he **is** the victim. The mocker is looking in a mirror.

> Ne suis-je pas un faux accord
> Dans la divine symphonie
> Grâce à la vorace Ironie
> Qui me secoue et qui me mord?
> ....
> Je suis la plaie et le couteau!
> Je suis le soufflet et la joue!
> Je suis les membres et la roue,
> Et la victime et le bourreau![43]

To the extent that Baudelaire has expressed the modern sensibility--who has expressed it better?--and influenced modern poetry--who has influenced it more?--to that extent post-Baudelairian poetry (and prose) is informed by an irony directly related to romantic irony.

* * *

When Verlaine speaks of modern man's "sens aiguisés" the epithet means not only "sharpened" but "set on edge"--they will become even more so with the passing of time. Baudelaire's disciple, Laforgue, and Laforgue's disciple, Eliot, will embroider on the master's moral irony and offer us disconcertingly rapid changes of mood and points of view; the ironic tone will become increasingly shrill.

C. A. Hackett has said that Laforgue's use of irony makes his work a complete contrast to that of the romantics.[44] This is not true since Laforguian irony is directly descended from romantic irony; in fact it _is_ romantic irony. As Henri Peyre states in his essay on "Laforgue among the Symbolists,": "Ever since the romantics. . .irony has served to convey the contrast between the author's assertion of his own freedom and his realization that he cannot reach the infinite of his dreams; his creation remains finite and paltry, and the creator can only look at it with mockery."[45] "Paltry" is precisely Laforgue's estimate of himself and his work.

> Ainsi donc, pâle et piètre individu
> Qui ne croit à son Moi qu' à ses moments perdus.

Laforgue will take a serious romantic theme, for example, disgust with everyday reality, and invest it with an irony that deflates both the theme and the paltry poet himself:

> Ah! que la vie est quotidienne
> Et du plus vrai qu'on s'en souvienne
> Comme on fut piètre et sans génie.

Laforgue's irony is informed by a feeling of the transience and futility of everything, including love and art. In a passage already quoted Vladimir Jankélévitch renders the feeling with precision: "Usure ou conversion--un sentiment n'est jamais éternel que jusqu'à nouvel ordre! Un voeu définitif n'est définitif que jusqu'à Pâques! Quelle créature ici-bas peut dire Toujours? Ainsi la conscience volage voit déjà le bout de son propre plaisir; elle le jauge en longueur, largeur et profondeur, elle le connaît, en d'autres termes, comme objet." [46]

An excellent example of this detached, "mathematical" view of love can be seen in the Pierrot amoureux of "Autre Complainte de lord Pierrot." The would-be lover does not allow himself to get overly excited about the prospect of meeting his First True Love; he already suspects that is is likely to be an ephemeral and trivial affair.

> Celle qui doit me mettre au courant de la Femme!
> Nous lui dirons d'abord, de mon air le moins froid:
> "La somme des angles d'un triangle, chère âme,
>   Est égale à deux droits."

The beloved is deflated by the periphrastic formula, the poet is deflated by the "we" that clashes grammatically with the "my", the passion is deflated by the negative superlative, and the protestation of love is deflated by the reductio ad theorem. As Warren Ramsey has correctly observed, the geometrical theorem has deeper implications than mere deflation; it is one of the symbols of Laforgue's sense of fatality: "The speaker of the poem is, among other things, telling the lady that what will be is bound to be."[47] But this sense of fatality is rendered in terms of self-parody. As with Corbière, the tone established is one of self-pity tempered by self-mockery. Pierrot's fear of overrating and overstating his love is clownishly squeamish; when addressing his Beloved he will replace romantic hyperbole by its more ridiculous opposite: the fear of expressing his emotion at all.

Pierrot's irony, his bitter smile, is not simply the result of a fear of overstatement or disillusionment. His emotions are constantly upended because they must compete with conflicting ones. In other words, the poet's contradictory impulses neutralize each other. The dissociation of sensibility, which so greatly impressed the younger Eliot, is expressed in a unique ironic style. In a typical poem of Laforgue there will be a conflicting counterpoint between theme and mood; or there will be a sudden reversal of sentiments; or the direct expression of a feeling will suddenly yield to a deflationary "objective correlative" of the feeling; or a deeply felt emotion will be controlled, chastened or canceled by an anti-climactic detail, or, as two recent critics have nicely put it, since the poet's difficulty seems insoluble, the issue will suddenly be suspended, the problem shelved.[48]

A muted form of the romantic irony refurbished by Laforgue will be offered by the Ecole Fantaisiste of the twentieth century: Paul-Jean Toulet, Francis Carco and Jean-Marc Bernard, among others. These poets will constantly oscillate between romantic sentimentality and enthusiasm on the one hand and bitter-sweet cynicism and distrust of lyricism on the other. Like Laforgue's Pierrot they will love without believing in love, hope while realizing there is no hope and generally look at themselves with ironic detachment.

* * *

In one compares the proud, aristocratic René to the heroes of contemporary fiction and drama, the differences at first glance may seem greater than the similarities, the main difference being that the modern sensibility has taken a self-deprecatory turn. This shift in sensibility did not arise spontaneously sometime around the turn of this century; it started with the playful-painful paradoxes and self-inflicted irony of the romantics. There is a direct line of descent from René to Lorenzaccio and Musset's black sheep, from the latter to the decadent hero of the fin de siècle, and from these to the contemporary anti-hero. The chief link between Musset's heroes and latter-day "heroes" is romantic irony. As I said a moment ago, this irony changed as it progressed through the nineteenth and twentieth centuries, mainly in the direction of increased shrillness. It develops into the demonic laughter of Baudelaire and Lautréamont, the "black humor" of Charles Cros, the "yellow" laughter of Corbière and Laforgue, the perverse laughter of the Decadents; the bitter-sweet laughter of the poètes fantaisistes; it is the predecessor of the modern tragic farce and the anti-hero, of the unreliable and imperceptive narrator in contemporary fiction, the sad clown is contemporary painting, the

Satie-like autoparody in contemporary music; it is also, as Morton Gurewitch has said, a prelude to the Absurd. In terms of the modern literary hero and modern tonality, I believe it is the chief legacy of romanticism.

chapter six

THE DECADENT HERO

In his good book on The Hero in French Decadent Literature
George Ross Ridge acknowledges the direct line of descent
between the decadent hero and the romantic hero but sees
the former basically as an extension of a single type: "The
decadent is the scion of the romantic dandy. As a matter
of fact, this is almost his exclusive lineage directly from
romanticism. He shares little with other types of romantic
hero." [1] In reality the decadent hero shares much with the
romantic hero, and in this chapter will be concerned with
establishing his many romantic connections.

A good place to start looking for links between the
romantic hero and the decadent hero is an important article
by A. Boutet de Monvel: "Postérité du Héros Romantique."
The author speaks first of the "profound continuity" that
extends from the Jeunes-France to the Surrealists ("la continuité
du Mal du Siècle") and then examines some decadent heroes
he considers to be direct descendents of the romantic hero,
especially those of Barbey d'Aurevilly, Lautréamont, Villiers
de l'Isle-Adam and Laforgue. Here is what he says about
Axel: "Le héros. . .avec sa carrure de tueur de loup, son
aisance hautaine. . .est lui aussi, comme d'ailleurs les autres
figures héroïques de Villiers, de la race byronienne des
forts, hantés par le désir de posséder un monde qu'ils
méprisent." [2] Of Les Chants de Maldoror he states: "Le Roman-
tism y est à la fois présent et renié. Héritier légitime,
il l'est assurément; paré lui aussi de toutes les défroques
d'antan" (p. 141). He goes on to say that with Maldoror
we witness a "secularization of the mal romantique": at
the beginning of the century spleen and the ideal were linked
to the religious perspective of the lost paradise (Chateaubriand,

Lamartine, Vigny). Maldoror abhors the human condition even more violently than the romantic hero, but rather than dreaming passively of escape (through revery) he attempts actively to escape through his multiple metamorphoses. "Ainsi donc, Maldoror occupe une place essentielle dans notre généalogie. Il y figure comme un dieu ou un monstre à deux têtes, accomplissant, sous les espèces traditionnelles du héros satanique, une mue intérieure qui dénonce le passé tout en en restant solidaire. En même temps, dans sa violence, il porte les revendications romantiques à leur extrême degré" (p. 142). On Laforgue: "Lui aussi veut laïciser le mal du siècle, en ne gardant des anciens thèmes d'évasion que ceux qui n'ont pas besoin de recourir à d'autres cieux: l'appel au néant, où les excès de la conscience et de la sensibilité trouveraient un apaisement . . . la nostalgie de la pureté, qui, ici encore, sous l'influence de la philosophie allemande, trouve chez Laforgue une expression renouvelée dans l'appel à l'inconscient, à la spontanéité primitive retrouvée dans la sensibilité et dans l'art" (p. 142). Of course, the secularization of the mal du siècle was actually accomplished early in the century.

Laforgue's most important incarnation of the mal du siècle is his Hamlet, a hero who was adopted by the romantics but whom Laforgue subjects to romantic irony: he reduces him to a decadent dandy. "Dérision du héros; mais il porte toujours les mêmes hantises, exaspérees sous la caricature. Nous voici loin cependant du déclamateur échevelé du début du siècle. Ce crypto-romantique de l'époque décadente s'est déguisé en dandy . . . un dandy maladif aux gestes étroits; cynique et vulnérable" (p. 143). But as de Monvel has already indicated, and as I shall attempt to show in more detail in the pages that follow, it is much more than mere dandyism that links the fin de siècle decadent to the romantic hero.

Almost every psychological trait of the decadent hero can be traced back to the romantic hero. Like the latter, the decadent tends to be introverted, solitary, misanthropic, melancholy and hypersensitive. He is often a pariah, and often by his own choice. The decadent hero feels surrounded by philistines; so did the romantic hero. Like the latter, the decadent is blasé and jaded and can be stimulated only by the extraordinary and the excessive. More importantly, there is a definite link between decadent world-weariness and romantic Weltschmerz. Romantic melancholy will take on many different forms in decadent literature. It may reveal itself in apathy or passiveness, or, at the other extreme, in very active perversity and perversion. Des Esseintes will experience both extremes. The original romantic hero felt that the world had nothing to offer him; he stood above its meanness and mediocrity. The decadent--in a tremendous shift of emphasis--feels caught up himself in the world's degeneracy and decay, much like the heroes of Musset. From the point of view of the history of the modern sensibility, the most significant word in Verlaine's famous line

> Je suis l'Empire à la fin de la décadence.

--is the first one. What sets the decadent apart from other men is his awareness of decadence (his own as well as that of the world at large) and his disconcerting actions, which are based upon that awareness. But this self-consciousness, which Arthur Symons correctly lists as an essential trait of the Decadence, is the very trait that George Ross Ridge considers to be the defining characteristic of the romantic hero. It is this self-conscious cultivation of depravity and perversity that distinguishes the true decadent from the degenerate heroes of Zola, whose pathology is involuntary.

There are many affinities between the prototypes of the romantic and the decadent hero: René and Des Esseintes. Both begin their adventure with the same spiritual itinerary, searching in vain for kindred spirits. Both quickly weary of everything and everyone around them and finally escape

into solitude, idleness and revery. Both go first to a Parisian
suburb. Both are momentarily tempted by the monastic life,
both reject it. Their hypersensitive and demanding natures
make them a prey to ennui and the death-wish. Des Esseintes
admits his lack of physical courage to commit suicide; René
rationalizes it. Des Esseintes's dandyism was merely a brief
phase during which he tried to cure ennui with eccentricity.
As Huysmans explicitly tells us, the phase died a natural
death after which the hero could look only with self-contempt
upon those "puerile" and "out of date" displays. He then
arranges a house whose rich and rare appointments are suited
to his peculiar tastes but only for his own gratification
and "no longer" to startle other people. The dandy performs
for the Other, Des Esseintes for himself. As with René,
the Other no longer interests him.

Decadent ennui is directly descended from Baudelairian
ennui, which in turn is directly descended from romantic
ennui, although here again there is a momentous shift in
emphasis. Romantic ennui was a sign of the hero's superiority,
his disgust with the quotidian, the daily round and trivial
routine. Baudelairian ennui is a sign of inner decadence
--spiritual apathy.

> Il ferait volontiers de la terre un débris,
> Et dans un bâillement avalerait le monde.

Mallarmé caught the same mood with the same image:

> Car j'y veux, puisqu'enfin ma cervelle, vidée
> Comme le pot de fard, gisant au pied d'un mur,
> N'a plus l'art d'attifer la sanglotante idée,
> Lugubrement bâiller vers un trépas obscur.

Romantic ennui contained already the germ of spiritual torpor:
although one of its principal causes was la hantise de l'absolu,
another was an often simultaneous feeling of the impossibility
of transcendence. Perhaps there is no better single way of
measuring the shifts in sensibility in nineteenth century
France than in studying these semantic shifts in the word

ennui. The romantic mal du siècle continues throughout the
century, but with a significant permutations, until it becomes
what a number of critic and historians, after Paul Bourget,
have called le mal de fin de siècle. It was a prophetic
label, perhaps a self-fulfilling prophecy.

Ridge declares that, unlike the romantic hero, the decadent
is "not really a man of fate, someone emprisoned in a social
and cosmic context, destroying either himself and/or others
as he writhes in anguish."[3] But Ridge himself has already
portrayed the decadent as "emprisoned" in his social context
by philistines and barbarians. The decadent is a man of
fate in a cosmic context as well, fate taking the form of
an organic or cyclical view of history. Civilizations are
born, they grow to maturity, they reach a peak, they decline
and they fall. The decadent tells us that we are in the
next to last stage of our cycle and that the final stage
of entropy is both inevitable and imminent.

Ridge's assertion that the decadent hero is unrelated
to the "fatal hero" of romanticism, is countered by A. E.
Carter, who sees three phases in the evolution of the decadent
movement.

> The first is the late Romantic phase. . .when the moody,
> introspective and fatal hero of 1830 adopts the cult of the
> artificial and the abnormal; then the Naturalist phase, marked
> by the influence of psychopathology, which leads to an interpre-
> tation of decadence in terms of nervous disease; finally the
> fin de siècle phase, when there is a return to the monstrous
> characters of late Romanticism.
> The cult of artificiality begins in the perversion of
> a Romantic legend, and decadent sensibility in the perversion
> of a Romantic type. Or rather, of two Romantic types, the
> languid, receptive character (Saint-Preux, René, Werther)
> and the dynamic "fatal man," who starts in the Don Juan tradition
> as the wicked Lord, borrows metaphysical lights from a variety
> of sources (including Milton's Satan) and runs lushly to seed
> in the melodramas of Byron, Hugo and Dumas.[4]

There is a "fatal" connection between heroes like the Gilles
de Rais of Huysmans's Là-bas ("Il ne pouvait plus toucher
à rien, sans le gâter") and Hernani ("Malheur à tout ce qui

m'entoure.") Elsewhere (p. 109) Carter submits that one can trace a line that runs without a break from the Don Juan type through the fatal man and the dandy to the decadent hero, to Gide's Prometheus, down to the existentialist hero and the mauvais garçons of Genet. That line will be traced in some detail in the final chapters.

Ridge feels that the decadent is basically different from the romantic hero in not being a rebel, but there is throughout the whole of decadent literature a definite moral rebellion, a delight in the perverse. Even during their most frivolous and farcical moments, when they were posing as Fumistes, Hirsutes, Hydropaths, Jemenfoutistes--and what have you--the decadents were launching a frontal attack upon bourgeois morality. Even the esthete Des Esseintes is a rebel of sorts. He flouts Nature and attacks Society. The very title, A rebours--against the grain--indicates such a rebellion. And Des Esseintes is related to the romantic outlaw by the criminal act of deliberately corrupting a young boy in order to create "an enemy the more for the odious society that wrings so heavy a ransom from us all." Here again, the shift in emphasis is significant. The romantic hero was a generous outlaw; the decadent has no pretentions to virtue. Note also that the many Satanic figures of decadent literature are variants of that untamed Rebel so admired by the romantics.

Ridge's least tenable assertion is that the decadent, unlike the romantic hero, is not a pathological hero (p. 49). But curiously enough, in another book Ridge himself asserts the contrary and acknowledges that the romantic hero fathered the decadent hero precisely because of his pathological tendencies: "Strong currents of pathology run through the romantic movement. . . . Consider Chateaubriand striking his pose, Gérard de Nerval dragging a lobster down the street, Baudelaire with his algolagnia, Barbey with his diabolical dandies, Hugo with his ouija boards; the list is limitless.

It is certainly not by chance that the Romantic hero sires the decadent hero."[5] If the term "decadent" has any usefulness in literary history, it is in conveying, both denotatively and connotatively, the notion of pathology. The decadent is the very incarnation of "modern man's morbid sensitiveness," as Des Esseintes says of the painter Moreau; he is the very symbol of civilization's decay, the emblem of its unhealth. François Livi says of the hero of A rebours: "Jean Des Esseintes est un névrosé qui cultive sa maladie."[6] This cultivation of neurosis is the chief literary method of the Decadence. It becomes an instrument of psychic exploration, even a badge of superiority. "Le dérangement nerveux," says Livi, "est désormais une expérience dont l'élite ne saurait se passer. . . . La névrose devient l'apanage des esprits supérieurs."[7] Des Esseintes may not be "sick" in a technical sense, but his morbid love of the pathological is itself pathological. He gives up active perversion in his retreat at Fontenay-aux-Roses, experiencing it now vicariously in all the morbid subjects treated by his favorite writers and painters. But this vicarious perversion produces no catharsis, only a stimulus to explore more and more novel perversities.

Again, it is curious that Ridge himself, like Mario Praz, has very thoroughly documented the pathological side of decadent heroes: their sadism, satanism, Schadenfreude, vampirism, masochism, coprophilia, necrophilia, profanation, blasphemy, abulia, sodomy, and incest. In a significant reversal of roles, the man--habitually effete and epicene--is now passive and dominated by the woman. The latter will take many forms: she may be a nymphomaniac, even a rapist; a witch or vampire; a transvestite or hermaphrodite, one of Walter Pater's "frail androgynous beings"; she is frequently frigid, frequently the opposite--either hypo- or hypersexual, never in between. Whatever specific shape the decadent heroine takes, she is always the incarnation of evil, a theme vividly expressed in the paintings of Gustave Moreau and Félicien

Rops. Female homosexuality, explored by Baudelaire and Verlaine,
as well as by a host of lesser decadents, may no longer be
classified by the American Psychiatric Association as pathological, but it was used by the decadents as a symbol of what
Spengler has called the sterility of modern civilized man.
Sterility is the major theme of the Decadence. It may take
the form of artistic impotence as in Mallarmé or in sterile
contemplation as in Des Esseintes or in sexual sterility
as found everywhere in decadent literature from the "stérile
volupté" of Baudelaire's lesbians to Mallarmé's Hérodias:
("J'aime l'horreur d'être vierge"). Both the decadent spirit
and the decadent style attest to the triumph of the pathological.
A new sense of beauty develops--actually an exacerbation
of the romantic esthetic--anticipating the convulsive beauty
of the surrealists, based on the loveliness of terror, the
fascination with horror, the attractiveness of evil, the
emergeance of the baser instincts, or in Freudian terms the
success of the id breaking through the censor and revealing
the repressed content of dreams.

Most of the major themes of decadent literature are
continuations of romantic ones. The spoiled relations between
the sexes had already been treated by Musset, hermaphroditism
by Balzac, vampirism by Nodier and Mérimée. The perverse
pleasure in destruction had already appeared in the Byronic
hero. The mixture of corruption and religiosity had already
been present in René and Amaury. The preference of art to
nature, the craving for the impossible (one of the most important
themes of the Decadence, inspired largely by the biography
and legend of Nero and Caligula), the attempt to counter
satiety with sadism, the tendency toward sexual inversion
and tranvestism--all this had appeared with a single late
romantic hero: d'Albert of Mademoiselle de Maupin, one of
the books that most marked Huysmans, Péladan and other decadents.
The hero of Gautier's Fortunio (1837) clearly anticipates
Des Esseintes, leading as he does a totally artificial existence
in a windowless home whose courtyard is inclosed in glass

and houses lush, bizarre tropical plants. The abuse of drugs, another important theme (and activity) of the decadents, is, as Baudelaire had noted, a depravation of the romantic passion for infinity and expansion of the ego. By his own admission, Lautréamont's song of evil was inspired in part by Mickiewicz, Byron, Southey and Musset. Praz would add another romantic to the list: Pétrus Borel, whose Contes immoraux also anticipate the Contes cruels of Villiers de l'Isle-Adam. Long before the decadents, lesbianism had been explored by Gautier and George Sand; long before naturalism, which in content at least can be considered as part of decadent literature in its broader sense, Hugo had suggested to his fellow writers that everything is a legitimate subject for art, that nothing is any longer tabou. The decadent fascination for the horrible, the disgusting as well as the wild and exotic has obvious roots in romantic literature.

The single most important progenitor of the decadent movement is none other than Chateaubriand himself. This may come as a surprise, and the Enchanter himself would deny the paternity. But we have it on the authority of the great critic of the decadent period, Remy de Gourmont, who said of Chateaubriand: "[Il] plane invisible sur toute notre littérature."[8] Chateaubriand had presented a witch-figure in Les Martyrs; the theme of incest is descretely present in both Atala and Les Natchez; the mingling of incest and sacrilege is found in René; sadism is an important theme of Les Natchez despite the often orthodox religiosity. Says Mario Praz: "Sadism and Catholicism, in French Decadent Literature, become the two poles between which the souls of the neurotic and sensual writers oscillate, and which can definitely be traced back to that 'épicurien à l'imagination catholique'--Chateaubriand."[9] Anatole France, speaking of Villiers de l'Isle-Adam, offers further corroborative evidence: "Il était de cette famille de néo-catholiques littéraires dont Chateaubriand est le père commun, et qui a produit Barbey d'Aurevilly, Baudelaire, et plus récemment, M. Joséphin Péladan. Ceux-là ont goûté par-dessus tout dans la religion les charmes du péché, la grandeur du sacrilège, et leur sensualisme a caressé les dogmes qui ajoutaient aux voluptés la suprême volupté de se perdre."[10] Praz adds other illustrious practitioners of "confused Christianity" to the list: Huysmans (Des Esseintes's admiration of the Church as the preserver of art is an echo of Le Génie du christianisme), Barrès, Léon-Bloy and, more recently, Montherlant. One might add that the fictional characters of Mauriac, Bernanos and Julien Green prolong the believer's facination with the charms of sin well into the twentieth century. It has been said that no one has cast a longer shadow on modern French literature than the bard of Brittany. It was not just his prestigious style nor his apparent orthodoxy that lengthened the shadow to the very end of his century and into our own. It was the thinly veiled tension between those two magnetic poles: mysticism and satanism.

We should add two final links to the chain binding romanticism and the Decadence. One is a question of style, the other of tone. Havelock Ellis has pointed out that a decadent style is only such in relation to a classic style and that it is usually the mark of an era of individualism. The greatest explosion of individualism in literature since the sixteenth century was of course the romantic period. The overripe side of decadent style--the complicated eccentricities, the contorted syntax, the strange vocabulary, the outlandish similes and remote analogies, the sustained and strained metaphors, the strident epithets and redundant decoration --all these stylistic features are simply exaggerations of romantic style.

Mario Praz has said this of decadent tonality: "A comic-heroic treatment . . . of the subject matter . . . constitutes, more or less, the common background of the whole of Decadent literature."[11] We find this half-serious, half-humorous tone in writers such as Laforgue, Péladan, Gourmont as well as that obstreperous English decadent, Oscar Wilde, a tone that deflates to some degree the importance of the very work in progress. Any work that does not take itself with complete seriousness as a work of art is informed by romantic irony. Des Esseintes himself was fond of a gruesome variant of romantic irony; he found it in the grim humor, the savage raillery, the cruel jeering and bitter irony of works like Corbière's Les Amours jaunes, Villier's Contes cruels and Charles Cros' La Science de l'amour. This sadistic or "decadent irony" grew out of the gentler romantic irony and will grow into the humour noir of the twentieth century. It no longer reflects a basically comic sense of life: we are approaching the realm of the Absurd.

chapter seven

NEO-ROMANTIC HEROES IN THE TWENTIETH CENTURY

I. The Romantic Legacy

Jacques Barzun has noted that romanticism, in the second
half of the nineteenth century, did not die out: it branched
out.[1] Realism, naturalism, symbolism and the Decadence--
all these movements were implicit in the romantic movement,
and all have continued into this century, either in their
original or in modified form. In 1907 the Revue Néo-Romantique
proclaimed: "Une renaissance du romantisme se prépare.
La littérature du XXe siècle continuera celle du XIXe."[2]
In 1924 Marcel Arland declared that the literature of his
time was still informed principally by the mal du siècle.[3]
In 1930 Edmond Sée submitted that if a participant in the
battle of Hernani had survived until that year, he could
have issued a Zola-like telegram: "Romantisme pas
mort . . . Pièces suivent."[4] In the June, 1939 issue of
the Mercure de France appeared two manifestoes: "Vers un
Romantisme intégral," and "Vers un Romantisme nouveau." In
1948, Julien Benda, bemoaning the fact, corroborated the
persistence of romanticism: "Une de nos thèses est que le
véritable romantisme date en France de la fin du XIXe siècle,
où il fait son entrée sous l'archet littéraire de Barrès
et philosophique de Bergson; on ne trouve rien chez un Chateaubriand, un Victor Hugo, un Lamartine, voire un Baudelaire
ou un Leconte de Lisle, d'analogue, fût-ce du plus loin,
au mépris d'un Barrès pour l'intelligence ("cette petite
chose à la surface de notre être!").[5] Benda finds the deepest
hiatus separating modern and ancient philosophy in the fact
that for the ancients the highest mode of being was immutability,
whereas for the moderns (the romantics) it is found in movement

and change. Modern romantic ethics takes its cue, he says, from the Gidian disponibilité, an openness to all moral possibilities, romantic esthetics from Gide's laudation of mobile, fluctuating emotions ("Mon émotion, sitôt fixée, n'est plus vivante"). The romantic impetus in modern painting and poetry is found in their intentional ambiguity, which creates a mobility of subject matter; in music it is found in the dissolution of the frontiers between major and minor keys and in sustained and unresolved dissonance; in the philosophy of history and of science, the romantic stance is found in the never-ending movement of the Hegelian dialectic; modern fiction from Proust onwards presents characters who evolve not according to some fixed essence but through their "libre dynamisme" (p. 76)--it is through their becoming that they choose their being. Misinterpreting Einsteinian relativity, he claims, modern writers from Gide to Sartre proclaim that Truth is Subjectivity, and he places existentialism at the very summit of this neo-romanticism.

In 1951 La Nef put out a special issue devoted to the contemporary mal du siècle. In 1952 Armand Hoog wrote: "Je me convaincs, devant la pensée du vingtième siècle, que les valeurs les plus importantes du romantisme y demeurent."[6] In 1954 Henri Peyre noted that the phrase le mal du demi-siècle had recently been coined to characterize the literature of the 50's.[7] In the same year M. Paribatra declared unequivocally: "La littérature contemporaine tout entière est romantique. De la fin du XVIIIe siècle, où il est né, jusqu'à nos jours, le romantisme suit un cours ininterrompu."[8] This romantic continuum was noted as early as 1908 by E. Seillière; it was analyzed by Albert Béguin in 1939, in 1959 by Germain Mason, who speaks of twentieth-century French literature as a whole as a "new-romanticism,"[9] in 1967 by Robert Emmet Jones (in The Alienated Hero in Modern French Drama), who declares that the French theater of this century is a continuation of the romantic drama and in 1971 by R.-M. Albérès, who claims that French literature of the first half of this century is not only a second romanticism but "our true romanticism." [10]   In 1977, thirteen distinguished scholars argued convincingly that not only modern French writers but Western writers in general have preserved much more than they have rejected from their romantic heritage (Romantic and Modern: Revaluations of Literary Tradition, edited by George Bernstein). In 1979 Gerald Graff (Literature Against Itself, especially chapter 2) claimed that the entire "postmodernist" literature of the 1950's, 60's, and 70's is a continuation of romantic premises. It is very possible that literary historians a century or two hence may lump the last two centuries together as "the Romantic Age." Such an assessment may be premature at this point, but it is already being made, and the evidence continues to come in, copiously.

Most of the major themes of twentieth century literature are romantic ones: despair and the denunciation of existence, solitude and the lack of communication, the search for sincerity and authenticity, freedom (from the gratuitous freedom of Gide to the committed freedom of Sartre), the writer as prophet and spokesman of mankind, the exceptional individual and hero, the alienated hero, the candid hero, the rebel and various types of anti-hero: the passive hero, the hero as outlaw and criminal, even the hero as coward and clown.

Many contemporary works camouflage a romantic theme with an "anti-romantic" tonality. Here for instance is Céline's description of the death-wish: "Tout notre malheur vient de ce qu'il nous faut demeurer Jean, Pierre ou Gaston coûte que coûte pendant toutes sortes d'années. Ce corps à nous, traversé de molécules agitées et banales, tout le temps se révolte contre cette force odieuse de durer. Elles veulent aller se perdre, nos molécules, au plus vite, parmi l'univers, ces mignonnes." In actual fact, it not just the theme here but the very tonality itself that is romantic: this jocular treatment of a profound anguish partakes of romantic irony.

The romantic ironist laughs bitterly at what he respects or fears most.

The romantic mythology lives on: for some it is the religion of history, for others it is some utopian social scheme; for many it is the myth of the superior individual, for even more it is the myth of rebellion or revolt.

I have just shown that a significant consensus has formed regarding the decisive influence of romanticism upon French literature in this century. The pages that follow will be confined to an analysis of a single aspect of this rich legacy, that bequeathed by the romantic hero.

* * *

The romantic hero was, in part, a reflection of political and historical instability. It is not surprising, then, that his twentieth-century heirs have been so numerous. This century has been an age of calamity and institutionalized violence. Wars and threats of wars, revolutions, brutally repressive political regimes--fascist, Nazi, communist, capitalist, Islamic--economic upheavals, collapse of empires and rapid shifts in centers of power, and a general confusion of values have been the dominant factors of twentieth century life.

Because of its geographical position, its once-important colonial possessions and its position at the very center of Western intellectual life, twentieth-century France has felt the shock of historical events more than any other country perhaps. To point up the analogy between the upheavals attendant upon the French Revolution and the upheavals experienced by twentieth-century France, it might be well to recall a few facts. In the First World War, 1,654,000 young Frenchmen were killed or missing in action. 2,888,000 were wounded, many of them permanently. It must be remembered that these four million men were from the most vigorous part of the population: its youth and its intellectual élite. Half of the school teachers, one third of the lawyers, two thousand writers and journalists who went to war never came back.[11] Of those young men who did return more than a million were crippled. Germaine Brée has spoken of the impact of the war upon the renascent romanticism of the twenties: "Le repliement sur soi ou l'anarchisme alimente un romantisme diffus qui colore l'époque."[12] The crise de l'élite or "brain drain" contributed greatly to the lack of political and social stability of the entre-deux-guerres. Also, the material damage, especially to France's northern industrial centers, and the financial crisis of the early thirties were largely responsible for the defensive-defeatist mentality that led to France's downfall in 1940.

The Second World War had an even more devastating effect upon the collective French sensibility. France lost 666,000 young men--in a very short time--out of a population of 40,000,000. When the armistice was signed, 2,550,000 Frenchmen were in Germany, either in prisoner of war camps or civilian concentration camps. France now knew the humiliation of invasion, defeat, occupation, deportations, the shame of defeatism, collaboration and the black market. A loss of international prestige was the price France had to pay for military defeat, the lost of its Colonial Empire and the political instability of the Fourth Republic.

In the twentieth century the very rhythm of life changed radically with the advent of the automobile, the airplane and the telephone. The acceleration of history was accompanied by the erosion of traditional values. Radio, then television, produced new generations of young people who could hear and see history being made right before them--and before being censored and interpreted by their elders, as Margaret Mead has noted. The Age of Technology eventually touched the lives of everyone. Relationships between man and his products

and between man and his associates became increasingly ephemeral.
It was not just a question of accelerating history but of
"future shock." Civilization seemed centerless and the young
were confronted with a plethora of experiences and conflicting
life styles. The time was more than ripe for producing an
updated version of the _puer_ _senex_. The new _puer_ _senex_ not
only goes through experience with the lightening speed of
a romantic hero, he has a concrete rather than a vague sense
of fatality. His world is hanging together by a thread,
a tenuous balance of Terror. He is frequently told that
a third world war is inevitable, given man's history, and
that the Fourth World War will be fought with rocks, bows
and arrows.

* * *

II. Neo-romantic Heroes in Fiction

Writing at mid-century in his Portrait de notre héros, R.-M. Albérès outlines the chief characteristics of the representative hero of contemporary French fiction; they can be summarized as follows:

1. Solitude: the contemporary hero avoids strong emotional ties with others. He feels himself to be a stranger not only among other people but in the universe, "un étranger devant sa destinée."

2. He is a wanderer, an unstable déraciné. "Comme le héros romantique, notre héros risque de devenir the wandering outlaw of his own dark mind."[13]

3. Although usually something of a ladies' man, he is devoid of the slightest trace of sentimentality. He is strictly honest in his dealings with women and does not use the word "love" loosely. But he also exhibits a tendency toward sadism.

4. He is cynical toward traditional and "ultimate" values.

5. Action is his chief remedy for ennui.

6. He is filled with a despair born of hyperlucidity. He is a puer senex in the romantic sense: "la lucidité vient trop tôt chez lui."

7. He does not dominate events, he endures them. He struggles and suffers in a violent world.

8. He is not above doing "evil," of displaying fear, of appearing egocentric. Authenticity and sincerity are his hall marks, not idealism, purity or perfection.

9. His every thought and action are informed by a tragic sense of life.

10. In another book, La Révolte des écrivains d'aujourd'hui Albérès adds another trait: Promethean Revolt--which he studies in writers such as Bernanos, Malraux, Camus, Aragon, Anouilh and Sartre.

Stating that this type of hero is the product of a highly "personal" novel and a littérature d'évasion, Albérès concludes:

"Peut-être notre héros a-t-il trop tendance à se détacher de son evironnement. La lucidité vient trop tôt chez lui, il ramène trop vite ses propres problèmes à lui seul, il reste autocrate et égoïste dans son aventure. Nul plus que le héros français n'est plus emmuré en lui-même. Dans ce petit cercle de lumière livide où se joue la tragédie du roman, un homme seul, sans amis, sans compagnons, sans amour."[14]

If Albérès' summary (and my summary of his summary) is accurate, it is clear that the romantic hero did not die with the romantic period and was still with us as late as the 1940's. Among the heroes studied by Albérès are Gille, Costals, Garine, Roquentin and Meursault (the last two are analyzed as neo-romantic heroes by René Girard in Mensonge romantique et vérité romanesque)--one could add, among others, Montherlant's Alban de Bricoule, Gracq's Allan (Le Beau ténébreux) and the pilot-heroes of St. Exupéry. If these neo-romantic heroes are somewhat less verbose, less prone to self-pity, more active and virile than their forebears, they still bear a striking family resemblance to them. They are not carbon copies of earlier romantic heroes but revealing palimpsests: the traces of the original are everywhere apparent.

Albérès finds these new heroes vastly superior to the original romantic hero whom he dismisses with a cliché of late nineteenth-century criticism: that he is a poseur. We know better now. We know that there is no posing in Adolphe or Obermann, in Lorenzaccio or Rolla, in the real Julien Sorel or even in René atop Aetna. On the contrary, it is in such heroes that contemporary "authenticity" began. Without fully realizing it, Albérès has been analyzing a good number of the romantic hero's legitimate heirs, that is, where he sees a superseding, I see a profound continuation.

The work of writers like Malraux, Saint-Exupéry, Gracq and Drieu la Rochelle is romantic in several respects. It is basically autobiographical: the heroes are stylized self-portraits of their creators, much as René was for Chateaubriand.

Their work is "escapist"--in the sense of a romantic turning away from banal and boring existence but <u>not</u> necessarily from responsibilities or matters of import. More importantly, the psychological makeup of many of their protagonists reveals a basic kinship with the romantic hero. I shall examine some of these latter-day romantics now, presenting a few exemplary figures rather than a broad survey. We shall be looking at some of the early heroes of Malraux and then at Drieu La Rochelle's Gille, who is an heir of both the romantic hero and the decadent hero and will thus serve as a transitional figure leading to the heroes of the next chapter.

* * *

Malraux's Early Heroes

La Voie royale is probably Malraux's earliest novel although it was published after Les Conquérants (1928). It is an uneven work, awkwardly constructed in parts, which is no doubt why Malraux excluded it from the Pléiade edition of his novels. Clearly romantic in conception, La Voie royale is an exotic novel of adventure, to a certain degree, even, a "Gothic" thriller, largely autobiographical and containing several lush, poetic descriptions of the wilderness worthy of Chateaubriand. René, disgusted with European society, went West; Malraux's adventurers go to the Far East.

The two heroes of the novel, the Dane, Perken, and Claude Vannec, are typical romantic "loners," having no family or social ties. Solitude in fact is the first striking trait of all Malraux's heroes: "Le premier trait de l'homme de Malraux est d'être seul. C'est que d'abord il a appris à l'être, il s'est défait de toutes les illusions, de tout le factice dont l'homme se masque sa solitude. Il a quitté la maison familiale, la vie facile, la patrie familière."[15] Perken and Vannec also perpetuate the romantic myth of the exceptional individual. Here, heroism takes the form of heroics and of great physical courage. And they share with the romantic hero an immense egoism and pride, the latter in their tremendous strength of will.

They are also related to the Fatal Hero and the Self-Conscious Hero. Both are engaged in a bitter struggle against their environment (here, hostile Nature) and are equally conscious of their impending doom (the inevitability and pointlessness of Death). Joseph Frank has noted that Malraux's heroes "were never simply engaged in a battle against a particular social or economic injustice; they were always somehow struggling against the limitations of life itself and the humiliations of destiny." [16] Self-consciousness and a sense of fatality go hand in hand in all Malraux's novels, man being constantly depicted as the only animal who knows he is going to die. Nietzsche had said that the hero of the future will be a man of tragic awareness. Malraux's heroes fulfill the prophecy, but their hantise de l'absurde, if seen in historical perspective, is in reality a new and more explicit version of the romantic hero's vague (i.e., tactful) hantise de l'absolu, his search for a bien inconnu--"unknown" because for him too the skies were empty.

Let me explain myself here with some concrete examples. Early in Adolphe, the hero tells us that the death of an elderly friend whom he greatly admired has filled him with a feeling of "uncertainty regarding human destiny" and with total "indifference" toward human life. The indifference extends even to his attitude toward himself: "tout en ne m'intéressant qu'à moi, je m'intéressais faiblement à moi-même." This total indifference caused by the fact of death is an early statement of the Absurd. An even earlier statement was made by Obermann: "Venir, s'élever, faire grand bruit, s'inquiéter de tout, mesurer l'orbite des comètes, et, après quelque jours, se coucher sous l'herbe d'un cimetière; cela me semble assez burlesque pour être vu jusqu'au bout." Obermann speaks of life as "burlesque"; Musset's Fantasio speaks of it as a "calembour"; Lorenzaccio and Gautier's d'Albert call it "comique"; Adolphe's systematic indifference announces that of Meursault. Romantic heroes made the same connection between death and the Absurd as did Malraux, Sartre and Camus. For Malraux, the absurd is not only the death of God but also the death of Man. As Cecil Jenkins explains in his essay on "Malraux the Romantic," the loss of the soul means the loss of identity, and so modern man is now forced to define himself "vertically" in terms of the one remaining absolute: death.[17]

Malraux's second novel, Les Conquérants, was also largely informed by the "Gothic" and exotic. So much so that the author felt the need to excise much of this romantic material in the 1949 edition. Much of it still remains. And the hero, Pierre Garin, called Garine, is still a genuine heir of the romantic hero. For one thing, he is a projection of the author himself (or as the author likes to see himself): "un type de héros en qui s'unissent l'aptitude à l'action, la culture et la lucidité."[18] Garine begins his career with the romantic disgust for ordinary life. He belongs, as Gérard tells the narrator, to those people "qui n'ont jamais pu accepter la vie sociale, qui ont beaucoup demandé à l'exis- tence."[19] He is an anti-social, misanthropic individualist.

> Je ne tiens pas la société pour mauvaise, pour susceptible d'être améliorée; je la tiens pour absurde. C'est bien autre chose . . . Qu'on la transforme, cette société ne m'intéresse pas . . . Je suis a-social comme je suis athée, et de la même façon. (p. 46)

> Je n'aime pas les hommes. Je n'aime pas même les pauvres gens, le peuple, ceux en somme pour qui je vais combattre . . . Ce qui est bien certain, c'est que je n'ai qu'un dégoût haineux pour la bourgeoisie dont je sors. Mais quant aux autres, je sais bien qu'ils deviendraient abjects, dès que nous aurions triomphé ensemble . . . Nous avons en commun notre lutte. (p. 51)

Unlike Malraux's later heroes, Garine finds in revolutionary action not solidarity but solitude; nor is it a means to social and political justice--the word "justice," he tells us, has no meaning for him. Revolution is principally an expression of the will to power, which is an end in itself.

> De la puissance, il ne souhaitait ni argent, ni considération, ni respect; rien qu'elle-même. (p. 43)

> Mon action me rend aboulique à l'égard de tout ce qui n'est pas elle, à commencer par ses résultats. Si je me suis lié si facilement à la Révolution, c'est que ses résultats sont lointains, et toujours en changement. Au fond, je suis un joueur. Comme tous les joueurs, je ne pense qu'à mon jeu. (p. 143)

Garine bears a close resemblance to Boutros, the communist agitator of Drieu la Rochelle's Une Femme à sa fenêtre. Both men are adventurers rather than idealistic militants. For both, fascism would have been as good an outlet for their energy as communism. Both scorn the Communists they work with as intensely as the capitalists they fight. For Boutros the revolution is simply something which risks death," and that's the only thing I love in the world." Garine could have said the same. He partakes less of the Promethean myth than of the Napoleonic legend: the rugged and ruthless individualist who uses the Revolution to become the Conqueror.

Edmund Wilson has said of the protagonist of Les Conquérants: "Malraux's hero, Garin, has a certain alloy of old-fashioned romanticism. There are moments when he gives the impression of being simply another René or Manfred, somber, tortured, terrifying, a solitary savage rebel, seeking in the revolution what René sought in the American forests, grasping at his bureau of propaganda with the same sort of desperation that Byron had brought to Greece."[20] There are also, I think, some interesting parallels with Julien Sorel. Revolution for Garine, as it would have been for the opportunistic Julien, is the chance to show one's energy and strength

of will, to prove one's freedom. For both, freedom is conceived
largely in negative terms: for Julien it consists in not
being scorned; for Garine in "not being conquered." The
vast scope of their unbelief and their one positive ethical
principle (energy) are identical. But in the end Julien,
with no future ambitions to worry about, becomes less self-
centered and learns to love. He even finds happiness. Garine,
on the other hand, remains a somber figure to the very end.
Even the decisive victory that he helped engineer gives him
no joy. He has lived his life according to romantic standards,
at its highest intensity, and dies as he had lived: a beau
ténébreux.

La Condition humaine (1933) is a metaphysical thriller
set like the first two novels in the exotic East. The lyrical
tone of certain passages and the over-all intensity of the
work make it romantic. Gaëton Picon finds the novel romantic
especially because of its revolutionary bias ("Revolution!
Everything that is not Revolution is worse than it!"), its
taste for the spectacular and the apocalyptic. The loosely-
knit panoramic structure is likewise romantic. Malraux indulges
in what some American critics have called "the fallacy of
imitative form":   the attempt to render a disordered world
by a disorderly book, for example by jerky cadences, rapid
transitions, startling juxtapositions and general dis-
jointedness.

Albérès simply calls this type of style "romantic." The
imagery in La Condition humaine is also romantic. First,
the frequent contrasts between sound and silence, revealing
a romantic love of dramatic antithesis. Then there are the
constant contrasts between light and darkness. The darkness
is often invested with a menacing quality and is symbolic
of man's fate, death. As one critic has noted, this type
of imagery is a development of the pathetic fallacy.

There is no central figure in La Condition humaine,
but all the important characters are related to the romantic

hero. Almost all are foreigners, exiles or expatriates,
and for all the antagonist is Destiny. All are characterized
by extreme self-consciousness and all are engaged in romantic
escapism, which for all of them is an attempt to avoid, transcend
or at least to forget for a time the horror of the human
condition. Most of the characters in the novel attempt to
escape through a Baudelairian paradis artificiel. The contemplative Gisors summarizes the situation:

> --Il faut toujours s'intoxiquer: ce pays
> a l'opium, l'Islam le haschich, l'Occident la
> femme . . . Peut-être l'amour est-il surtout le
> moyen qu'emploie l'Occident pour s'affranchir
> de sa condition d'homme . . . .
> Sous ses paroles, un contre-courant confus
> et caché de figures glissait: Tchen et le meurtre,
> Clappique et sa folie, Katow et la révolution,
> May et l'amour, lui-même et l'opium . . Kyo
> seul, pour lui, résistait à ces domaines.[21]

If Albérès' definition of romanticism as the expression
of an anguish and a freedom is valid, then La Condition humaine
is a romantic novel par excellence. There is more to romanticism, of course, than anguish and freedom, but these themes
are indeed eminently romantic. The word angoisse appears
on nearly every other page. Anguish is the realization of
the fact of death which, for Malraux, is the supreme proof
of the absurdity of life: if a man's life were worth anything,
it would go on. It is also the realization of man's psychological and metaphysical solitude, his inability to establish
genuine and lasting contact with others and with the universe.
Malraux shares Schopenhauer's view that thought can lead
only to unhappiness. Gisors again serves as mouthpiece:
"Tous souffrent, songea-t-il, et chacun souffre parce qu'il
pense. Tout au fond, l'esprit ne pense l'homme que dans
l'éternel, la conscience de la vie ne peut être qu'angoisse"
(p. 400).

When one looks at Malraux's fictional heroes as a group,
one sees certain pathological tendencies of the romantic
hero, especially sadism and the fascination with death. Garine

and Perken torture and kill their victims with obvious relish.
Ferral's erotic imagination likes to dwell on women being
flagellated, humbled or humiliated. An unconscious death-
wish seems to motivate many if not most of Malraux's heroes.
The willing acceptance of death on the part of Hernandez,
Garine, Tchen, Kyo and Vincent Berger comes suspiciously
close to suicide--especially when viewed collectively.

> --Je serai bientot tué.
> N'est-ce pas cela surtout qu'il veut? se
> demandait Gisors. Il n'aspire à aucune gloire,
> à aucun bonheur. Capable de vaincre mais non
> de vivre dans sa victoire, que peut-il appeler,
> sinon la mort? Sans doute veut-il lui donner
> le sens que d'autres donnent à la vie. Mourir
> le plus haut possible. (p. 75)

Pierre de Boisdeffre has noted that Malraux's heroes seem
to be looking for reasons to die: "Ils meurent en contemplant
leur solitude, avec une sorte de délectation amère, demandant
à la mort cette délivrance que Gisors recherche dans l'opium.
Ne meurent-ils pas grisés par cette mort, où ils voient un
moyen d'échapper à eux-mêmes et à leur destin, ne vivent-
ils pas _pour_ cette mort qui transformera leur vie en destin?"[22]

Denis Boak summarizes the romantic psychology of Malraux's

heroes: In the novels . . . the contemptuous rejection
of ordinary life and the refusal to allow any
sense of limitation to affect the challenge to
destiny are equally typical of the Romantic Hero,
dividing his life between grandiose and flamboyant
gestures and metaphysical introspection. Looked
at from a viewpoint radically opposed to Malraux's
own, the whole idea of anti-destin might be viewed
as escapism; and the same might be said of many
other facets of Malraux's work: the exoticism,
obsession with mythomania--the Romantic symptcm
par excellence--and with revolution and rebellion.[23]

Boak's trenchant anti-romanticism and his preference for
the more varied characterization of the traditional novel
make him a rather stern judge of Malraux's fiction. Only
La Condition humaine finds real favor. His view no doubt

needs to be corrected by the more enthusiastic one of Picon, Albérès, Boisdeffre and Mauriac. The latter stated in 1961 that Malraux was the greatest living writer. The truth probably lies somewhere in between the view of Malraux's detractors and his supporters. But Mauriac's further contention that Malraux represents "the arrival of romanticism to power" can hardly be disputed.

* * *

Gille

Posterity has yet to determine the final status of Drieu La Rochelle in the history of French literature, but, as Frédéric Grover has correctly observed, his testimony is indispensable to any historian of the contemporary French sensibility.[24] Drieu is unmistakably a romantic writer, witness his anti-rationalism, his admiration for and production of confessional fiction, his proclaimed disregard for "style" (and at the same time his exuberant, "romantic" handling of it), his concept of the writer as prophet, his quest for the absolute, his death fixation and, indeed, his death. He belonged to that group of young men in the Twenties who were bent on self-destruction, who not only preached suicide but practised what they preached--men like Jacques Rigaut and René Crevel. The suicide of the latter was followed by that of Alain, the hero of Drieu's Le Feu follet and still later, in 1945, by that of Drieu himself ("Le suicide, c'est la ressource des hommes dont le ressort a été rongé par la rouille, par la rouille du quotidien").[25] Claude, the auto-biographical hero of La Comédie de Charleroi, also had the urge to commit suicide and his reasons were romantic ones: melancholy and profound ennui. The first generation of romantics had brooded about not being able to aspire to the military

glory of an earlier era. Claude's generation, too: modern
warfare, he complains, has become too mechanized and dehumanized
to permit of individual glory. Saint-Exupéry had similar
feelings about the development of modern aerial warfare:
well before the Second World War the daring improvisations
and aerial acrobatics of the individualistic, romantic "air
barons" of the First War--colorful men in colorful uniforms
and scarves flying in the breeze--had become a thing of the
past; pilots now had to fly "in formation." A romantic hero,
Claude suffers at having to share his war experience with
the mediocre men around him, officers as well as enlisted
men. His misanthropy, like René's and Manfred's, is universal.

As many critics have noted, the first of Drieu's three
"Gille" novels, L'Homme couvert de femmes (1925), illustrates
the main symptoms of what Marcel Arland had called the year
before "un nouveau mal du siècle." Gille Gambier is a lonely
figure in a hostile world, an "outlaw" with respect to bourgeois
morality and conventional society. His melancholy is decidedly
romantic in nature, at least according to his friend Luc
who compares him implicitly to René: "Il a l'air triste,
comme ça, de loin en loin, mais c'est une tristesse très
vague, dont il s'accommode, qui va avec un bon petit égoisme,
bien organisé."[26] Note too the touch of romantic irony:
the hero, who is treated seriously, is not immune to the
sarcasm of other characters and even that of the narrator.
Gille has the romantic's sense of moral solitude and being
seul de son espèce.

> --Je suis toujours seul.
> --Mais tout le monde, sot.
> --Ah! pas comme moi. (p. 99)

A Don Juan of the romantic school, he is seeking, he tells
us, the perfect woman and is motivated not by sensual but
by "esthetic concupiscence"--an interpretation the reader
has difficulty accepting since Gille seems more sensitive
to the flesh as flesh than as pure form. He excuses his

idleness in terms of the romantic disgust with everyday reality
and the concomitant yearning for the absolute: "Je ne fais
rien, mais qu'on me laisse suspendre à cette seule parole
de vie, à ce hameçon déchirant: 'que ne mérite de vivre
que l'absolu.' Peut-être qu'un absolu se forme en moi, laissez-
moi à mon attente" (p. 154).

The Gille Gambier of Drôle de voyage is now 35, still
the Don Juan "covered with women," and still just as lonely.
Women, he explicitly tells us, are nothing but sex-objects:
"Décidément, les femmes n'existent pas. A quoi bon leur
façonner laborieusement une apparence de solidité semblable
à celle de l'homme? Il vaut mieux les considérer comme des
objets, des fragments de l'univers qui ne vivent que sous
le regard de l'homme." [27] The voyage in the title refers
to his constant wanderings from woman to woman in his futile
search for that perfect one, that "créature tout à fait réussie."
His solitude arises also from his alienation within a materialistic, decadent and moribund society, and his relations
with that society are characterized in romantic terms: he
is once again the "outlaw."

Gille's lack of direction has made of him a rather passive,
docile person. He is eager to please others, and his actions
are frequently dictated by their will and whims. His lack
of ambition (cf. René, Obermann, Adolphe et al) makes his
colleagues at the Quai d'Orsay consider him a failure--a
judgment partly shared by the protagonist and the not-always
admiring author. The latter admits (through his narrator)
that his hero's life is spent in "une songerie qui n'en finissait
pas" coupled with a persistent "bouderie": a latter-day
René, admired but also chastened by romantic irony. As he
had in the previous novel, he strikes others as sad-looking,
and on two different occasions he is referred to as "un vieux
jeune homme," the omnipresent puer senex of modern French
literature. He also shares the romantic hero's egoism and
emotionalism: "Il ne se rappelait jamais les noms, ni des

lieux, ni des gens, il ne se rappelait que l'émotion que les uns et les autres lui avaient donnée" (p. 37).

Pierre Barbéris has said of René that his real secret was a political one. This is even truer of Gille than of René. His political boutade at the end of the novel is premonitory. To animate a languishing dinner table conversation, someone asks him if he is a Bolshevik:

> Oh non. Comment voulez-vous qu'un Européen soit bolchevik? Nous avons été beaucoup trop bien élevés par notre mère Europe. C'est nous qui avons inventé le socialisme--des Anglais, des Français et des Allemands--il fallait des Russes pour y croire. Non, même les Allemands sont beaucoup trop bien élevés pour être bolcheviks. Tout au plus sommes-nous capables d'être fascistes, c'est-à-dire de mettre un peu de démagogie dans notre conservatisme. (p. 309)

At the time of the novel's publication (1933) Drieu had been observing Italian fascism with great interest and was also eagerly following Hitler's rise to power (Hitler is mentioned in the novel)--although he was not yet sure what fascism was.

The third and final of the Gille novels is Gilles--with an s that may refer, as some critics think, to the fact that Drieu's last Gille is a composite (and a new synthesis) of the others. Just as plausible an explanation is the fact that there are two distinct Gilles in the final novel: the first is still the beau ténébreux treated with a touch of romantic irony; the second is not subjected to irony now that he has become a militant with a mission: fascism. During the Spanish Civil War Gilles will fight against Malraux's men who have also evolved from egotistical adventurers to militant activists with a cause. For convenience we will distinguish between Gilles I and Gilles II.

Gilles I is still the ladies' man. There is Alice, Antoinette, Dora, Mabel, Myriam, Pauline . . . it is indeed tempting to put them in alphabetical order. He sleeps with

all kinds and conditions of women, from common whores to
the daughter of the President of the Republic. His frenetic
sexual comportment suggests a <u>coito</u> <u>ergo</u> <u>sum</u> erotomania.
Sex is his only pleasure, alcohol his only opiate. Enmeshed
in the decadence of his century (he is as much a decadent
hero as a neo-romantic hero), he nevertheless stands apart
from it through his anguished lucidity. Like René's, his
"fate" is utter solitude.

> Il fallait accepter la solitude, c'était
> la réalité même de sa souffrance; la solitude
> prenait des proportions fantastiques, c'était
> décidément sa destinée: "C'est un don inestimable
> qui m'est fait, prononçait-il avec une gravité
> dérisoire, que de connaître le sort humain dans
> toute sa nudité. Les solitaires sont riches de
> tout l'aveu de la véritable situation humaine."
> Cette fatalité dominait aussi inexorablement ses
> rapports avec les femmes que ses rapports avec
> les hommes.[28]

This is not the only passage where Gille's romantic brooding
about solitude and fatality is labeled "dérisoire," and the
iterative past tense ("prononçait-il") suggests that his
conceit is as frequent as it is gratuitous.

As with René, cynicism and misanthropy drag Gilles into
the wilderness: "Gilles avait été attiré par une zone encore
plus profonde parmi les zones infinies et diaprées de la
solitude: il était parti dans le désert. De la grande ville
au désert, passage facile, lucide; du sable humain au sable"
(p. 350). This echoes René's "la foule, vaste désert d'hommes!"
And like René he contemplates suicide as the only way out.
Possessing the same <u>état</u> <u>civil</u> as Didier and Antony, he will
at times indulge in their self-pity: "Je suis né dans la
solitude, moi l'orphelin, le bâtard, le sans-famille, et
je retournerai à la solitude" (p. 425). Frankly marrying
Myriam Falkenberg for her money, he affects the dress, insolence
and cynicism of the dandy and treats his wife with sadistic
cruelty. His life is characterized by the "inept frivolity"

of the Roaring Twenties, the Années Folles, in which he lives like some hero of a Hemingway or a Fitzgerald.

> Gilles n'aimait guère qu'on se souciât de cuisine, mais il aimait boire. Tous les soirs ils étaient gris, comme tant d'autres à ce moment-là à Paris. Ils se levaient tard, sortaient pour déjeuner, rentraient pour faire l'amour, ressortaient pour traîner aux bords de la Seine qui sont tout Paris. Ils buvaient, dînaient, allaient au cinéma, rebuvaient dans les boîtes. (p. 148)

The feverish pace of his frivolity cannot hide an urge to self-destruction: "Il n'était pas fait pour vivre. La vie telle qu'elle s'offrait à lui, telle qu'il semblait pouvoir seulement la vivre, était inattendue, décevante, de façon incroyable. Il n'était capable que d'une seule belle action, se détruire" (p. 37).

His first step out of this impasse is the founding of a political journal appropriately called L'Apocalypse, informed by a cyclical view of history and the conviction that Society and History have reached their "Winter." The journal advocates the destruction of democracy, capitalism, mechanism and scientism and the renascence of the idea of aristocracy. Modern man, incarnated by the Jew unleashed from his ghetto in 1789, will be remade in the image of the "virile catholicism" of the Middle Ages. Gilles flirts with communism but only as a destructive agent. The notions of equality and progress are actually to be demythologized.

Gilles sees hope for the eventual triumph of his political program in the rise of the fascist movement. Since the movement is still young and amorphous, Gilles thinks he can help shape it, especially in encouraging a rapprochement of fascism and the Church. He then takes the final step, commiting himself to political activism. Gilles I becomes Gilles II. The decadent hero becomes a virile one, loving not only the "catholicisme viril" of the Middle Ages but the fraternité virile of combat. The earlier Gilles was already ripe for fascism not only intellectually but temperamentally. He had always thought that the law of life was the law of combat and that the only thing that counts in love and war is strength. "La pathétique aventure de Drieu, et de ses héros délégués a été de ne trouver de fondement à son action que dans la mystique romantique de la force, reflet sublimé de sa solitude crispée, et produit désespéré de l'égotisme."[29]   Gilles I had discovered as a soldier in the First World War that no idea or sentiment has any reality if it is not tested by the risk of death.   Gilles II discovers that true friendship can exist only between men facing a common danger.   The new Gilles sins no more, we are told.   He no longer has time for women, and, exaggerating the misogyny of some of Malraux's heroes, he despises even speaking to them!

* * *

III. Neo-Romantic Heroes on Stage

After careful study of a forty-year period of French drama a critic offers the following summary of its most typical protagonists: "The heroes and heroines of almost all the major French playwrights of this period are subjected--by themselves or by society--to exile from the quotidian world. Often this alienation is forced upon them because of their inability to adjust to the conventions of society; often they force themselves to become exiles because they will not accept. . . the laws and conventions which make an orderly if mediocre world."[30] The period discussed is not 1830-1840, as would have seemed plausible out of context, but the years 1920-1960. The passage is from The Alienated Hero in Modern French Drama by Robert Emmet Jones, who goes on to say that these protagonists are "spiritual brothers" and "siblings" of the dramatis personae of nineteenth-century romantic plays: "We might almost say that today's theatre is a culmination of the romantic, that its themes, essentially the same, have been broadened . . . that its characters are as egocentric and eccentric as those of the last century, that even its outlook is basically romantic and adolescent, and that the effects which it achieves, its feeling of confusion and despair, are exactly the same."[31] Jones' assessment is corroborated by Michael Goldman, who speaks not just of the French theater but of all modern drama from Ibsen and Strindberg through --of all people--Brecht ("Brecht's . . . artistic career is a brilliant, hopeless struggle to be free of the Romantic legacy") to the present: "Characters in modern drama are typically haunted by a feeling of being cut off from the joy of life, or indeed from life itself, a feeling of being dead. This is a Romantic feeling, and in this essay I wish to put forward the notion that the history of modern drama is essentially that of adapting this feeling to dramatic representation."[32]

Jones concentrates on the aristocratic heroes of Montherlant, who portray the isolation of the superior individual
[he might also have studied, like John Fletcher, [33] their
scepticism and world-weariness], the pathological heroes
of Lenormand, the "black romanticism" of Anouilh's rebellious,
"doomed" but pure sauvages--a modern variant of the Noble
Savage--the implacable heroines of Giraudoux (whom Jones
relates to the force qui va type) and the existentialist
and absurdist hero. I shall not repeat what Jones has ably
said, but in the interests of concreteness, I should like
to add a few remarks of my own on the heroes of Anouilh and
Sartre. The romantic connections of the Theater of the Absurd
will be discussed in the chapter that follows.

* * *

On the connections between the Anouilhian hero and the
romantic hero I want to make a half-dozen points as succinctly
as I can.

1. Anouilh's protagonists, just like their romantic
forebears, seek an absolute, a state of perfection or purity,
that does not and cannot exist in this finite world. Thoughtful,
sensitive men, and even callous men in their rare sensitive
moments, entertain hopeless aspirations that are doomed to
be crushed by the cruel exigencies of Life. Their tragic
situation resides precisely in this impossibility of reconciliation between the baseness of everyday life and these idealistic
aspirations. Another trait that the Anouilhian hero shares
with René in this same connection is the puer senex motif:
"Anouilh's attitude throughout his plays is that of an idealist
of twenty, with more than the usual experience of life and
marked from the beginning with the pessimism of maturity."[34]

2. Implicit in nearly every play and especially in
the cumulative effect of the entire opus, is the assumption

that a malevolent fate rules over the destiny of Anouilh's heroes. This assumption is made explicit in the cynical formulas of Lucien in Roméo et Jeanette, who tells us that everything good is "prohibited" on this earth and that "God hates happiness." Love, man's only hope for salvation, is doomed to deteriorate under the crushing weight of Time and the pressure of material circumstance. Solitude is man's essential condition, and this condition is exacerbated by the painful lucidity of the Anouilhian hero. This world view is another manifestation of what some critics call "negative romanticism" and others "black romanticism." But the stubborn refusal of bovine contentment and the "happiness" of the mediocre [cf. "Vous me dégoûtez tous avec votre bonheur!" --uttered by Thérèse (in La Sauvage) and by Antigone] partakes of Romantic idealism.[35]

3. Since the surrounding world can only defile and degrade, the Anouilhian hero, as Jacques Guicharnaud has said, "has no recourse but flight"[36] that is, romantic escapism, which more often than not takes the form of the death-wish. Anouilh's Orpheus, for example, considers suicide the noblest step he can take.

4. Like that of the romantic hero, the Anouilhian hero's relationship to his family is always problematic. The family represents a sordid attempt at self-preservation through compromise of high principle and even common decency and is ultimately disowned by the hero (e.g., Jacques-Gaston in Le Voyageur sans bagages and Georges in Le Rendez-vous de Senlis). Anouilh, with modern candor, is making explicit part of what was implicit in the orphan topos of romantic literature.

5. One of Anouilh's major themes, the interplay of purity and corruption within a single character was also part of the original romantic program for the drama, witness the Préface de Cromwell. Like Hugo, Anouilh endeavors to present man's irreducible dualism, his nostalgia for purity

and innocence but also his <u>nostalgie</u> <u>de</u> <u>la</u> <u>boue</u>, not only through characterization but also through a mixture of tonalities, as in the bitter farce and the <u>pièce</u> <u>noire</u> relieved by comic interludes and fantasy. One of the basic characteristics of Anouilh's dramaturgy, then, is the romantic <u>mélange</u> <u>des</u> <u>genres</u>.

One must keep in mind that when critics speak of Anouilh's "anti-romantic" tendency to deflate the grandeur of sorrow (e.g., Guicharnaud, p. 116), this "anti-romantic" animus is <u>not</u> non-romantic. Romanticism has many moods, and many of them are contradictory. To Musset's "Rien ne nous rend si grands qu'une grande douleur" can be opposed Vigny's "Gémir, pleurer, prier est également lâche." Anouilh's mixture of tonalities, his ironic counterpoint, partakes not only of the Hugolian <u>mélange</u> but, more profoundly, or romantic irony.

6. The stubborn, prideful, "no" that the Anouilhian hero says to compromise of any sort in life and ultimately to life itself, is fundamentally a romantic stance. This romantic "no" is beyond good and evil (but not sincerity and authenticity) and beyond logic and common sense, the classical <u>raison</u>. "I'm not here to understand," says the misologistic Antigone to Creon, "I'm here to say no." "I shall not try to convince you," says Thomas à Becket to the King, "I shall only say no." When the King insists: "But you must be logical, Becket!" the latter says: "No, it's not necessary . . . One has only to do, absurdly, what one has been entrusted with doing--and to the very end." This Anouilhian <u>jusqu'au</u> <u>boutisme</u> is eminently romantic. His heroes are rebels without a cause, they remain frozen, as one critic has put it, in an attitude of gratuitous revolt. In Anouilh, and in the original romantics, we have a basically similar appraisal of the human predicament. The differences between the various authors lie largely in their individual response to this predicament. Anouilh's answer is that there can be no affirmative or effective counter-response, no noble

rebellion. The Anouilhian hero merely spits in the eye of his Fate and complains, not without some self-pity, that all the cards are stacked against him.

* * *

There is a very similar identification, in both romanticism and literary existentialism, with modern tastes and preoccupations, and there is also a significant resemblance between the littérature engagée of the latter and the humanitarian phase of the former. The two basic phases of Sartre's philosophy, that propounded in L'Etre et le néant and that of the Critique de la raison dialectique, curiously resemble the two waves of French romanticism. In both the romantic movement and in Sartrean philosophy the first phase insists on the uniqueness, primacy and total freedom of the individual, the second on the primacy and freedom of the group; the first phase insists on individual revolt, the second on the revolution of the group against political and economic oppression. In both phases of Sartre's work, the aim of philosophy is liberation. "La liberté dans l'art, la liberté dans la société, voilà le double but," we recall, is Hugo's definition of romanticism. In his first phase, Sartre was concerned with the authentic individual; in his second phase, with an authentic society. Since it is in the first phase that Sartre's theatrical work is mainly located, it is with the original themes and emphases that we are primarily concerned. These themes are romantic: individual freedom and Angst, estrangement and alienation ("L'enfer, c'est les Autres."), frustration, homelessness, loneliness, ennui, revolt, sadism, masochism, "flight," the negative, "nihilating" consciousness and the irreducible distance between the individual and the world. The futile romantic urge to unite the self to some absolute finds a correlate in the urge of the pour soi to merge with the en soi, man's futile aspiration to "become God." Such a synthesis cannot develop dialectically, Sartre tells us, and therefore man is a "useless passion," a theme whose many variations have been eloquently expressed from pre-romanticism to neo-romanticism, from Chateaubriand's René to Anouilh's Antigone.

The extreme insistence upon the primacy of the individual self on the part of practising existentialists such as Asher Moore ("As an existentialist . . . my primary object is myself and my own life.") has been called a "romanticism" by fellow philosopher Rollo Handy [37] --and quite properly, I think. I am not confusing Sartrean existentialism with the many so-called "romantic philosophies of life" which propose a guide for living based on egotism, freedom, instinctual behavior etc., nor am I calling it romantic simply because of its connections with German philosophy--as Anglo-American philosophers are wont to do. I am calling existentialism a romanticism because its basic themes and concerns are virtually identical with those of the original romantic movement in France. If I am overstating the case, and existentialism is not a romantic philosophy, it is certainly a philosophy for romantics.

Serge Radine thought himself "audacious" when in 1950 he called Sartre's philosophy a latter-day romanticism, but Julien Benda had arrived at the same conclusion two years earlier, and by now a sufficiently large consensus of critics, historians and philosophers has been established to consider such an interpretation as an established fact of intellectual history. [38]

If romanticism is the expression of an anguish and a freedom, as Albérès has defined it, then the inescapable conclusion is that literary existentialism is indeed a romanticism and that the Sartrean hero is a neo-romantic hero par excellence. Freedom and anguish are the two basic components of the Sartrean hero's "situation." Another constant is solitude. Sartre's self-conscious heroes (cf. Ridge's definition of the romantic hero) are all solitary figures who reject or are rejected by their milieu. They are all orphans or bastards or feel that they are. In both his philosophical and literary works, Sartre focusses on equivocal, frustrating relationships. Love inevitably turns sour and perverse in its futile attempts to appropriate the self-hood of the Other. As were the romantics, Sartre, from Les Mouches to Les Séquestrés d'Altona, has been fascinated with the theme of incest ("Even today, this is the only form of relationship which I have any feeling for" [39]), largely because of the psychological and sociological obstacles it presents. His heroes also seem to be harboring a romantic death-instinct. Critics have noted the resemblance of the Sartrean hero to Heidegger's "être-pour-la-mort" (Sein zum Tode), his tendency either to be executed, to let himself be executed or to take his own life.

Such a figure is Hugo Barine of Les Mains sales. His killing of Hoederer was and forever will be ambiguous: there are at least a dozen possible motives and combinations of motives that might explain his original impulsive act, his "crime passionnel" (the title Sartre had originally proposed for the play). His choice, at the end of the play, of the present and future meaning of that past act is ambiguous too. It is indeed idealistic, courageous, "authentic," that is, performed in existentialist good faith--but it is also suicidal. Hugo had admitted to Olga early in the play that he had no desire to live. And later: "Je ne suis pas fait pour vivre, je ne sais pas ce que c'est que la vie, et je n'ai pas besoin de le savoir. Je suis de trop, je n'ai pas ma place et je gêne tout le monde, personne ne m'aime, personne ne me fait confiance." [40] This is the melancholy romantic hero, out of place in any society, unloved and misunderstood. He is a romantic rebel in revolt against his own social class and misunderstood by his adopted one. His communist comrades, mistrusting his wealthy background, prefer to see in him an effete bourgeois intellectual, an undisciplined anarchist, rather than a potentially effective man of action, as Hugo,

like Garcin of _Huis clos_, prefers to picture himself. Hugo's
communist ideology cannot check his romantic misanthropy:
"Les hommes" Pourquoi les aimerais-je? Est-ce qu'ils m'aiment?"
(p. 387). His facetious _and_ symbolic remark about not being
his father's son makes of him still another in the long line
of Sartre's bastard heroes, who, as Victor Brombert has noted,
represent the intellectual pariah, condemned to narcissistic
lucidity and eternal alienation--a condition which Brombert
has properly called "Sartre's _mal du siècle_."[41]   Another
obvious romantic theme of the play is the inevitable antagonism
between the individual and "the system," here the fickle
political tactics of the Communists.

Hugo's final act is, I think, analogous to that of Anouilh's
Antigone: a refusal to compromise with a principle that
he has freely--even gratuitously--chosen.   Gratuitously,
because, as one critic has noted, the existentialist hero
accepts a mandate that no one has given him; in a value-less
universe he must invent his own values as he goes along.
Hazel Barnes says that Hugo's final decision may "smack of
romanticism,"[42] but I would say rather that is reflects romanticism's nobler side: the defiant gesture is not a pose; it
is a profound expression of a man's desire to give subjective
meaning to a world that is objectively absurd.

* * *

I have a bit more to say about the contemporary theatre
and will say it in the following chapter. This chapter's presentation of several neo-romantic heroes is not meant to be exhaustive; but enough evidence has been presented to demonstrate
the continued centrality of the romantic hero, or more properly,
his heirs, in the literature of this century.   Corroborating
this centrality is the fact that many of the themes associated
with the romantic hero and the decadent hero are precisely

those that have dominated, in this century, not just French
literature but Western literature in general. The individual
frustrated by the institutions of modern society has been
portrayed by writers as different as Boris Pasternak and
Saul Bellow. The impotence of the lone individual in a hostile
world has been portrayed from Joyce's Bloom to the heroes
of Anthony Burgess. Ellin Horowitz has spoken of the modern
hero as seen in Conrad, Hemingway, and Lawrence as "the alienated
passive hero in a de-personalized world who must become an
exile in order to search for 'the reality of experience'
and of the Faulkner and Hemingway heroes as lonely figures
on the shady side of the law.[43]   Ihab H. Hassan calls contemporary American literature a "literature of opposition" and
claims that "The central and controlling image of recent
fiction is that of the rebel-victim. He is an actor but
also a sufferer. Almost always, he is an outsider, an initiate
never confirmed in his initiation, an anarchist and clown,
a Faust and Christ compounded in grotesque or ironic measures.
The poles of crime and sainthood define the range of his
particular fate, which is his character."[44]   Gore Vidal says
that the obsessive concern with sexuality which informs so
much of contemporary writing is partly the result of a wish
to épater le bourgeois and that much of the despondency and
apparent confusion in the world of letters derives in part
from "the nervous, bloody age in which we live" and partly
from "a hunger for the absolute."[45]

This centrality of the romantic hero will be even more
conspicuously evident when we add the contributions of his
more distant heirs, the scions of the decadent hero.

chapter eight

SONS OF THE DECADENT HERO

The protean anti-hero of twentieth century literature
may at first glance seem far removed from the original romantic
hero, but the latter's self-proclaimed superiority could
not conceal the several weaker sides of his nature, some
of which he was aware of (and proud).   The weaker sides,
the perverse, passive and even pathological tendencies of
the romantic hero, have never disappeared from the modern
literary scene; they have been preserved, even exacerbated,
in his progeny.   As shown earlier, there is a direct line
of descent from the romantic hero to the decadent hero of
the fin de siècle and, as I will attempt to show now, there
is a direct line of descent from the latter to the anti-hero
of this century.   As the analysis of the anti-hero proceeds,
I will be looking for his ties of kinship not only with the
decadent hero (this, after all, is not hard to prove) but
also and especially his family resemblance to the original
romantic hero.

Just as modern painting shattered the portrait and disposed
of its elements in other ways, modern fiction and drama have
often shattered the original portrait of the romantic hero
while preserving his individual features in a variety of
novel ways.   One way is to isolate a single trait, say passivity,
and make it the sole defining characteristic of an allegorical
hero.   Another way has been to shatter the image of a unified
psyche and the "well-rounded" character of traditional fiction
in favor of the stream of consciousness with its seemingly
incoherent succession of thoughts, moods, memories, anticipa-
tions, phantasies and even hallucinations.   Victor Brombert,
quoting Irving Howe, has said that it is the problematic
nature of experience that has transformed the modern protagonist
from a definable entity into "an occasion for a flow of

perceptions and sensations."[1] This is, for example, the basic method (and philosophical bias) of the nouveau roman. The breakdown of the unified psyche began in romantic literature, from the zwei Seelen of Goethe's Faust to the ambivalent heroes of Musset, Stendhal and Gautier.

I am thinking especially here of an important remark by Walter L. Reed, who says in his Meditations on the Hero: "I should like to argue . . . that in the case of the Romantic hero it is not simply a case of decline or eclipse or overshadowing by the antihero (all along, the ironic critique of heroes continues to coexist with more positive treatments, as is the case of Julien Sorel or the Underground Man). Rather I would say that the image of the Romantic hero is shattered in the modern novel, and its elements are disposed in new ways. The elements are dispersed in one of two directions, either backward into the substratum of myth (from which the human heroic form originally emerged) or forward, as it were, into the multiple ambiguities of the narrator who celebrates the hero's achievement. Unable to maintain his precarious middle ground--precarious even in the mid-nineteenth-century meditations--the Romantic hero in the twentieth century is absorbed into the background and/or foreground that he originally tried to stand apart from."[2]

In this chapter I want to consider three basic types of the "decadent" anti-hero--the passive hero, the hero as clown, and the hero as criminal--in order especially to point up their kinship with the romantic hero. The latter's genealogy will then, I think, be complete.

* * *

I. The Hero as Clown and the Passive Hero

Michaux's Personae

No two writers could seem further apart than Henri Michaux and Chateaubriand. The latter's enthusiasm in talking about himself is as extreme as Michaux's reticence. But a study of their lives reveals some interesting parallels. Both writers spent a lonely childhood, feeling uncomfortable in their own family and withdrawing into themselves; both felt the lure of mysticism, even the monastery, despite a largely irreligious nature; both felt the lure of the sea and ships and became world travelers. Like René, the personae of Michaux's obliquely personal poetry express a radical incompatibility between themselves and the world surrounding them. They share René's disgust with ordinary, routine, material life, the moral mediocrity of the herd and the false values of modern civilization.

For Michaux poetry is both self-exploration and self-preservation. As self-exploration it is, as Malcolm Bowie has shown, an ontological adventure, an exploration of the poet's inner space: "J'écris pour me parcourir." [3] As self-preservation, it is catharsis, a sudden release of pent-up emotions, anger especially. It is also magic: a hostile and recalcitrant world is brought under the practitioner's power. [4] Michaux's entire poetics is summed up in a word: exorcism. The word expresses a romantic desire to keep the hostile powers of the surrounding world at bay. The word also betrays a romantic esthetic: poetry is not a craft, it is a spontaneous, immediate and violent response. The poet does not proceed with carefully preconceived plans, his spur is the spur of the moment. Ordinary language alone does not suffice to express Michaux's anger and (defensive) aggression. He will often compose rasping, grating cacophonies and pugilistic neologisms to express his savage revenge on the hostile world with which he struggles:

```
Il l'emparouille et l'endosque contre terre;
Il le rague et le roupète jusqu'à son drâle;
Il le pratèle et le libucque et lui barufle les ouillais;
Il le tocarde et le marmine,
Le manage rape à ri et ripe à ra.
Enfin il l'écorcobalisse.⁵
```

Michaux's melancholy has reminded at least one critic of the romantic hero: "Il y a chez Michaux un côté plaintif, pathétique (et même un côté 'regarde comme je souffre,' un côté voyeur et montreur de soi, une certaine complaisance, un amour de son mal, une délectation morose, une certaine passivité, un certain égoïsme mélancolique."⁶ Exactly the same reproaches have been leveled of course at René and the romantic hero in general. But Michaux's romantic melancholy and misanthropy and even his violent anger are tempered by a sense of humor and self-parody.

Michaux's most important literary self-portrait is the prose-poem "Clown"--a title that is significant both as autobiography and as an expression of the modern sensibility. The sad clown has become one of the chief heroes of modern art and literature. He has figured in modern French poetry from Banville's Odes funambulesques (1857), through Laforgue and Jacob, to Apollinaire and Cocteau. He has figured even more prominently in modern painting, notably in the works of Picasso, Rouault, Chagal and Buffet. Most of the paintings of clowns and harlequins have revealed or suggested the tragedy behind the comic mask. But Michaux, while exploiting this now conventional association, has given the subject an ironic twist. His clown is not the tragic man behind the comic mask; the grotesque mask of the clown is the real man as he really is: "ras . . . et risible." Michaux's clown does not possess a shred of tragic dignity; the absurd figure he cuts is the true picture.

Michaux's most sustained presentation of the clown-hero is Plume. The very name of his "hero" suggests a Chaplinesque, Thurberesque and Kafkaesque vulnerability and the lightness of mind and body of a Stan Laurel. As world-traveler (the

symbolic significance of this role should not be overlooked)
Plume is the uncomplaining victim of gratuitous insults and
aggression. "Les uns lui passent dessus sans crier gare,
les autres s'essuient tranquillement les mains à son veston.
Il a fini par s'habituer. Il aime voyager avec modestie."[7]
If he asks a waiter for something that is not on the menu
(or even on the menu), he is immediately accosted and accused
by authorities of greater and greater rank: the maître d'hôtel,
the manager, the police commissioner, the head of the Sûreté
and finally the chief of the forbidding Secrète. Each encounter
ends with the same refrain: "Plume s'excusa aussitôt." In
restaurants he is constantly refused the meal he has ordered,
in hotels he is refused a room, on ships he is relegated
to the baggage hold. If he gets on a train he is immediately
thrown off ("Bien, bien. Je comprends parfaitement. J'étais
monté, oh, pour jeter un coup d'oeil.") In Rome he is not
allowed to even look at the Coliseum ("Bien, bien. C'était . . .
Je voulais seulement vous demander une carte postale, une
photo, peut-être.") In Berlin five pimply prostitutes force
him to accept their wares, take all his money and throw him
out ("Tiens, pensa Plume, ça fera un fameux souvenir de voyage
plus tard.") The first section of the work, entitled "Un
homme paisible," would have been better placed at the end.
It summarizes Plume's placidity and passiveness and suggests
deeper implications. Plume has become so accustomed to hostility, his hopelessness is now so total, that he has become
dehumanized into an unfeeling vegetable. Plume awakens to
discover that all the walls of his house are missing ("Ants
must have eaten it . . . anyway, the thing is over and done
with"). And he goes back to sleep. Shortly he is re-awakened
by a train rushing at him and his wife at full speed, but
after expressing mild annoyance he goes back to sleep. Finally,
awakened by the cold, he finds himself dripping in blood
and his wife lying in pieces next to him: "I sure wish that

train hadn't passed through here like that, but since it
has . . . ." And he goes back to sleep.

> --Voyons, disait le juge, comment expliquez-vous
> que votre femme se soit blessée au point qu'on l'ait
> trouvée partagée en huit morceaux, sans que vous,
> qui étiez à côté, ayez pu faire un geste pour l'en
> empêcher, sans même vous en être apercu.   Voilà le
> mystère. Toute l'affaire est là-dedans.
> --Sur ce chemin, je ne peux pas l'aider, pensa
> Plume, et il se rendormit.
> --L'exécution aura lieu demain.   Accusé, avez-
> vous quelque chose à ajouter?
> --Excusez-moi, dit-il, je n'ai pas suivi l'affaire.
> Et il se rendormit.[8]

Earlier, I traced the sad clown topos forwards from
Banville to Cocteau ; it can also be traced backwards: to
Musset.   Like the antics of the romantic <u>bouffon</u>, Plume's
clownish passivity has disturbing overtones.   He partakes
of the twin twentieth-century myths of the Little Man as
Tragic Hero and the Passive Hero, both overwhelmed by forces
beyond their control, bewildered by a hostile, decadent and
polluted environment, the victims of cosmic indifference
or malevolence.   We certainly have moved a great distance
from the Cornelian Hero, master of himself and of the universe,
and from the confident anthropocentrism of pre-Copernican
days.

* * *

Samuel Beckett and the Theater of the Absurd

To future historians of art and literature the twentieth
century will undoubtedly be the Age of Experimentation. Artists
have tried everything. They have imagined and explored everything. They have succeeded and failed in everything. The
avant-garde theater is but another manifestation of this
esthetic freedom that began with the romantic revolt.

There is an avant-garde beauty. Like that of the surrealists, it is a convulsive beauty consisting largely of
shock, surprise, and wonder. This basically romantic esthetic,
implicit in so much of today's music, painting, even architec-
ture, has been explicitly expressed by the writers, especially
in France. One thinks of Baudelaire saying that next to
the pleasure of being surprised, there is no greater pleasure
than to cause surprise. Apollinaire, seeking to explain
the new spirit of modern art, claimed that the new resides
wholly in surprise. Apollinaire's motto was: "I astonish."
Cocteau spent his entire career trying to satisfy the request
of Diaghilev: "Astonish me."

Since the appearance of Alfred Jarry's Ubu roi in 1896,
a new attitude toward farce has been forming in the West,
especially in France. Originally, farce was intended as
the lowest form of theatrical humor. Its principal device
was singularly unsubtle: exaggeration. The dramatic action
was remote from meaningful human activity, and the characters
were less than ridiculous human beings: more often than
not, they were subhuman. Everything to be enjoyed in the
old farce was more than obvious. The spectator could be
inattentive and still get the gist of the play. The similarity
between the new farce and the old one is largely superficial.
Laughter is now a means as well as an end in itself. The
exaggerations, as David Grossvogel has pointed out, are really
understatements--the innocuous surface is accompanied by
a "dangerous undertow."[9] The characters remain poorly drawn

psychologically, but their activity is meaningful in the sense that it has philosophical implications. The new farce is especially characterized by its latent tragedy: the comic mode is used to convey a tragic sense of life.

Taking its cue from such plays as Apollinaire's cubist farce Les Mamelles de Tirésias, Cocteau's fantasy, Les Mariés de la Tour Eiffel, the tragic farces of the Belgian playwrights, Crommelynck and Ghelderode, the exteriorizations of both expressionism and surrealism, and especially perhaps, the plethora of cinematographic techniques, the contemporary farce exploits the tangible dimensions of the "visual" or "total" theater. The aim of dramatists such as Ionesco, Beckett, and the early Adamov, is what Grossvogel (in an exciting graduate seminar at Harvard) called "the physical representation of tragedy" and what Jacques Guicharnaud calls "the actualization" or "the concrete realization" of metaphors, that is, a kind of poetry of the theater.

Backed by the authority of Aristotle and Artaud, these playwrights feel that in the theater actions speak louder than words and that the stage is a concrete place that demands to be filled. Boileau's classical dictum on decorum (that what should not be seen on stage--and the restrictions were legion--should be revealed by narrative exposition) is reversed: the narrative tendency of the classical stage is rejected in favor of the concrete, visual stage. Whether the content of contemporary farce be called irregular tragedy or irregular metaphysics, it is presented as a visual art, a poetry for the theater, by the theater, and in terms of the theater.

One of the essential traits of the avant-garde theater that is usually overlooked by critics and spectators alike is its modesty. If the farcial exaggerations are really understatements, the seeming braggadoccio is really humility. Both the romantic drama and the classical tragedy had at least this much in common: the heroes made no attempt to conceal their sorrow. It was made painfully explicit in the classical monologue and the romantic tirade. If the classical hero showed some restraint when talking of his sorrow, the "hero" of the modern farce is even more modest: he never talks about it directly at all. "There's something wrong somewhere" is the most explicitly tragic remark made in William Saroyan's My Heart's in the Highlands, a comic play filled with tragic understatement and overtones. The groan of the grand manner has become a whimper.

To understand the modern farce one must keep in mind that it is essentially romantic not only in its esthetic bias (shock, surprise and wonder) but in subject-matter (revolt and the mal du siècle) and in structure (the mélange des genres and the visual theater--compare Hugo's stage directions, for example, with Racine's) even though it seems anti-romantic in tonality, any residue of "romantic" sentimentality or even pathos being cleansed and chastised by laughter. But this supposedly anti-romantic tonality is itself romantic in origin; it is a new form--an extension really--of romantic irony: the dramatist not only deflates the significance of the universal scheme of things but also his own sorrow and anguish, which are genuine, however, and deep.

While it is easy to see the filiation between the "hero" of the new farce and the decadent hero, the kinship with the romantic hero is obscured by the deliberate ambiguity. The new farce moves by indirection. Neither the action nor the dialogue treat the play's subject explicitly. The "plot" is not a concatenation of incidents linked causally and which move toward an inevitable dénouement. It is usually a single incident or series of incidents that simply mark time or beat around the bush (a perfect metaphor, by the way, of modern man's passivity). The dialogue too is periphrastic, forcing the spectator to figure out the subject for himself. Once the subject is discovered, one usually finds that it is related to a romantic theme, especially the denunciation of the human condition and metaphysical anguish.

In a number of subtle ways, Hamm, in Beckett's _Fin de Partie_, is a comic version of the romantic hero. He certainly has the latter's egocentrism and is in fact a thoroughgoing solipsist. His very first words are "A moi." And all the other characters and indeed the entire universe--for what its worth--revolves, or should, he thinks, around him. His partner, Clov, is not treated as an end in himself but as a means to Hamm's many selfish ends. Ruby Cohn says of him: "Hamm's self-centered lines and striking costume suggest the residue of a heroic mode." [10] Like the romantic hero, he is both miserable and proud of it:

> HAMM (. . . Il s'éclaircit la gorge, joint les bouts des doigts.) Peut-il y a--(bâillements)--y avoir misère plus . . . plus haute que la mienne?[11]

Like the fatal hero of romantic literature he both predicts his doom and ambivalently yearns for it: "Je te donne la combinaison du buffet si tu jures de m'achever" (p. 175). Romantic ennui is translated into the comic mode by his frequent fits of yawning, romantic escapism by his frequent requests for a pain-killer.

Basically _Fin de partie_ belongs to the literature of neo-décadentisme: Beckett's world is reaching its end, in fact the end was there at the very beginning, we are told. But if one listens carefully, one can hear distant echoes of romantic literature.

> HAMM.--La nature nous a oubliés. (p. 152)
> . . . .
> NELL.--(élégiaque).--Ah hier!
> HAMM (avec lassitude). . . . . Nature!
> HAMM . . . . Seul, je m'embarquerai seul!
> Prépare-moi ce radeau immédiatement. Demain je serai loin. (p. 172

And in this exchange a few pages later (Hamm asks if Nagg is still alive), one hears an ironic restatement of the romantic lacrimo ergo sum:

```
CLOV.--On dirait que oui.
      ....................
HAMM.--Et Nagg?
      ....................
HAMM.--Qu'est-ce qu'il fait?
      ....................
CLOV.--Il pleure.
HAMM.--Donc il vit.  (pp. 195-96)
```

In fact, one can very easily see in Hamm (who is a ham actor among other things) a parody of the romantic hero. But ever since Byron, Musset, Stendhal and Gautier we have become used to an author making fun of his own distress and his hero's misery.

```
    NELL (sans baisser la voix.)--Rien n'est plus drôle
que le malheur, je te l'accorde. Mais--
    NAGG (scandalisé).--Oh!
    NELL.--Si, si, c'est la chose la plus comique au
monde.  (p. 158)
```

Structurally and stylistically, Beckett's work can be, and has been, related to classicism, especially the tendency toward understatement and the stringent, make-a-play-out-of-nothing economy. But he has also given comic and ironic treatment to many basic romantic themes. He is the artist of despondency and desolation, of anguish and despair. For Beckett, to be is to be bored or to be suffering; these are the two poles of his romantic ontology. Like Hamm, the Unnamable utters the lacrimo ergo sum lament: "I, of whom I know nothing, I know my eyes are open, because of the tears that pour from then unceasingly." Beckettian man is a self-conscious and dying animal. Solitude is his basic lot. His encounters and conversations with others serve mainly to underscore his fundamental isolation. Malone tells a story of Sapo, who lives "in the midst of strangers," and Malone himself means, among other things, Man Alone. A romantic variant on the theme of solitude is, as we have frequently seen, the orphan topos, which frequently recurs both explicitly and by implication, in Beckett's work as well. The protagonist of Not I is an old woman who was an orphan at birth, and the characters of the trilogy, Malloy, Moran, Malone, and the Unnamable, as well as all those that follow, belong to what A. Alvarez calls "Murphy's world": "that of the utterly deprived, of those who seem orphaned at birth."[12] The hero of L'Expulsé is expelled from the house in which he was born and raised, and Malone, who has only a blurred memory of his mother, seeks a home town he can't even name.

Beckett's heroes are also related to the puer senex. For classical antiquity this meant maturity and sagacity in a very young man; for the romantics it means precocious disillusionment and cynicism. Beckett, who continues the romantic version, translates the theme into symbolic terms, that is, in terms of physical decrepitude. His decaying characters are either octogenarian, like Malone, or, like the narrator of Comment C'est, they have "the feeling . . . of having been born octogenarian." For Beckett this motif is informed mainly by an excruciatingly painful awareness of the fragility and evanescence of human life, a theme which in Breath has been given its most concentrated theatrical expression in Western literature:

Curtain
1. Minimum light on stage littered with miscella-
neous rubbish. Hold about five seconds.
2. Faint brief cry and immediately inspiration
and slow increase of light together reaching maximum
together in about ten seconds. Silence and hold
for about five seconds.
3. Expiration and slow decrease of light together
reaching minimum together (light as in 1) in about
ten seconds and immediately cry as before. Silence
and hold about five seconds.

Curtain
RUBBISH No verticals, all scattered and lying.

CRY Instant of recorded vagitus. Important that
two cries be identical, switching on and off
strictly synchronized light and breath.

BREATH Amplified recording.

LIGHT   If 0=dark and 10=bright, light should move
from about 3 minimum to 6 maximum and back.[13]

This is the entire text.   It is to be performed in 35 seconds,
without actors or words.   If the focussed structure can be
called "neo-classical," the rubbish that litters the stage
can be called "neo-decadent" and the anguished cries neo-
romantic.   This "play" is at once the summary of an individual
life, then of human life in general (As Pozzo puts it in
Godot: "One day we are born, one day we die, the same day,
the same second.") and even perhaps of the entire race (section
2 could be interpreted as homo sapiens evolving from the
primordial rubbish to which he will shortly return in section
3 through the inexorable second law of thermodynamics: entropy).
Like the romantics Beckett is ambivalent about death.   It
is seen as a mockery of human life and as a relief from torture
and boredom.   The death-wish is an insistent in Beckett's
work as it was for any of the romantics.   As A. Alvarez notes,
"In Beckett's work the death instinct wins: it is as though
the force of life were too fragile and uncertain to withstand
the overwhelming pull toward death."[14]   Not nihilism but
nihilotropism [15] is what impels Beckett's protagonists inexorably
yet asymptotically toward Nothingness.

* * *

If contemporary critics were asked to pick the one play
written since the Second World War that best represents modern
man's way of feeling, the critical consensus would probably
select En attendant Godot.   Beckett's tramps, like the romantic
hero, are solitary outcasts.   However, the romantic outcast lived
outside society because he was overqualified, or at least
thought he was.   Beckett's heroes are mere derelicts, bums,
clowns, who cannot be taken with total seriousness (cf. romantic
irony).   Beckett goes to some pains to establish his protagonists' participation in the clown myth.   In the second act,
Estragon's shoes are arranged in Chaplinesque fashion--heels

together and toes splayed--and all the characters wear Chaplin's
bowler hat. Similarly, Ionesco will allude to Laurel and
Hardy.

Several romantic themes are immediately apparent in
Godot: solitude and estrangement; the Charlot-like "miser-
abilism," a comic variant of romantic melancholy; then there
is ennui ("We are bored to death," laments Didi)--this romantic
theme par excellence is still a very important one in the
contemporary theater, although it too has been largely transposed
into the comic mode. Here is one example among many in Godot.

> VLADIMIR.--Si tu les essayais?
> ESTRAGON.--J'ai tout essayé.
> VLADIMIR.--Je veux dìre les chaussures.
> ESTRAGON.--Tu crois?
> VLADIMIR.--Ça fera passer le temps. Je t'assure, ce
> sera une diversion.
> ESTRAGON.--Un délassement.
> VLADIMIR.--Une distraction.[16]
> ESTRAGON.--Un délassement.

The allusion here is to Pascal's divertissement, man's emptiness
and wretchedness without God and his desperate attempts to
fill the void. But, as Jacques Guicharnaud has pointed out,
"What Beckett's man has that Pascal's free thinker lacks
is lucidity, the consciousness of his own condition . . .
Vladimir and Estragon know that they act in order to avoid
thinking about their condition."[17] This acute self-consciousness is one of the defining characteristics of both the decadent
hero and the romantic hero. The death-wish motif occurs
twice in Godot. Suicide is first contemplated as another
Pascalian divertissement; the second attempt is thwarted
by a mechanical failure (the rope breaks)--leaving the question
of suicide unanswered, although it remains a possible option.
The extreme passiveness of Vladimir and Estragon is seen
not only in their endless waiting but in their physical im-
mobility. Both acts end identically:

> VLADIMIR.--Alors on y va?
> ESTRAGON.--Allons-y.
>
> Ils ne bougent pas.

Their passiveness translates helplessness rather than hopelessness. If they don't move, it is because there is no place to go. But they haven't given up hope of finding Godot one day. Or rather finding Him again. Both Vladimir and Estragon have vague memories of having talked with Him before. As they try to recall their conversation with Him, one can hear echoes of the romantic nostalgia for a paradise lost and desperate yearning for a paradise to come, the bien inconnu and the unattainable Absolute. Estragon's "vague supplication" is directly related to René's vague à l'âme.

> ESTRAGON.--Qu'est-ce qu'on lui a demandé au juste?
> VLADIMIR.--Tu n'étais pas là?
> ESTRAGON.--Je n'ai pas fait attention.
> VLADIMIR.--Eh bien . . . Rien de bien précis.
> ESTRAGON.--Une sorte de prière.
> VLADIMIR.--Voilà.
> ESTRAGON.--Une vague supplique.
> VLADIMIR.--Si tu veux.
> ESTRAGON.--Et qu'a-t-il répondu?
> VLADIMIR.--Qu'il verrait.[18]

Beckett, astutely, has refused to pin a specific symbolic label on Godot, leaving this up to the individual spectator and reader. He would no doubt subscribe to Tolkien's remark that what often passes for allegory is really "applicability": if the symbolic glove or grid fits, use it. Godot has been variously interpreted as the Almighty God, a diminutive god, happiness, immortality, Love, Death, Silence, Hope-That-Springs-Eternal, etc. The ambiguity that Beckett deliberately creates allows a romantic reading as well. The romantic hero, too, yearned for, waited endlessly for, but never found his vague and unknown Good. (Cf. the silent t in Godot, a Joycean pun.)

I am not trying to reduce Beckett's work to romanticism; I am simply attempting to show its romantic residuum. If twentieth century literature is at bottom romantic, as so many critics and historians agree, it should not be surprising to find romantic resonances in one of its most representative writers.

* * *

II. The Hero as Criminal: Genet

The romantic hero was not just an outsider, he was often an outlaw--either a literal one sought by the authorities or a conscious breaker of laws, written or unwritten. The decadent hero of the _fin de siècle_ is not just recalcitrant but perverse, and perversion is often pushed beyond the limits of legality. In the twentieth century the literary crime rate has increased almost exponentially. Rather than multiply examples, I should like to focus on the work of one writer, Jean Genet.

The romantic hero tells us often that he is an orphan. Jean Genet does too, and he has the credentials to prove it: his early years were spent as a ward of the National Foundling Society--the Assistance Sociale. A homeless soul, he had to invent a family for himself, preferring, much like Julien Sorel, one of royal blood. He begins to steal, according to Sartre, his hagiographer, at the age of ten and by the age of sixteen he was an authentic outlaw, moving from one romantic institution to the other: from the orphanage to the reformatory. (Looking back years later at the Mettray prison, Genet tells us in _Miracle de la Rose_ that time had softened its hard edges and made of it a "romantic stele.") A kind of Vigny without dignity, Genet identifies with all the pariahs of the modern world: the black man, the Arab, the servant, the prostitute, the homosexual and especially the criminal. From 1932 to 1940 he goes on a "pilgrimage" in which his goal is to reach the lowest possible state of degeneracy; our budding romantic hero deliberately becomes a decadent one. Like Michaux's clown he wants to show himself as "ras et risible." Unlike Michaux's clown, he succeeds. He indulges in thievery, begging, prostitution and dope-peddling and is in and out of jail from one end of Europe to the other. He succeeded then in alienating a world that had first alienated him. Seldom has the "épatez le bourgeois" been pushed to such lengths, and seldom has an incurable romantic created such a buffer zone of solitude between himself and "honest folk."

Lewis Cetta has said: "It is Genet's purpose, in part, to reassert and reaffirm this Other within the Self. To that end, he has become a dedicated irrationalist in a society still perversely clinging to eighteenth-century rationalism, and in that sense he is a romantic."[19] I think the case for Genet's romanticism can be put in much stronger terms. More than any other major French writer of this century, Genet has not only continued but exacerbated the romantic revolt against the "straight" world, its attack on and flight from everyday reality. More significantly, he has revived, in very original fashion to be sure, most of the great myths of the romantic age: Satan, Faust, Prometheus, Don Juan, the pariah, the puer senex, the somber and fatal hero and especially the sublime criminal.

The satanic in Jean Genet's life and work stems in part from a sacrilegious urge (and perhaps a psychological need) to betray that which he reveres (cf. again, romantic irony). We read at the end of the Journal du voleur: "L'idée de trahir Armand m'illuminait. Je le craignais et l'aimais trop pour ne pas désirer le tromper, le trahir, le voler. Je pressentais la volupté inquiète qui accompagnait le sacrilège. S'il était Dieu . . . et qu'en moi il eût mis sa complaisance, il m'était doux de le nier."[20] Similarly, Erik in Pompes funèbres dreams of shooting God, wounding Him and making of Him a mortal enemy. Genet both seeks God and seeks to deny Him. One can feel this ambivalence in nearly every passage in which God is named. Aspiring to reach Heaven "in spite of God," Genet respects God's power but his inordinate (romantic) pride makes him recalcitrant; he fancies himself as a "Lucifer fencing with God":

> Si l'orgueil est la plus audacieuse liberté--Lucifer ferraillant avec Dieu--si l'orgueil est le manteau merveilleux où se dresse ma culpabilité, tissé d'elle, je veux être

> coupable. La culpabilité suscite la singularité (détruit la confusion) et si le coupable a le coeur dur (car il ne suffit pas d'avoir commis un crime, il faut le mériter et mériter de l'avoir commis), il le hisse sur un socle de solitude. La solitude ne m'est pas donnée, je la gagne."[21]

This short passage is heavily laden with romantic themes: fierce pride; audacious freedom; the noble criminal; the primacy of the singular self (Genet's heroes are all highly conscious of their gesturings and posturings that set them apart from others: Querelle's poses, we are told, are a kind of "terrifying dandyism."); the solitary figure perched high above ordinary mortals (hissé sur un socle de solitude); and finally what concerns us most here: the Satan-Lucifer myth. In Notre Dame des Fleurs we are told that Mignon's bitter sneer partakes of "satanism" and that the author would have liked, in a romantic antithesis, to model Divine on Lucifer.

Another reason why Satan fascinates Genet is the latter's romantic thirst for the Absolute, in this case absolute Evil, la hantise du mal: "Tuer un homme est le symbole du Mal. Tuer sans que rien ne compense cette perte de vie, c'est le Mal, Mal absolu. Rarement j'emploie ce dernier mot, car il m'effraie."[22] Querelle, in betraying Gil, views himself as a latter-day Faust, entering into a non-verbal pact with the Devil in which the soul offered is not his own but that of a precious friend.

To his dismay Genet discovered that Absolute Evil is unattainable, and that his revolt against God was doomed to fail. Thus several critics have invoked the figure of a beaten Prometheus rather than a triumphant Satan lurking in the shadows of Genet's work. Sartre tells us that Good is the vulture that gnaws at Genet's liver. And Richard Coe, extrapolating from Genet's implicit attitude, says: "If the commandment: 'Thou shalt not kill' does in fact emanate from a Divine Authority . . . then consciously to defy the supreme law of God is the act at least of a Prometheus, if not a martyr. It is the revolt of human dignity and human liberty--a tragic, hopeless and doomed revolt . . . against the degrading servitude imposed by a superior will or a transcendental determinism."[23] One of Genet's characters, Lefranc in Haute Surveillance, is explicitly called a Prometheus.

That other rebel against God, Don Juan, makes his appearance in Les Nègres, in which the actors dance to a minuet from Mozart's Don Giovanni, celebrating thus the "unrepressed, unrepenting, elemental pleasure principle--the dark, erotic force."[24]

Satan and Faust, Prometheus and Don Juan appealed to the Romantic imagination because they are archetypal figures of the Rebel. Another Romantic rebel was the sublime criminal. For Genet all criminals are sublime because crime is sublime in itself. "I love the act of stealing because I find it elegant in itself."[25] A murder, we are told in Querelle de Brest, is a work of art. "Sublime" is the very epithet Genet uses to describe both the petty criminal Stilitano and the arch-criminal, Hitler. The Gestapo, if it could combine pederasty with its thievery and betrayal, would become "étincelante." Criminals to Genet are "beautiful," their work ennobling, they walk on water like gods. Through a miraculous transsubstantiation the criminal's sackcloth can become, like Harcamone's, silk and brocade. Genet admires the ritual beauty of the thief's repeated gestures, his crowbar becomes his scepter, the symbol of his "enthronement."

Other details too reveal a romantic conception of the criminal. For one thing a criminal career allows one to escape the monotony of everyday life. Somewhere in the Journal Genet says that the thief is the most estimable of the characters that inhabit him, that through his criminal heroes he is led far from life's "banal paths." The thief is also a solitary creature for whom normal human relationships are foreign. Solitude, for Genet no less than for the romantics, is a man's surest badge of glory. It is automatically conferred upon the criminal: the greater the solitude, the greater the criminal, so that the trio, thief-murderer-traitor, forms a hierarchy. "C'est peut-être leur solitude morale--à quoi j'aspire--qui me fait admirer les traîtres et les aimer."[26] The murderer especially is related to the fatal hero in two ways: he is an instrument of fate in the lives of others, and he lives in the expectation of his own condemnation.[27] We are told in _Querelle de Brest_ that the criminal knows that his criminal act is suicidal.

Genet's male protagonists may be "gay" in the new sense of the word, but certainly not in the old one. Neither their criminal activities nor their forbidden sexual ones produce real joy. Genet's heroes strike us rather by their gravity. They resemble the _beau ténébreux_ of romantic lore. "Terne", "triste", "sombre", "funèbre" are the epithets most frequently used to describe the physiognomy of fictional heroes such as Bulkaen, Métayer, Harcamone, and Divers. As for Pilorge:

> Son visage découpé dans _Détective_ enténèbre le mur de son rayonnement glacé, qui est fait de son mort mexicain, de sa volonté de mort, de sa jeunesse morte, et de sa mort. Il éclabousse le mur d'un éclat qui ne peut s'exprimer que par la confrontation de ces deux termes qui s'annulent: lumière et ténèbre. La nuit sort de ses yeux et s'étend sur son visage . . . O Pilorge! Ton visage, comme un jardin nocturne seul dans les Mondes où les soleils tournent! Et sur lui, cette impalpable tristesse . . . Ton visage est sombre, comme si au grand soleil une ombre s'était portée sur ton âme [28]

Genet tells us in the _Journal_ (p. 209 and pp. 211-12) that it is to "gloomy and somber" heroes that he is attracted; and in _Pompes funèbres_: "Je reste attiré par les êtres qu'on appelle ténébreux, ceux en qui quelque chose me révèle la nuit, ceux qui sont enveloppés de nuit" (p. 53). Sometimes these dark faces are made even darker still by dirt (Bulkaen) or coal dust (Querelle). Even the laughter of Genet's heroes is somber (e.g., _Miracle de la Rose_, p. 422). The handsome captain of Genet's imaginary pirate ship is loved especially for his increasing melancholy and solitude (ibid. p. 288).

In <u>Pompes funèbres</u>, Eric is explicitly called a "beau ténébreux" (p. 143).

Genet has even given us his version of the romantic <u>vague à l'âme</u>: free-floating anxiety can be "greater" than a precise sorrow.

> Est-il bien sûr que le chagrin est plus grand si l'on en a davantage conscience? On a conscience de son chagrin quand on garde l'esprit braqué sur lui, quand on l'examine dans une tension qui ne fléchit pas: il vous dessèche alors comme un soleil regardé en face, son feu vous dévore à tel point que j'éprouvai longtemps une brûlure à mes paupières. Mais il arrive aussi que le chagrin désagrège les facultés, disperse l'esprit . . . . Nous souffrons de ne pouvoir fixer notre chagrin; nos actes s'enveloppent d'une aura de lassitude et de regret qui fait paraître les actes faux--faux de très peu, vrais en gros, mais faux puisqu' ils ne nous comblent pas. Un malaise les accompagne tous." (<u>PF</u>. p. 73)

It is not surprising then, given Genet's propensity for somber heroes and for vague melancholy that his favorite season ("la saison de base de ma vie," <u>MR</u>, p. 327) is late autumn. "Autumn is the season nearest to Genet's own emotions, the most familiar to him, the least oppressive. As a true, if belated romantic spirit in the vein of Ossian and Senancour, his melancholy, his "despair," if it finds peace anywhere in the world, finds it among the drippings of dark branches and the mouldering of dead leaves."[29]

In <u>Pompes funèbres</u> (p. 67) we read of Pierrot who forced himself to swallow a worm: "Il se trouva pris entre s'évanouir d'écoeurement ou dominer sa situation en la voulant. Il la voulut. Il obligea sa langue et son palais à éprouver savamment, patiemment, le contact hideux. Cette volonté fut sa première attitude de poète, que l'orgueil dirige. Il avait dix ans." Do we find the <u>puer senex</u> in Genet and his heroes? I am convinced that we do. Sartre has said of Genet: "He is not an old child, he is a man who expresses a man's ideas in the language of childhood."[30] But Sartre is thinking of Genet the established man of letters. I am thinking of Genet the adolescent and pre-adolescent who, between the ages of ten and fifteen--according to Sartre's own reckoning--and definitely by the age of sixteen according to Genet's (Journal du Voleur, p. 186) had already made his fundamental existential choice: I will be a thief. Sartre himself says of the young Genet: "We are not lumps of clay, and what is important is not what people make of us but what we ourselves make of what they have made of us. By virtue of the option which they have made on his being, the decent folk have made it necessary for a child to decide about himself prematurely . . . I deeply admire this child who grimly willed himself at an age when we were merely playing the servile buffoon."[31]

Querelle is only fifteen when he "chooses" to live among thieves and speak their argot. Dédi in the same novel is but sixteen when he starts consciously and gravely to create his essence, his "self-imposed-therefore-ethical-dereliction." Another child-criminal, Bulkaen, a precocious hero destined to die young, makes exactly the same type of ethical decision: "L'insulte la plus grave parmi les durs--elle se punit de mort très souvent--c'est le mot 'enculé', et Bulkaen avait choisi d'être cela justement qui est désigné par le mot le plus infâme. Il avait même décidé que le plus particulier, le plus précieux de sa vie serait cela." (MR, p. 329; our emphasis).

Genet's type of puer senex is both hardened and saddened by a precocious knowledge of the facts of life and a commitment to sin: "L'enfance qui a été mise très tôt au courant des choses de l'amour est grave, ses traits sont durs, sa bouche gonflée par un chagrin rentré qui la fait délicatement palpiter, ses yeux sont de glace. Je l'ai remarqué chez les mineurs de Fresnes" (MR, p 329). Genet says of himself and his very young hoodlum friends that they are "la descendance juvénile et nativement doctes" (MR, p. 346; our emphasis) of those angels described in the Old Testament who descended to earth to spread corruption and fornication. That Genet's puer senex is negatively precocious is precisely what makes him romantic.

Let us focus now on one of Genet's hero-heroines, Louis Culafroy, alias Divine. He is one of Genet's many beaux ténébreux, those "êtres ternes et tristes que je lâche parfois pour les beaux danseurs et voyous" (NDF, p. 146). At the end of Notre Dame des Fleurs the author expresses some surprise that he has not given "her" or even the younger Culafroy a single smile (p. 195). Her career as girl queen, as Sartre has shown, gives her no real joy and no real communication with her partners; she is condemned to romantic solitude. "Tout concourt à établir autour d'elle--malgré elle--la solitude" (p. 197). Rejected by human society, her goal is to attain the "superhuman" and "sainthood," by foul means rather than fair: "sortir de l'humain par l'abject voulu" (p. 69). Nearing the end of her life, she sums it up romantically: "Ma vie? Je suis désolée, je suis une vallée de la Désolation" (p. 196). She lives now only to hasten toward Death. But even as the younger Culafroy, suicide was her great preoccupation. And like the romantic hero, it is from a high place that she plunges headlong to her doom: "Elle a passé sa vie à se précipiter du haut d'un rocher" (p. 198). When she dies, it is from a romantic ailment: la phtisie. Deliberately emptied of all hope and happiness by the author, she thus qualifies for romantic sainthood.

Genet has also made of Divine a fatal hero-heroine. Both as Culafroy and Divine, she has been constantly awaiting the moment of death, the "moment choisi par la Fatalité" (p. 42), which she knows will come early, and she marches toward death "selon une fatalité supérieurement agencée" (p. 204). The romantic hero, by definition, is an être d'exception. Often, as is the case of the Hugolian Hero, this exceptionality is more verbal than visible; he is simply the locus of exceptional circumstances, that is, his fate.

This is true also of Divine: "Ce n'est pas d'ailleurs que Culafroy, enfant, et Divine, eût une finesse exceptionnelle; mais des circonstances d'une exceptionnelle étrangeté l'avaient choisi comme lieu d'élection" (p. 189).   "It is important to realize," says Richard Coe, "that Genet's characters-- and Genet himself--feel themselves to be the object of a fatal conspiracy; they are beings predestined for damnation, not by a personal God, but by the very natural order of the universe.   They belong to the Elect, but they are chosen to be plunged headlong into humiliation and evil . . . . Divine believes that the entire natural order of the universe is specifically aimed at "her" destruction and, like the typical Romantic hero, the Byronic âme damnée outlawed and exiled by the whole of creation, feels that this selectivity, which has ordered the very stars in their courses in such a way as to accomplish the downfall of one single being, raises her so far above the common run of humanity that she is Queen, Archangel, and Saint rolled into one: the Elect among the Elect, for whom all miracles are possible."[32]

Genet was tempted to make of Divine a fatal hero in the other romantic sense as well: doomed not only to live and die unhappily but also to harm all those near and dear to him: "S'il ne tenait qu'à moi, j'en ferais un héros fatal comme je les aime.   Fatal, c'est-à-dire décidant du sort de ceux qui les regardent, médusés" (NDF, p. 25).   Yeux Verts (in Haute Surveillance) is another héros fatal in this sense: fatality, we are told, takes the shape of his muderous hands.

That Genet is a true son of the decadent hero is obvious to everyone.   Richard Coe sums up nicely:

> His cult of evil would have been familiar to Baudelaire; his satanism belongs by rights to the epoch of Huysmans and Lautréamont . . . In the circles of Wilde and 'Bosie', he would have felt himself at home; it was Wilde who brought to the fore the underworld of homosexual voyous . . . it was Wilde and Whistler who preached Genet's own doctrine of aestheticism . . . . If the characteristic of the nineties is to

> be decadent, precious and anarchic, no writer is more
> blatantly ninety-ish than Genet. When the murderer
> Ravachol was caught and tried, it was the fin-de-siècle
> novelist Paul Adam (and not Genet) who cried out:
> "A saint is born among us!"; and less than a decade
> later it was the young Marinetti (and not Genet) who
> argued that "art can only be violence, cruelty and
> injustice." Genet's symbolism is as fin-de-siècle
> as his politics; it was in the nineties that that
> wooly-minded demicharlatan, Joséphin (Sâr) Péladan,
> exalted the sacred image of the Mystic Rose above
> all other symbols."[33]

One might add that Genet's flowers-from-filth esthetic (a bowel movement, for instance, is described as "My two bouquets of violets" or "I've got a cigar on the tip of my lip") is a development of the romantic-decadent esthetic.

Genet admits on several occasions that it is his own decadent raiment that he has draped on the shoulders of Divine and his other hero-heroines and, as is always the case, upon close examination one can see the many romantic threads of the decadent garment. To reduce Genet to a romantic pure and simple would be folly: among the many creatures inhabiting him there is also a classicist. But to ignore the romantic dimension of his work would be an even more savage reduction since romanticism--eternal romanticism--informs his work so decisively; it is his mainspring. More vividly perhaps than any other contemporary writer, Genet has articulated the negative side of the romantic imagination.

chapter nine

Some Concluding Remarks:

The Romantic Hero and the Modern Sensibility

The pessimism of the original romantic hero was a reflection of the uncertainties of contemporary history; this is true too of his heirs, but the pessimism of the latter has also been greatly reinforced by certain negative and negative-seeming philosophies, from Schopenhauer to Sartre, and especially by some of the philosophical implications of modern science. The many nineteenth-century discoveries in heredity, genetics and morphology were beginning to explain in mechanistic terms the nature and behavior of living creatures, including man. Astronomy was revealing a universe much vaster in size than had ever been imagined before, the corollary of which was the increasing smallness of man. Geologists, examining river erosion, and Darwin, pondering the origin of biological species, suggested that Biblical time was grossly inaccurate and that the Biblical account of creation was in need of revision or rejection. Cultural anthropology was disclosing a bewildering variety of religious beliefs, of myths and mores, and was suggesting that the key concept in ethics was relativism. William Lecky (<u>History</u> <u>of</u> <u>European</u> <u>Morals</u>) was asserting that there is no act which cannot be shown to have been for-bidden as a sin at one time and place and enjoined as a duty at some other. [1] Conte was developing a positivism which recognizes no reality beyond that which is revealed to the senses. Taine's determinism applied as much to man's intellec-tual, moral, even esthetic efforts as to the physical efforts of crabs and lobsters. Renan, having de-deified Christ, was telling Western man to put faith only in Science.

But to many thoughtful men the implications of science were not uplifting at all. Man, once the King of creation,

Center of the universe, and Captain of his soul, now seemed dwarfed by the immensity of space and time in which he moved like an insignificant and almost invisible ant. Man's cherished "values" seemed to be mere products of local custom, genetic inheritance and the vicissitudes of history. Darwin's theory of evolution suggested that Reason, once man's glory and one of the cornerstones of French classicism, is a mere survival tool. Freud suggested that man's rational and artistic activities are mere sublimations of his sexuality. Behaviorism was soon to posit that man's "consciousness" is a mere epiphenomenon accompanying his conditioned behavior. Recent research in DNA (deoxyribonucleic acid) has led many biologists to conclude that the various species have developed by purely accidental modifications, from pressure exerted either by the external environment or from within the organism; all creatures, man included, would then be the product of a "cosmic lottery," creatures of Chance.

The most disturbing thing of all, I think, is that this relentless attack on the dignity of man, has been coming from all directions: geology, astronomy, biology, psychology, anthropology. For many in search of a humanism, there has seemed nowhere to turn for empirical comfort. Little wonder then that the passive hero, the little man as tragic hero, the clown and the anti-hero have become four of the central figures in modern literature. It is not enough to speak of this in terms of a purely literary tradition. This is the dominant intellectual atmosphere we have to breathe. Although the twentieth century has produced a very large number of talented Christian writers, this has not been a Christian century. The modern sensibility, for better or worse, is a lay sensibility. T. S. Eliot once observed that the result of modern culture has been to obscure what we really are and feel, what we really want. Chateaubriand and his hero, René, had said much the same more than a hundred years before. The vague à l'âme and ambivalence are still basic facets of the modern ego. Twentieth century man is not sure of his place in the cosmic, the historical or even the local scheme of things. His état d'âme has ranged between free-floating anxiety or quiet desperation to that rather precise form of metaphysical anguish called "consciousness of the Absurd." The romantic hero's sense of alienation and his often morbid melancholy have, if anything, increased in intensity and have produced a Literature of Despair.

This despair has not produced tragedy or truly tragic heroes. Tragedy, as Joseph Krutch reminds us in The Modern Temper, deals with reconciliation to life and with the greatness of man symbolized by noble heroes whose outward calamities are the occasion for inward victories. Modern works tend to present an accusation of life and a belittlement of man's significance. Contemporary history is seen as an "immense panorama of futility and anarchy" (Eliot). This attack on the essential goodness of life and the essential greatness of man was begun by the romantic hero, and the work has been continued, diligently, by his heirs.

* * *

How are we to appraise the romantic hero's appraisal of the human condition? I believe that it is both surprisingly accurate in many ways and grossly inaccurate in others.

It is accurate in its description of the human predicament: man's self-consciousness automatically alienates him from the rest of nature, making him restless, often bored and discontent, and drives him to a search or at least a yearning for a higher, transcendent harmony. This romantic appraisal is not only in basic accord with an ontology such as Sartre's but a psychology such as Erich Fromm's (see Excursus I).

The romantic hero's appraisal of the human situation is also in line with Freud's, especially the irreconcilable conflict between the demands of instinct and individualism on the one side and the restrictions of civilization on the other; the contention that civilization is largely responsible for our misery and that we would be happier if we gave it up and returned to primitive conditions; the urge for freedom against rules imposed from without, especially regarding man's sexuality and his inherent aggressiveness; the struggle against the super-ego and the sense of guilt (Freud would have an easy explanation for the secret remorse of the Byronic hero and the rather frantic attempts to reject the sense of guilt by French romantic heroes); the recognition that while happiness requires as a precondition an integration into a human community, there is in man an egoistic urge to avoid union with others. These views, which coincide exactly with those of the romantic hero, are summarized in Civilization and its Discontents.

Although the romantic hero's estimate of the human predicament seems accurate, his estimate of himself, of his fellow man and of Life itself, seems inadequate. As a puer senex his disenchantment and cynicism are precocious but also premature and somewhat immature. Before really exploring life and learning fully about himself, the romantic hero rather leaps to the conclusion that the two are incompatible. Before really getting to know other people, he concludes that they are brutish and mean. His pessimism is not the bitter fruit of long experience; it is rather a facile and largely untested presupposition with which he enters adult life and which becomes not a true Fate but simply a self-fulfilling prophecy.

A critic, we recall, has said this of Michaux's melancholy: "There is in Michaux's work a plaintive, pathetic side (and even a 'look how I'm suffering side,' a voyeur and exhibitionist side), a certain self-satisfaction, a love of one's mal, a masochistic pleasure in one's sorrow, a certain passivity, a certain melancholy egoism." Exactly the same charges have been leveled at René and the romantic hero, and with a good deal of justification. Might they not be leveled also at the modern ego?   There are, to be sure, solid historical reasons for our modern discontent, our Age of Anxiety and Anguish, such as the proliferation of catastrophe and negative philosophies or philosophical implications, the acceleration of history, future shock--all of which began with the French, romantic and industrial revolutions. (The ebb of Faith began earlier, with the philosophes of the Enlightenment, but it was not until the romantic period that "Voltaire's sons were born" [Musset] i.e., when metaphysical anguish set in.) However, it would be damaging or deflating to the modern ego if its weaker or pathological sides were diagnosed as cause rather than effect. When one looks at Western literature of the last two centuries as a block, one can easily get the feeling that writers have taken almost for granted, they have concluded too aprioristically that the human condition is not just difficult but utterly unbearable. This view has attained, almost, the status of a dogma that is not to be questioned; it is presented not as something to be demonstrated but as one of the givens. It seems to a certain extent, then, unearned.

Man, whose dignity has been relentlessly deflated for over two centuries now, is a much maligned animal. In a universe that may be radically irrational, man is the only known animal capable of impressive exercises in reason. In a universe that may be objectively absurd, man is the only animal capable of projecting subjective meaning into it, that is, human values. Man is the only animal capable of converting matter into spirit, stone and clay into statues, sounds into song. He is the only animal endowed with a sense of beauty, a sense of honor and justice (and their important correlative: guilt), the only animal capable of real and not just instinctual courage, the only one capable of disinterested contemplation, compassion and unselfish love. If man is measured not by averages but by his greatest past accomplishments and by his present potential (e.g., the most highly evolved individuals now living), then his future need not seem bleak. Sometimes man takes giant steps forward, more often he only stumbles forward, sometimes his movement is that of an agonizingly slow spiral in which there is little discernible forward movement, but this is man, even more than the tramps of Beckett and the perverts of Genet. When one stops and thinks that our stumbling man is, in terms of geological time, still only on the lowest rungs of the evolutionary ladder, there is surely cause for cautious hope. A noted scientist has described our species recently as young and curious and brave and as holding much promise.

The very centrality of the romantic hero and his heirs in French and Western literature speaks eloquently and convincingly of a crisis of the modern spirit, a crisis that can be analyzed in Christian or in Marxist terms. Ultimately the analysis of the modern crisis will have to be done in humanist terms. If man is not worth saving, he is not even worth condemning.

APPENDICES AND EXCURSUSES

APPENDICES

* * *

EXCURSUSES

* * *

During the course of my research on this book I have encountered some passages dealing with neo-romantic heroes that might have been included in earlier chapters, but I did not want to burden the text with a tiresome and repetitious survey. I have relegated these passages and some very brief discussions of them to appendices. I have also encountered some passages from psychologists and sociologists that, while not bearing directly on the romantic hero do bear on the romantic hero's expression of the modern sensibility. These passages have been relegated even further back, to excursuses, since they will likely be of more interest to some readers than to others.

APPENDIX I

Montherlant's Alban de Bricoule

"S'il existe des classes sociales pour distinguer les uns des autres les romantiques," says Pierre Moreau of Montherlant, "la sienne est celle de Chateaubriand, de Vigny."[1] Several of Montherlant's most frequently recurring themes are romantic ones: the isolation and solitude of the superior individual, the mediocrity of the "herdsmen," the magnificence of pride and the drama of contradiction within a single personality. The Montherlantian hero, as Robert B. Johnson has shown, is a "sensitive and sensual creature existing in an alien environment (alien because it is ignoble); he is in constant struggle with himself and is inevitably doomed to destruction."[2] As it was with the romantic hero, there is a cause and effect relationship, in Montherlant's heroes, between their misanthropy and their solitude, between their egocentrism and their "doom."

The prototype of the Montherlantian hero appears in the author's very first novel, Le Songe (1922). The novel is not one of Montherlant's best efforts, but a brief discussion of its protagonist might be of interest to those readers curious to know other neo-romantic heroes than those presented in chapter seven. The setting of Le Songe is the First World War, and the subject has been called by one critic "a vast romanticized culte du moi" on the part of the protagonist, Alban de Bricoule. Alienated from society, Alban is indeed a model of self-reliance and self-confidence.

> Je ne compte que sur moi et ne consulte que moi.[3]
> Tout, tout, j'ai tout fait tout seul, toujours. (p. 54)

He fully realizes however, that his egoism is an intellectual limitation, that it causes a fundamental inability to understand adequately anything or anyone that is not himself. Others

inspire in him ennui and antipathy, and he is always doing
something different from the crowd.

> Tout lui semblait facile, comme en ce temps du
> collège, où il était toujours à part, dans la cour
> pendant l'étude en étude pendant la récréation, à
> la schola pendant la promenade, à la bibliothèque
> pendant le salut, jamais comme les autres, et néanmoins
> jamais puni, pas une fois en sept ans, de même qu'aujour-
> d'hui, sachant bien qu'il avait en somme abandonné
> son poste, pourtant il n'avait pas envisagé une fois
> qu'on pût le punir. (p. 150)

The fact that he is never punished implies a recognized superiority.   Montherlantian man does not follow the herd, nor
does the awed or admiring herd expect him to.

As a soldier, Alban initially looks forward to the war
for several reasons including patriotism and a disinterested
sense of duty; but the central one is a desire for glory
achieved through a display of energy, intelligence and courage
--like the young Lorenzaccio.   A good exemplar of what some
critics call the T.E.L. Prototype (for T. E. Lawrence), he
has a keen appetite for danger; action for him is even a
form of "repose."   He thinks the death most worthy of him
would be a violent one.   He sees himself as an _homme fort_,
as a _conquérant_ (a word that may have caught Malraux's eye);
one can imagine him using his strength in the service of
fascism just as well as for democracy.   As with the other
adventurer heroes of the T.E.L. Prototype, the cause is less
important than the test of strength, the proof of one's freedom:
"J'ignore l'utilité de mon sacrifice, et dans le fond je
crois que je vais me sacrifier à quelque chose qui n'est
rien, qui est une de ces nuées que je hais.   Croyant mon
sacrifice inutile, et peut-être insensé, sans témoin, sans
désir, renonçant à la vie et à la chère odeur des êtres,
je me précipite dans l'indifférence de l'avenir pour la seule
fierté d'avoir été si libre" (p. 110).

Pierre Moreau sees in Montherlant's fiction many implicit
allusions to Stendhal and in Alban many analogies of detail
with Julien Sorel.

Il arrive à Alban des aventures et mésaventures
pareilles à celle de Julien Sorel et de Lucien Leuwen. . .
Ce qui impose le souvenir de Stendhal, c'est surtout
le dédain du public, cette volonté de se réserver
aux happy few . . . et cette morale . . . que l'on
voudrait oser appeler le stoïcisme des épicuriens.
S'imposer tel geste hardi et décisif à tel moment
déterminé, comme un devoir, regarder telle timidité
comme une lâcheté à laquelle on ne saurait survivre,
se donner à soi-même une des recettes contre le malheur,
ne souffrir que le naturel, se refuser à omettre les
traits de vérité sous prétexte qu'ils blessent les
convenances et aliènent les sympathies: attitude
commune à Beyle, à Julien, à Alban, à Dominique, à
Costals, et au moraliste de Mors et Vita. (Stendhalienne
aussi, cette anatomie idéologique des sentiments,
cette précision dans les catégories de l'amour, cette
chimie qui décompose dans l'éprouvette une souffrance,
une colère, une poussée de fierté . . .⁴

Moreau might have added one more trait to the list: the
thirst for power and glory.

Alban is a fascinating and disconcerting character because
of his contradictory nature. In battle he displays great
courage at certain times, abject fear at others. He is capable
of a camaraderie of epic proportions with his one friend,
Prinet, willing to die with him and for him, even begging
God on one occasion to take his life for his friend's. But
in ordinary life he is condescending and patronizing. Friendship, for Alban, does not imply equality, nor does it prevent
his sadistic streak from expressing itself. In a fit of
pique he kills his friend's cherished dog and thereby a friendship. His relationship with Dominique Soubrier is equally
puzzling. It evolves from a deeply platonic to an equally
deep sensual feeling but never develops into true love. She
excites him mainly as the victim of his insensitivity and
mental cruelty: "Il ne répondit pas. L'agrément de la faire
souffrir montait de sa sensualité. A songer qu'il avait
pouvoir sur elle par ce moyen si simple de garder le silence,
il était réjoui dans son coeur."⁵ This side of Alban will
be developed into near-monstrous proportions in the person
of Costals of the Jeunes Filles tetralogy (1934-39). Here

egocentrism borders on the psychopathic and subtle sadism becomes a habit, an expression of Montherlantian machismo.

That Montherlant, despite the classical tendency of his dramaturgy, is a legitimate heir of the romantics should be clear; indeed he has explicitly called himself "leur fils ingrat."[6]

APPENDIX II

The Pilot as Romantic Hero

The name of Malraux is inevitably linked with that of Saint-Exupéry. Both men sought in action a virile fraternity and the opiate of their anguish. The fiction of both men is largely romantic in tone and texture. Saint-Ex's prose is lyrical, at times sentimental, and poetic--his aeronautical metaphors would have been especially appreciated by those original romantics who were defining romanticism in terms of modernism. And he furnished French literature with a new exoticism: "non plus celui du là-bas mais celui du là-haut."[1] Both Saint-Ex and T. E. Lawrence have compared aviation to a monastic life; not only did it represent a rigorous discipline, it was also an escape from a detested epoch ("Je hais mon époque de toutes mes forces," wrote Saint-Ex in his "Letter to General X".)[2] Michel Quenel gives a succinct appraisal of this "monastic" side of their careers; it has decided romantic overtones: "Refus définitif des mesquineries de la vie sociale, goût d'une existence structurée autour d'une croyance vigoureuse, désir obsessionnel d'atteindre ici-bas l'absolu, l'élan de l'âme y est, il n'y manque que la foi."[3]

The airplane is perhaps the romantic hero's ideal machine. He is ever fond of looking with condescension upon the earth below from a high vantage point, witness René on Aetna, Manfred on the Jungfrau, Julien Sorel on a high beam, a mountain top, a tall prison tower. The plane is a natural symbol of moral and intellectual superiority; it represents an art of living at a high altitude, as Pierre Moreau has said in connection with Malraux and Saint-Exupéry; and, as Georges Moulin says in connection with the latter, it is "opposé à ce monde où l'on vit si bassement."[4] Jules Roy, another author-pilot and disciple of both Malraux and Saint-Ex, has

spoken of the fighter pilot as belonging to a "new race":
"Les médiocres et les impurs n'ont jamais été taillés pour
cette tâche réservée à quelques-uns."[5] The bomber pilot,
like the pioneer postal pilot, knows that he is tied to his
machine for life, that is, death. It is his "fatality."
The airplane is also a natural symbol of the romantic yearning
for an unknown absolute. Finally, it is a solitary machine,
perfectly suited to the heroics of a solitary hero and offering
a peculiarly romantic form of uprooting and voluntary exile.

Even as a child Jacques Bernis, like his narrator-friend
in Courrier Sud, was fond of three romantic modes of escape
from routine existence; travel, elevated sites, and death.

> Nous savions déjà que voyager, c'est avant tout
> changer de chair . . . . Fuir, voilà l'important.
> A dix ans, nous trouvions refuge dans la charpente
> du grenier.[6]

> Des lézards bruissaient entre les feuilles, que
> nous appelions des serpents, aimant déjà jusqu'à l'image
> de cette fuite qui est la mort. (p. 60)

Years later, as a pilot, Bernis sees how different his life
is from that of other men. Seeing some old friends after
a prolonged absence, he sees them as "prisonniers d'eux-mêmes"
and himself as a "fugitif" and a "magicien." The pilot's
feeling of superiority with regard to former buddies is also
reported by Jules Roy.

> Il semble moins paradoxal de noter, que, si
> l'apparence du pilote n'a pas changé, son âme par
> contre a subi une profonde métamorphose, et qu'on
> ne saurait, en aucun cas, la comparer à celle d'un
> homme de même culture et de même rang social: deux
> camarades de collège dont l'un est devenu pilote se
> retrouvent aussi séparés que deux animaux d'espèce
> différente, élevés par la même mère.[7]

The pilot hero of Courrier Sud is clearly a romantic hero,
expressing his scorn for "Ces coutumes, ces conventions,
ces lois, tout ce dont tu ne sens pas la nécessité, tout
ce dont tu t'es évadé" (p. 33).

The solitude of the superior individual is found not only in Saint-Ex's pilots but in men like Rivière who send them on their dangerous missions. Somewhat exaggerating his situation, as romantic heroes are wont to do, Rivière sees his responsibilities as cosmic in scope and as automatically alienating him from the herd: "Ce soir avec mes deux courriers en vol, je suis responsable d'un ciel entier. Cette étoile est un signe qui me cherche dans cette foule, et qui me trouve: c'est pourquoi je me sens un peu étranger, un peu solitaire."[8] Saint-Ex's heroes have a romantic as well as aristocratic scorn for the médiocres and fully expect, like the hero of Citadelle, to be misunderstood and rejected by them. If the hero's superiority were not misunderstood, he would of course have to turn in his romantic badge.

APPENDIX III

Julien Gracq's Beau ténébreux

The influence of Chateaubriand on Julien Gracq is enormous, as Gracq himself admits: "Nous lui devons presque tout."[1] It affects every aspect of his fiction: his heroes, his settings, the "correspondences" between the heroes and the settings, the very rhythm of his often poetic prose. The atmosphere of Le Beau ténébreux is "théâtral," "irréel"-- two of the novel's key words; it resembles the romantic atmosphere of the Argol estate, "dont la caractéristique essentielle," says Léon Roudiez, "est d'être la négation de la vie de tous les jours."[2] (The fifteen-year old hero of Au Château d'Argol, published eight years earlier, in 1937, is a puer senex and a "second docteur Faust," devoting his life to the "démon de la connaissance.") Gracq even goes to some pains to make explicit the Chateaubriandesque atmosphere and subject of Le Beau ténébreux. The title, for one thing. Then the narrator, Gérard, reads La Vie de Rancé and is overwhelmed: "Livre étonnant . . . Livre entièrement fait d'harmoniques . . . C'est bien le Nunc dimittis le plus pathétique de notre littérature."[3] And when an orchestra plays "Stormy Weather," he is suddenly seized with "un incroyable vague à l'âme." Finally, at the bal travesti which ends the novel, Christel is disguised as Atala, while Allan is dressed as a young romantic. Even before this episode she had intimated that she wanted the protagonist to serve as her Chactas and attend her at the hour of her death.

The Gracquian hero is a direct descendent of René. He shares the latter's love of solitude, his sense of superiority, his restlessness and taste for travel, and especially his obsession with death: "Sans Chateaubriand, le héros gracquien n'eût pas été exactement ce qu'il est. Une certaine qualité d'âme humaine, une tonalité de l'ennui, une obsession

du suicide qui n'est que la forme aiguë de la présence de
la mort . . . C'est dans cette confrontation avec la mort
que se révèle la qualité propre des personnages de Gracq,
leur façon très moderne, certes, . . . d'être nos René du
XXe siècle."[4]

Gérard is less the narrator than the annonciateur:
he establishes a mood of "fascinated" expectation in connection
with the arrival of the Hero, whom he does not even know.
(Indeed, Allan's character is revealed mainly by the effect
he has on others.) Gérard is attracted to the romantic qualities
of the dark, mysterious, prince-like stranger ("jeune prince
romantique"), because he, too, is a romantic soul. Like
René, Gérard is deeply moved by the sound of Church bells
and the sight of lofty belfries. The following passage
seems to be a direct allusion to René:

> Tout endimanché à travers les allées du beau
> jardin, j'attendais le son des cloches des vêpres--
> derrière un repli de la Loire on voyait un clocher,
> si fin sur la ligne d'horizon, et vers le nord, on
> entendait le bruit d'un train. C'est tout, et j'ai
> le coeur prêt à crever. Que m'arrive-t-il? (p. 40)

The answer is probably found in René: nostalgia and a premonition of death. As in Mauriac's novels, the train here is
a modern memento mori, as is the lonely spire silhouetted
against the horizon. Long before Gérard, René had spoken
of a solitary spire kindling in him "a secret instinct" and
suggesting to him that he was only a voyageur on this earth.

I said a moment ago that Allan's character is revealed
not so much by what he does or says as by the effect he has
on others. These reactions reveal the presence of a romantic
hero.

> Il est un peu volcanique, votre ami. (p. 41)

> Il se manifestait en lui par périodes une humeur
> triste et sauvage, une sorte d'humeur lugubre. (p. 59)

> L'idée de la mort, et plus encore, l'apparat funèbre
> qui l'entoure d'habitude, semblait exercer sur lui
> une étrange fascination. (p. 63)

> Il me semble qu'il est triste. Tout le monde
> le déteste ici, je veux dire que personne ne le com-
> prend, ne l'aime comme il mérite d'être aimé. (p. 141)

> Vous êtes un être très étrange, Allan, un être
> peut-être exceptionnel. (p. 155)

Others speak of his "air de Werther perpétuel," or see him as "un homme du destin." Like the romantic hero he seems always to be looking down upon others from a high vantage point. His room gives off an "atmosphère de haute montagne" (p. 129) of "je ne sais quelle idée de haut lieu" (p. 30); he likes to overlook a city from a hill top "comme un aigle planeur" (p. 101) or an ocean beach from the high balcony of his hotel. Irène, whose advances toward Allan have been rejected, calls him, sarcastically, "l'homme fatal." But there is a double irony here for she doesn't know how right she is. And Allan himself likes to speak of his "trajectory" upon this earth.

Allan's fascination with death is not presented as a case of morbid maladjustment to life; it is related rather to the yearning for the absolute. Like René's, Allan's precocious imagination has quickly exhausted the joys of this earthly life--he is still another puer senex. Dolores, who will join Allan in a double suicide, like that of Vigny's "Amants de Montmorency," looks at death not as the end but as a beginning: "J'ai lu quelque part que la mort était une société secrète. Le mot donne, n'est-ce pas, à réfléchir. Ce qui n'est qu'une fin, un pis-aller, et c'est peu dire, pour la plupart des êtres, ne peut-il devenir pour d'autres une vocation?" (p. 80). For many heroes, from the romantic period to the present, death indeed seems less an accident to be avoided or postponed than a vocation.

APPENDIX IV

Schopenhauer and the French Romantic Hero

In a number of significant ways, German philosophy contributed to the rise of the French romantic hero and assured
him of a numerous progeny. Kant exalted sentiment, conscience,
instinct and intuition above the reason. Hegel encouraged
the cult of the Hero, Fichte and Schelling the cult of the
ego. The apotheosis of egotism is found in the philosophy
of Stirner. The philosophy of Leibnitz, Kant, Fichte and
Schelling were popularized in France by Mme de Staël. The
two qualities she admired most in these philosophers were
the importance given to the emotions and the supreme value
they place on the Self. [1] But the philosopher who best reflects
the romantic malady of the spirit and who, with Nietzsche,
most contributes to the continuance of the malady in the
romantic hero's heirs, is Schopenhauer. The World as Will
and Idea was published in 1819, but its influence was not
greatly felt until the second half of the nineteenth century.
What is even more interesting than the influence is the nearly
exact equivalence between the world view expressed by Schopenhauer and that expressed or implied by the romantic hero.

By accepting Kant's theory that space and time are a
priori subjective forms of intuition and concluding that
the entire world is man's idea, Schopenhauer expressed his
own version of romantic subjectivism. His conception of
the noumenon is also "romantic": the Will, that timeless,
spaceless, uncaused activity that expresses itself in the
individual as incessant impulse, blind instinct, endless
striving, craving, yearning. The analogy with the Faustian
spirit is obvious.

Schopenhauer turned philosophical optimism upside down,
rejecting both the concept of infinite secular progress and
Hegel's idea of infinite spiritual progress, the dialectical

process of the Absolute. Like Senancour, Schopenhauer believes human existence to be futile, even senseless. Man agonizes in the face of cosmic absurdity. Happiness is a mirage. Like the romantic hero, Schopenhauer's man is a creature of infinite desires in a world that can offer only limited fulfillment. Since the Will is an endless striving, it can never find satisfaction nor attain tranquility.[2] When one desire is satisfied, ten others take its place. Even if it were possible to have all one's desires satisfied, the result could only be boredom. Like the romantic hero, Schopenhauerean man is a fatal hero, painfully aware of the inevitable defeat of his aspirations. The higher the organism the greater the suffering, the man of genius suffering most of all. Pain is the positive force in the world, pleasure is a negative principle, the momentary relief from pain. Human life swings "like a pendulum" backwards and forwards, between pain and ennui.

Like his pessimism, Schopenhauer's misanthropy resembles that of the romantic hero. The average man is seen as a "dull scoundrel," his life is base, trite and selfish. It is only fear that makes him honest, only vanity that makes him sociable. The only way to succeed in this world is to be as grasping as the rest. Julien Sorel, Lucien de Rubempré and Eugène de Rastignac learned early this lesson in cynicism.

The world is seen then as a living hell in which, as in Sartre's Huis clos, each man is a devil to his neighbor. One refuge from this living hell is the disinterested contemplation of the esthetic experience. Another is the moral life, which Schopenhauer identifies with pity for one's fellow sufferers (Mitleid); a third means of escape is the renunciation of the Will-to-live. This renunciation is not suicide, but the leading of a passionless, ascetic life in the Buddhist manner--a negative nirvana viewed mainly as an end to torment and striving. Suicide--the romantic death wish--is listed as another means of escape, as is still another romantic flight from ugly Reality: madness.

In our initial chapter we had occasion to outline some striking similarities between the romantic hero and Hegel's world-historical individual. There are some even more striking parallels between the romantic hero and Schopenhauer's famous portrait of the genius. The main difference is that the latter is 2/3 intellect to 1/3 will (these are Schopenhauer's figures), whereas in the romantic hero the proportions are roughly reversed. The genius is a man of knowledge, his mind is fixed on universals, whereas the romantic hero is a perpetual seeker, the universal eludes him. But the resemblances are many, and they are significant. The genius's knowledge is intuitive rather than discursive. His greatest tool is his imagination. He is a paradoxical being, a mixture of serenity and melancholy but with a proponderance of melancholy. The brighter a man's intellect, the more distinctly does he perceive the misery of his condition. The genius, like the romantic hero, has pathological tendencies: his very intellectual superiority and hypersensitivity are contrary to nature, that is, the normal primacy of the will. From all this arises a disposition akin to that of the Byronic hero or the heroes of Musset: "that extravagance of disposition, that vehemence of the emotion; that quick change of mood under prevailing melancholy." At times the genius will exhibit the "dreamy absentness" of a René, at other times the passionate excitement of an Hernani. In romantic and post-romantic literature these rapid changes of mood have been expressed through various forms of romantic irony. The world view implicit in romantic irony is shared by Schopenhauer: "The life of every individual, if we survey it as a whole . . . is really always a tragedy; but gone through in detail it has the character of a comedy."[3] Life, Schopenhauer seems to say, is pathedic.

Another essential characteristic shared by Schopenhauer's genius and the romantic hero is solitude. The genius is too different from other men to be their companion; he is "not adapted for thinking in common, i.e., for conversation with the others; they will have as little pleasure in him and his oppressive superiority as he will in them."[4]   The genius is for the most part an alienated being, in contradiction and conflict with his age, destined to be misunderstood by his contemporaries. He is maladapted in the world of practical everyday living dominated by mundane strivings of the will, and he strikes others as "strange." He is, like the romantic hero, a stranger in their midst.

APPENDIX V

Zarathrustra: a Bridge between the Romantic Hero

and his Heirs

The romantic conception of the Hero finds its most lyrical expression in the philosophy of Nietzsche. The concept of the Superman has its roots not only in Fichte's transcendental ego, Stirner's individualistic ego, Hegel's world-historical individual and Schopenhauer's "genius" but also in the romantic hero himself. Will Durant notes that Nietzsche's Übermensch looks suspiciously like Schiller's Karl Moor and Goethe's Götz.[1] He also, I think, looks suspiciously like Stendhal's Julien Sorel. Nietzsche, who was an admirer of Stendhal's work and thought, put into his Superman most of Julien's essential traits: pride, energy, the will to power, egotism, self-discipline, the search for intensity of experience, the penchant for living dangerously as well as beyond good and evil. To sum it up: the emulation of Napoleon, the Superman's great precursor.

Nietzsche's analysis of the "resentment" of the herd toward the superior individual echoes that endured by the romantic hero. The latter's unwholesome melancholy and misanthropy and his wholesome longing for a transcendent life are echoed by Zarathrustra: "I love the great despisers because they are the great adorers, they are arrows of longing for the other shore."[2]

A self-acknowledged romantic, Nietzsche places instinct above the intellect, the individual above society, the Dionysian above the Apollonian. He has been called the culmination of the romantic movement, "the last great scion of the lineage of Rousseau."[3] (To show that the lineage extends well beyond Nietzsche, however, has been one of the aims of this book.) Three other important romantic traits of Nietzsche are his Weltschmerz, which he believes to be even more intense than

that of Leopardi and Schopenhauer, his hatred of the bourgeois
and his insistence on the decadence of contemporary civilization.[4] Decadence for Nietzsche is democracy, "the counting
of noses," and the herd-morality of Christianity and socialism.
He felt that the most obvious sign of nineteenth-century
decadence was the worship of the rich bourgeois, those unimagin-
ative, unintelligent, undiscerning men of money with their
vulgar tastes and ambitions. "Swift apes," he called them,
climbing greedily over one another and dragging themselves
into the mud.

Just as man, for Nietzsche, is a rope stretched between
the animal and the Superman, so Zarathrustra is a rope stretched
between the original romantic hero and many of the latter's
heirs. Zarathrustra is working for heroes, the "higher men"
of today who are still all-too-human, still too similar to
the average man. He is fighting to conquer their pessimism
and nihilism so that they may remain bridges to the higher
race of men yet to come. As a commentator writes: "Nietzsche
is still dealing with pessimism here; but it is the pessimism
of the hero--the man most susceptible of all to desperate
views of life, owing to the obstacles that are arrayed against
him in a world where men of his kind are very rare and are
continually being sacrificed. It was to save this man that
Nietzsche wrote."[5]

Zarathrustra is not only a poet-prophet and seer working
for romantic heroes, he is a genuine romantic hero himself,
since he, although still unworthy of the One who will come
after him, is higher even than those "higher men" for whom
he works. Zarathrustra is the solitary and misunderstood
hero, the "lonesome one," the mountain-dweller living well
above the heads of the herdmen. To the self-righteous he
is "a robber," a "devil," and a "law-breaker"; in fact he
is a Noble Outlaw, a Promethean figure who not only defies
God but pronounces Him dead. Although he brings a message
of hope for the future, the present fills him with disgust

and melancholy; at times he even resembles the beau ténébreux: "Gloomy is the night, gloomy are the ways of Zarathrustra" (p. 11).

Zarathrustra preaches the innocence of the instincts and the mere instrumentality of the intellect, that "little sagacity" used in the service of the higher Will. He preaches the importance of the ego and sings of selfishness, wholesome and "blessed." Like the romantic hero he believes that "the only possible way in which the great man can achieve greatness is by means of exceptional freedom--the freedom which assists him in experiencing himself" (p. 431).

Below are some specific passages that show Zarathrustra's curious kinship to various romantic heroes, especially French ones. The passages speak for themselves and need no analysis.

Zarathrustra has urges similar to those of Faust--

> Would that I were wiser! Would that I were wise from the very heart, like my serpent!
>
> But I am asking the impossible. (Prologue)

at times he reminds one of the Byronic hero--

> Hungry, fierce, lonesome, God-forsaken: so doth the lion-will wish itself.
>
> Free from the happiness of slaves, redeemed from Deities and adoration, fearless and fear-inspiring, grand and lonesome . . . . (II, xxx)

I said a moment ago that just as man, for Nietzsche, is a rope stretched between the animal and the Superman, so Zarathrustra is a rope stretched between the French romantic hero and many of the latter's heirs. At one end of the rope one can clearly see René--

> Flee, my friend, into thy solitude! (I, xii)
>
> Ah! whither shall I now ascend with my longing! From all mountains do I look out for fatherlands and motherlands.
>
> But a home have I found nowhere: unsettled am I in all cities, and decamping at all gates.
>
> Alien to me, and a mockery, are the present-day men, to whom of late my heart impelled me; and exiled am I from fatherlands and motherlands. (II, xxxvi)

> I am a wanderer and mountain-climber, said he
> to his heart, I love not the plains, and it seemeth
> I cannot long sit still.
> Summits and abyss--these are now comprised to-
> gether! (III, xlv)

> Me, the lonesomest one. (XXX, xlviii)

> To some, lonesomeness is the flight of the sick
> one; to another, it is the flight from the sick ones.
> (III, ix)

At the other end of the rope one can see people like
Malraux's Garine--

> The happiness of man is, "I will." (I, xviii)

> Hail to thee, my Will! (II, xxxiii)

and the aristocratic pilots of Saint-Exupéry--

> For this is our height and our home: too high
> and steep do we here dwell for all uncleanly ones
> and their thirst. (II, xxviii)

> And as strong winds will, we live above them,
> neighbors to the eagles, neighbors to the snow, neighbors
> to the sun: thus live the strong winds. (Ibid.)

> All my wandering and mountain-climbing: a necessity
> was it merely, and a makeshift of the unhandy one:
> --to fly only, wanteth mine entire will . . . .
> (III, xlviii)

and the Anouilhian Nay-sayer--

> To create itself freedom, and give a holy Nay
> even unto duty. (I, i)

> . . . a holy Nay-sayer, when there is no longer
> time for Yea. (I, xxi)

and the existentialist hero--

> To create new values--that, even the lion cannot
> yet accomplish: but to create itself freedom for
> new creating--that can the might of the lion do. (I,i)

> This--is now my way,--where is yours? Thus did
> I answer those who asked me "the way." For the way
> --it doth not exist! (III, lv)

and even the decadent heroes of Genet--

> I know not the happiness of the receiver; and
> oft have I dreamt that stealing must be more blessed
> than receiving. (II, **xxxi**)

> A hunger ariseth out of my beauty: I should
> like to injure those I illumine; I should like to
> rob those I have gifted:--thus do I hunger for wickedness!
> Such revenge doth mine abundance think of: such
> mischief welleth out of my lonesomeness. (II, **xxxi**)

> "Man must become better and eviler."--so do I
> teach. The evilest is necessary for the Superman's
> best. (IV, lxxiii)

> I rejoice in great sin as my great consolation.
> (ibid.)

APPENDIX VI

The Main Bridge Between 19th and 20th-Century

Romanticism: Barrès

As Julien Benda, quoted earlier, and many others have suggested, Maurice Barrès--for better or worse--is the single most important figure in leading romanticism from the nineteenth century into the twentieth. Indeed, Barrès, whose career was situated at the crossroads of the two centuries, was himself a crossroad of nearly all the romanticisms of both. Gide will condemn him for the staid traditionalism of the Roman de l'énergie nationale but will underplay his own debt to Barrès and to the radical romanticism of the Culte du moi. In 1921 the dadaist-surrealist group will put Barrès "on trial" for subverting the human spirit, but it was he, thirty years before they, who emphasized the relative unimportance of Reason and who proclaimed the supreme importance of the unconscious. One of the works that marked him most as a child was that of Walter Scott. At the beginning of his literary career, when he was developing the Culte du moi, harking back philosophically to Fichte, Schopenhauer and Nietzsche, his literary "intercessors," among others, were Benjamin Constant, the young Sainte-Beuve, Rousseau and Byron; other authors he admired at the time were Gautier, Baudelaire and Huysmans. Later in his career, when he attempted to free himself of his inveterate romanticism, he will at the same time try to become the twentieth century's Chateaubriand by composing, as Henri Bremond suggested he do, a new Génie du christianisme. Like Chateaubriand he will emphasize not the truth of the Church's dogmas but the beauty of its pomp and ceremony, the glory of its history (selectively recalled), the stability and rootedness it offers its adherents. Gide, rather petulantly, suggested that all that is most impressive in Barrès' work was already contained in that of Chateaubriand.

The exaggeration does point up the many similarities: the importance of sentiment, even sentimentality, the belief that deep emotion and passion come closer to the truth than intellectualism; the demi-croyant mysticism ("I cannot say if religion is true or not, but I love it."); the lure of exoticism; the distrust of innovation (as opposed to the creative evolution of the Hegelian and Bergsonian dialectics); the melancholy that pervades the early novels and that is never entirely absent from the later works; the thirst, especially in the declining years, for the infinite; the decadent attraction to themes of decay and dissolution; the fascination with death. Barrès will exert a direct and profound influence on neo-romantics like Montherlant, Malraux, Mauriac, Drieu la Rochelle and Camus and, through them, indirectly on many others.

The novels of the Culte du moi trilogy, especially the first one, Sous l'oeil des barbares (1888), are the nineteenth century's last great paean of romantic individualism and solipsism. The Self alone is important, the Self alone is really real. All that is not-self, the non-moi, is an inferior and dangerous sub-reality, the realm of the Barbarians, not just the living but the dead ("notre malaise vient de ce que nous vivons dans un ordre social imposé par les morts, nullement choisi par nous. Les morts, ils nous empoisonnent."). Barrès' Culte du moi contains already the disponibilité and déracinement, the emotional fervor and fluidity of Gide's Nourritures terrestres. A good system of living, we are told, is to have no home and to have no fixed or settled emotions: "nulle fièvre ne me demeurera inconnue, et nulle ne me fixera." Already present also is Bergson's intuitionism. The Self, through its own dynamism, must capture the movement of the universe and unite itself to it intuitively; thus will be finally resolved the antinomy of subject and object.

Philippe, the hero of Le Culte du moi, is at the outset a young decadent, weaker even than the barbarians he looks down upon "from on high." They at least enjoy the élan vital of primitivism. Stifled by his mal de fin de siècle, his goal is to regenerate his life. The first stage of his development is the recognition of his inalienable Self as the one undeniable reality. He lives "under the eyes" of the Barbarians, under the look of the Other, and resists the attempts of the others to bend him to their image of him. He retreats into himself to ward off the alien invaders and to preserve his individualism. He is, then, a decadent hero striving to make himself into a romantic hero and is also a forerunner of the existentialist hero (the latter will call the Barrésian Barbarians salauds). André Maltère, the romantic "outlaw" hero of L'Ennemi des lois (1893), will, like Philippe, struggle against society's attempts to restrict his freedom and individuality by opposing the instinctual life to its "stuffy rationalism."

Philippe fails to find in solipsism and uprootedness a constant source of energy and vitality. He is still prone to ennui, lethargy and depressions; thus he considers reestablishing contact with the Barbarians. In Un homme libre (1889) and Le Jardin de Bérénice (1891) there is a growing thematic tension between individualism and traditionalism. Philippe finally realizes that his moi can be revitalized only through direct contact with everyday reality, with political "commitment" and especially with his "roots." The self is now situated within an ontology of Being, not Becoming; it is a distinct and unchanging essence acquired at birth. Here of course the Barrésian hero and the existentialist hero will part company. They will also quarrel about the proper object of political commitment and about the relative limits of freedom and determinism.

Barrès' intellectual (or anti-intellectual) evolution from the individual to "national energy" did not bring an abrupt end to his romanticism. In the first place, nationalism is narcissism writ large. His political engagement is still

egocentric: it is not the cause that really interests him,
it is adventure and high-pitched emotions he seeks ("I am
only interested in being moved.")   He is also interested
in moving others, in the will to power.

In the second place, much space is devoted to the romantic-
decadent phase (i.e., before his "conversion") of François
Sturel, the profoundly autobiographical hero of Les Déracinés
(1897).   Sturel exhibits many resemblances to the dynamic
side of Julien Sorel, not the least of which is the mutual
admiration of Napoleon, "professeur d'énergie."   In other
respects, however, especially at the beginning of his career,
he more closely resembles Musset's Octave.   He is described
as "un jouisseur délicat. . . un nerveux à la recherche de
son bonheur. . . au net, un débauché."   He resembles Octave
more profoundly in his masochistic propensity to spoil a
happy moment ("sa volupté la plus fine, dans le secret de
son coeur, semble être de gâcher un bonheur.")   Like René,
Sturel is a lover of solitude and revery and is a rather
passive seeker of perfection.   Although avid for happiness,
he rejects it in all its forms because he is too fastidious
to accept the mediocrity that ordinary happiness entails,
in the end "enjoying only his melancholy."   But like Philippe
and like Drieu La Rochelle's Gille, he will eventually find
his way out of the decadent impasse through a nationalism
that borders on--that announces in fact--fascism.

While acknowledging his romantic inheritance, Barrès
was always wary of its weaknesses and its dangers.   He rejected
its esthetic ("le souci perpétuel d'étonner, le virtuosisme,
l'outrance et le bavardage qu'on nomme lyrisme") and its
aimlessness; he saw it as both an exciting and a dangerous
power ("un excitateur sans frein, ni orientation").   His
great effort, revealed as early as Un homme libre, was to
attempt a synthesis of romanticism and clear-sighted realism,
to create what might be called a disciplined romanticism.
Romantic hyperesthesia was to be used as an instrument of
"positive knowledge."   Barrès' goal, in short, was to harness

romantic energy and to "regulate" romantic emotivity. Thus, for instance, the preface to Amori et dolori sacrum (1903):

> Ces pages sont, à vrai dire, un hymne. Je n'ignore pas ce que suppose de romantisme une telle émotivité. Mais précisément nous voulons la régler. Engagé dans la voie que nous fit le dix-neuvième siècle, nous prétendons pourtant redresser notre sens de la vie. J'ai trouvé une discipline dans les cimetières où nos prédécesseurs divaguaient, et c'est peut-être à l'hyperesthésie que nous transmirent ces grands poètes de la rêverie que nous dégagerons des vérités positives situées dans notre profond sous-conscient.
> (OEuvre, VII, 9-10)

The final phase of Barrès' career cannot be considered simply, as some have labeled it, a "Catholic romanticism." To the end, he was a precursor of the Absurd. Barrésian man, like Schopenhauer's and Sartre's, will complain of being a useless passion, and like the man of the Absurd he will complain that the thirst for the eternal and the absolute is an impossible dream: life is endless flux and fragmentation.

> La Vie n'a pas de sens. Je crois même que chaque jour elle devient plus absurde. Toujours désirer et savoir que notre désir, que tout nourrit, ne s'apaise de rien! Ne vouloir que des possessions éternelles et nous comprendre comme une série d'états successifs! De quelque point qu'on les considère, l'univers et notre existence sont des tumultes insensés."
> (Les Amitiés françaises, "Le Chant de confiance dans la vie." OEuvres, V, 559-60)

But, says Barrès, we must make some sort of accommodation to this absurd universe, we must put down some anchor within the universal flux. His traditionalism as a cure for alienation is to a certain degree, even a surprising degree, a pis-aller-faute-de-mieux, a defensive mechanism ("it's a question of finding. . . a refuge against the mediocrity of the universe.").

> La France a construit une tradition qu'il faut maintenir et développer. . . faite de moeurs, de délicatesses, d'expériences préalables, les plus propres à nous protéger et à faire digue contre les brutalités poussées de la vie, qui est une inventrice, jamais lasse, de douleurs.
> (Ibid.)

Again, there are many romanticisms in Barrès, and if they contradict each other, even attack each other, this very contradiction in itself profoundly romantic.

EXCURSUS I

Some Support for the Romantic Hero's World-View:

Freud and Fromm

Since it is bad form to annoy and distract the reader with lengthy quotations embedded in remote footnotes, I shall place two of my longest quotations here.

In my concluding remarks I acknowledged that the romantic hero's assessment of the human predicament is, to a certain degree, quite accurate. If one accepts Erich Fromm's description of the human predicament, then the romantic hero's world-view is uncannily accurate.

> The first element which differentiates human from animal existence is a negative one: the relative absence in man of instinctive regulation in the process of adaptation to the surrounding world . . . .
> Self-awareness, reason, and imagination have disrupted the "harmony" which characterizes animal existence. Their emergence has made man into an anomaly, into the freak of the universe. He is part of nature, subject to her physical laws and unable to change them, yet he transcends the rest of nature. He is set apart while being a part; he is homeless, yet chained to the home he shares with all creatures. Cast into this world at an accidental place and time, he is forced out of it, again accidentally. Being aware of himself, he realizes his powerlessness and the limitation of his existence. He visualizes his own end: death . . . .
> Reason, man's blessing, is also his curse. . . Man is the only animal that can be bored, that can be discontented, that can feel evicted from paradise. . . .
> Having lost paradise, the unity with nature, he has become the eternal wanderer . . . He must give account to himself of himself, and of the meaning of his existence. He is driven to overcome this inner split, tormented by a craving for "absoluteness," for another kind of harmony which can lift the curse by which he was separated from nature, from his fellow men, and from himself.[1]

The romantic hero is the expression of that torment, of that craving, of which boredom and discontent are only two of the symptoms.

The romantic hero also anticipates--and again rather uncannily I think--some of the reproaches the Freud was led to make against the super-ego.

> In the severity of its [the super-ego's] commands and prohibitions it troubles itself too little about the happiness of the ego, in that it takes insufficient account of the resistances against obeying them--of the instinctual strength of the id, and of the diffi- culties presented by the real external environment. Consequently we are very often obliged, for therapeutic purposes, to oppose the super-ego, and we endeavor to lower its demands. Exactly the same objections can be made against the ethical demands of the cultural super-ego. It, too, does not trouble itself enough about the facts of the mental constitution of human beings. It issues a command and does not ask whether it is possible for people to obey it. On the contrary, it assumes that a man's ego is psychologically capable of anything that is required of it, that his ego has unlimited mastery over his id. This is a mistake; and even in what are known as normal people the id cannot be controlled beyond certain limits. If more is demanded of a man, a revolt will be produced in him or a neurosis, or he will be unhappy.[2]

This passage is significant: it throws considerable light upon the romantic hero's revolt, his frequent neuroses and his perpetual unhappiness; it also corroborates, in the light of empirical data and with the aid of new concepts, the romantic hero's agonizing appraisal of the human situation.

EXCURSUS II

The Romantic Hero and the Modern Sensibility:

Some Insights from Sociology

In 1960 Norman Mailer (<u>Advertisements</u> <u>for</u> <u>Myself</u>) sketched an intuitive description of the contemporary sensibility by listing "hip" concepts and feelings along with their "square" opposites. Induction for instance is hip, deduction is square. The self is hip, society square. Crooks are hip, cops are square. Saints are hip, clergymen square. Questions are hip, answers square. The body is hip, the mind square. Mailer's celebration of the nonrational is, quite appropriately, not accompanied by a logical explanation of the grounds of his choices. But César Graña, a perceptive and articulate sociologist, correctly guesses at them.

> We can perceive, for instance, that induction speaks for boldness of mind, for unfolding and many-sided possibilities, for gaining understanding through ambivalence, and touching with the aid of feeling on the pulse of the concrete and the living. There is in it the freedom, the excitement, and the taste of a personal appropriation of experience. Deduction, on the other hand, suggests a cramped, rigid, and naked intellectual style--"safe," reductionistic, and impersonal, dependent on accumulated fact. The crook is hip because he is a nay-sayer to market values and utilitarian regularity (he is a taker, not a producer, buyer, or seller), but beyond that because he is among those who believe in self-assertion at the risk of everything else, even self-destruction. Cops, on the other hand, are the officious servants of social conformity. Saints are hip, because they are men "infatuated with self-perfection," sacred eccen-trics. . . . The body is hip because it represents the breathing, total reality of life impulses with all their secrets and irresistibility. The mind is square because it represents what Freud calls the "procrastinating factor of thought," that is, caution, calculation, and the element of distance and control which comes with abstraction. . . . A question is hip because it is in itself disquieting, unfinished and beckoning, and when truly a pure question, does not go beyond the flow and counterflow of wondering.

> An answer kills suspended experience by reducing the
> question to measurable terms. It forecloses the state
> of wondering. It deindividualizes and socializes
> experience by solving the problem and, therefore, creating
> the possibility of pragmatic action.[1]

As Graña adds, one can replace "hip" and "square" by "romantic" and "bourgeois," and the equation will be the same. The point I want to make here is that the romantic hero is "hip," both he and his many heirs are "in" in the sense of being in tune with the modern sensibility. And not just the literary sensibility, for I interpret "hip" as applying also to those non-intellectuals who are endowed with a certain self-awareness and a general awareness of the temper of the times.

Graña asks the inevitable and important question: what is it in the spiritual scene of modern society that can account for the intellectual touchiness, the willfulness and frequent bitterness of modern man's romantic sensibility? He finds the answer, as do other sociologists, in the modern historical process which, in the main, has been a progressive rationalization of social experience. Mailer's aphorisms, says Graña, are really a restatement of the romantic rejection of rationalism: rationalism as a philosophical method--the reduction of all experience to analytical terms--and rationalization as a social process, which tends to reduce all of human experience to consistently predictable results.

Both Max Weber and Thorstein Veblen believe rationalization to be the dominant bias and drift of modern society. Veblen sees this process of rationalization mainly in technology, especially its capacity to weigh, measure and manipulate the environment. Weber sees it mainly in institutions such as the legal foundations of the modern state (as distinguished from ancestral, sacred or purely personal forms of public authority) and modern bureaucracy (with its insistence on fixed administrative formulas, regular duties, and authority based on trained skills rather than personal obligation or favor).[2]

Pointing out frequently the "rationalist" character of bureaucracy (rules, means, ends, matter-of-factness, rigid order etc.), Weber outlines briefly in his Essays in Sociology the vast extent to which modern civilization has become bureaucratized. Inevitably, for example, the modern democratic insistence on "equality before the law" and the demand for legal guarantees against arbitrariness and "privilege" has led to a demand for "formal and rational 'objectivity' of administration as opposed to the personally free discretion flowing from the 'grace' of the old patrimonial domination."[3] Then there is the necessarily bureaucratic structure of modern standing armies; the inevitable bureaucratic organization of interurban and interregional transportation and long-distance communications systems; the bureaucratization of modern capitalism with its demands for expertly trained technicians, clerks etc., and the reduction of modern office management to rules and routine in the interests of efficiency.

Although Weber speaks briefly of the bureaucratization of education and of training in general, he does not mention what I believe to be an even more significant facet of contemporary life: child rearing. Not only does the tender 6 year-old child have to endure the rationalization process of what in America is called "the first grade," the 5 year-old and increasingly the 3 and 4 year-olds of bourgeois families have to endure the "socialization" process of kindergarten, nursery schools and even day care centers. Socialization means enforced conformity to the norms, "logic" and unwritten rules of adult behavior patterns (e.g., putting things away, being cooperative when one is not in a cooperative mood). So, the rationalization process does not hit a young person simply with his first encounter with government, military service or the office where he or she may work but not long after learning to walk. Recently, mothers of 2 to 4 year-olds have been reading more and more books on "how to" raise children "rationally" rather than spontaneously with the

old-fashioned trial and error method based on common sense
and a non-system of tenderness mixed with the "right" dosage
of discipline.

The benefits obtained from rationalized child-rearing
are undoubtedly offset to some extent by some long-lasting
psychological stress (cf. Freud's insights into toilet-
"training") that expresses itself in rebellion, often displaced
rebellion: the child or adolescent who has been successfully
stifled in one area may choose another terrain in which to
express his rebellion. The terrain may be becoming increasingly
fertile for future romantic rebels.

But let us relate all this to the original romantic
hero.

The first massive effort to rationalize modern life
came with the French Revolution. The old unwieldy divisions,
the provinces, were abruptly abolished so as to create instantly
a rational, tightly unified organization. The country was
divided into departments, departments into districts, districts
into cantons, cantons into communes. The system of weights
and measures was rationalized by the introduction of the
metric system. Primary, secondary and higher education were
reorganized, primary education becoming free and in principle
obligatory. Although it was obligatory in principle only
(there were no funds to create enough schools for universal
education), the principle was significant. An attempt was
even made to rationalize religion, that is, to do away with
it. The Cathedral of Notre Dame was re-dedicated to "the
cult of Reason." The old "parlements"--venal and favoring
inequality before the law (the interests of the aristocracy)
--were abolished. In their place were established three
types of tribunal: a criminal tribunal in each department,
a civil tribunal in each district and a "tribunal de paix"
in each canton. A decree of 12 September 1791 proclaimed:
"Il sera fait un code de lois civiles commun à tout le royaume."[4]
This project was finally and brilliantly realized in 1800-
1804 by Napoleon and his Conseil d'Etat. A supreme rationalist,

Napoleon supervised the editing of a code that guaranteed all the basic rights demanded by the revolutionists, such as freedom of conscience and equality before the law. The latter, as we have seen, is dependent upon a very large and meticulously organized bureaucracy. Napoleon's reorganization of the bureaucracy, like his masterful military planning, was a model of rationality. The conservative side of the Napoleonic code, especially the preoccupation with the rights of private property and ownership, turned the now minutely regulated marriage contract into a business contract. Napoleon's subsequent reform of the judiciary and the university were done along the same general lines, that is, rational ones. This Napoleonic organization was left intact by the Restoration and was largely preserved well into the twentieth century. Its effects are still felt today.

While for René the Revolution meant emigration, exile and ostracism, it affected most of his immediate heirs in other ways. Any sympathy felt for revolutionary ideals was tempered by second-hand reports from elders and historians of the period's cruelty and violence and first-hand evidence of the intellectual and social confusion that the last years of the eighteenth century bequeathed to the nineteenth so that even among the more liberal-minded of the young romantics the prevalent attitude toward the Revolution was one of ambivalence. But the Revolution unleashed powerful forces that were soon to gain momentum thanks to Napoleon and also to the mercantile ethos of the nascent Industrial Revolution, that were tending to rationalize nearly every facet of the social structure. I submit that these forces represent another significant impact of the Revolution upon the romantic hero. Although they could not have been fully conscious of the new rationalization of human society that was taking place, romantics like Musset, when they would exclaim things like "il faut déraisonner," were reacting in some measure to precisely this situation and not simply to the (already-defunct) Age of Reason. The rationalization of marriage into a commercial venture provoked a very conscious rebellion that took the form of a radically new phenomenon: "romantic love." The increasing pressure toward uniformity and conformity helped produce, by reaction, the dandy. The romantic hero's rebellion involves these issues and others such as bourgeois morality --including the new work ethic that interpreted "real work" in terms that excluded writers and artists like Chatteron --hypocrisy (the high inflation of which was the result of the increased pressure to conform), the new religion (Money) and in general the increasing uniformity, regimentation and rationalization of everyday life. If the romantic hero did not rant specifically against "bureaucratization" (in his time bureaucrate was not even standard French but a neologism spawned precisely during the Revolution), his rebellion, which surely involved some measure of displacement, was often a conscious rebellion against "authority," a term both broad and abstract enough to take in some, in fact much, of what we have been discussing.

The romantic sensibility is in revolt against the measurable, the regulated, the predictible, the uniform, the utilitarian. The revolt has taken many forms: not just romantic love and the dandy, not just the late romantic esthetic (ars gratia artis), and movements like the Decadence, Dada (whose main target was l'anti-poétique Raison) and surrealism; but especially--because of the very long continuity which this book has been attempting to outline--the romantic hero and his many rebellious heirs. The latter have not always (or ever perhaps) been totally admirable characters, but they have reflected rather admirably, that is, accurately, the modern sensibility--not just its ideals and wholesome yearnings but its polymorphous perversity.

EXCURSUS III

A Counter-Perspective from Humanistic Psychology

While praising the romantic hero for reflecting quite
accurately many facets of the modern sensibility and even
the basic human condition, I chided him for his somewhat
facile and unearned negativism, especially with regard to
his fellow man. In the interests of seeing the romantic
hero with some perspective, I offer here a counter-perspective,
that of the so-called "Third Force," the American-based school
of humanistic psychology or "growth psychology."

Writers like Karen Horney, Kurt Goldstein, Rollo May,
Gordon Allport, Carl Rogers and Abraham Maslow postulate--
as do Adler, Jung and Fromm--a positive growth tendency in
the human organism which drives it to fuller development.
For all these writers--except Fromm--the healthy organism
develops from within by intrinsic growth tendencies in the
Bergsonian sense, rather than from without in the behavioristic,
Skinnerian sense of environmental determinism. Jung, one
recalls, had rejected Freud's exclusive emphasis on man's
lower animal nature and recognized an inherent human tendency
toward higher values, believing that there was in man a strong,
instinctual need for spiritual satisfaction. Adler, seeing
man's primary motivation as an innate striving for superiority,
spoke of man's "great upward drive." Carl Rogers, after
many years of clinical experience, came to the conclusion
that the innermost core of man's nature is positive, "forward-
moving." Karen Horney posits the existence of evolutionary
tendencies inherent in man which urge him to realize his
given potentialities. Fromm believes that man's upward drive
results not from innate tendencies, but from the very dialectical
nature of his human situation: "There is no innate 'drive
for progress' in man; it is the contradiction in his existence
that makes him proceed on the way he set out. Having lost

paradise, the unity with nature, he has become the eternal wanderer (Odysseus, Oedipus, Abraham, Faust); he is impelled to go forward and with everlasting effort to make the unknown known by filling in with answers the blank spaces of his knowledge."[1]

This belief in man's basic urge to grow in a positive, healthy direction is the basic tenet upon which rests the theoretic and therapeutic approach of the entire Association for the Advancement of Psychoanalysis. Lawrence Le Shan has spoken of a major revolution that has taken place in the field of psychoanalytical-oriented psychotherapy, involving a critical re-examination, among other things, of the notion of psychic determinism and the Freudian assumption or implication that human nature is bad.[2] In 1961 appeared the first issue of the Journal of Humanistic Psychology, and in 1962 was founded the American Association of Humanistic Psychology; both the journal and the association represent a revolt against psychoanalytic and behaviorist orthodoxy. By the mid 1960's the association numbered over 1200 members.[3] Such a number of specialists represents a consensus not to be taken lightly.

Abraham Maslow, one of the prime movers of the Third Force, has taken as one of his specialized areas of inquiry not neurotic or abnormal types but the above-normal, the self-actualizers, the happy, healthy, creative and productive people of this world as well as average people during their "peak experiences," those privileged moments during which they experience a fullness of being. His conclusions are in sharp contrast to the view of man represented by the romantic hero and the latter's heirs. Self-actualizers, says Maslow, exhibit an especially pronounced tendency toward psychological growth and health found in all normal human beings: "We can certainly now assert that at least a reasonable, theoretical and empirical case has been made for the presence within the human being of a tendency toward, or need for growing in a direction that can be summarized as self-actualization, or psychological health . . . i.e., he has within him a pressure toward unity of personality, toward spontaneous expressiveness, toward full individuality and identity, toward seeing the truth rather than being blind, toward being creative, toward being good and a lot else."[4] This is a startlingly hopeful statement in an Age of Anxiety! Healthy people, says Maslow, yearn for what is good for them and for others; for them virtue is its own reward in the sense of being enjoyed in itself. "They spontaneously tend to do right because this is what they want to do, what they need to do, what they enjoy, what the approve of doing, and what they will continue to enjoy."[5] When the healthy subject is also endowed with high intelligence, there is an inward pressure to grow intellectually, a need to know. Research by one of his professors, E. L. Thorndyke, on a group of children with I.Q.s of over 180 revealed that every single child in the group showed an almost insatiable curiosity, which needed no encouragement, but manifested itself as a powerful hunger or drive or need. Here the cliché "thirst for knowledge" reveals a profound truth.

When one compares this view of man with that of the romantic hero, one cannot help thinking back to Goethe and Sainte-Beuve's identification of classicism with health and romanticism with disease. The judgment is grossly unfair when applied to the romantic movement as a whole, which was a period of great energy, creativity, even humanitarianism in its later stages, but when applied specifically to the romantic hero, there is, alas, much truth in it. The romantic hero is endowed with high intelligence, keen sensitivity, sincerity, a wholesome yearning for the absolute, and yet his urge toward self-realization is always blocked somehow, he is a case of arrested development. One need not even compare the romantic hero to Maslow's above average self-actualizers to see that there is something lacking in him. Compare him for instance to the economically and intellectually impoverished "Oakies" of Steinbeck's Grapes of Wrath, and the romantic hero is still found wanting.

The last clear definite function of man--muscles
aching to work, minds aching to create beyond the
single need--this is man.   To build a wall, to build
a house, a dam and in the wall and house and dam to
put something of Manself, and to Manself take back
something of the wall, the house, the dam; to take
hard muscles from the lifting, to take the clear lines
and form from conceiving.   For man, unlike any other
thing organic or inorganic in the universe, grows
beyond his work, walks up the stairs of his concepts,
emerges ahead of his accomplishments.   This you may
say of man--when theories change and crash, when schools,
philosophies, when narrow dark alleys of thought,
national, religious, economic, grow and disintegrate,
man reaches, stumbles forward, painfully, mistakenly
sometimes.   Having stepped forward, he may slip back,
but only half a step, never the full step back.   This
you may say and know it and know it.[6]

chapter one

1. Frederick Garber, "Self, Society, Value and the Romantic Hero," Comparative Literature, 19 (1967), 321.

2. Raney Stanford, "The Romantic Hero and that Fatal Self-Hood," The Centennial Review, 12 (1968), 430.

3. George Ross Ridge, The Hero in French Romantic Literature (Athens, GA: University of Georgia Press, 1959), pp. 5-6.

4. José Ortega y Gasset, Meditations on Quixote, trans. Evelyn Rugg and Diego Marín (New York: Norton, 1961), p. 141.

5. Walter L. Reed, Meditations on the Hero (New Haven: Yale University Press, 1974), p. 6.

6. Søren Kierkegaard, Either/Or, trans. David F. Swenson and Lillian M. Swenson (Garden City: Doubleday, 1959), I, 141.

7. David H. Miles, "Portrait of the Marxist as a Young Hegelian: Lukács' Theory of the Novel," PMLA, 94 (1979), 23.

8. Reed, p. 5.

9. Stanford, p. 33.

10. Ridge, p. 33.

11. François-René de Chateaubriand, OEuvres romanesques et voyages (Paris: Gallimard, 1969), I, 128. Subsequent references are to this edition.

12. Henri Peyre, What is Romanticism?, trans. Roda Roberts (University, Alabama: University of Alabama Press, 1977), pp. 77-83.

13. Manuel de Dieguez, Chateaubriand ou le poète face à l'histoire (Paris: Plon, 1963), chapter one.

14. Quoted by Fernand Baldensperger, Goethe en France (Paris: Hachette, 1904), p. 72.

15. Ibid., p. 113.

16. Pierre Barbéris, Balzac et le mal du siècle (Paris: Gallimard, 1974), I, 53. Barbéris distinguishes between two types of mal du siècle: (a) that of 1820--aristocratic, contemplative and exactly synonymous with the vague des passions described above; cf. Max Milner's paraphrase of Barbéris: "il s'agit d'un état d'âme qui s'exprime dans les mêmes termes que celui de René. A la plénitude du coeur répond un univers où rien n'est possible ni concevable de ce qui donnerait à l'homme ce plus-être auquel il aspire" [Le Romantisme: Paris, Arthaud, 1973, I, 97]; (b) that of 1830, bourgeois rather than aristocratic, concrete rather than vague,

the result of the disenthrallment that ensued when the July Revolution failed to create a new society. In my view Barbéris's two categories are not enough to embrace all forms of romantic melancholy, and his mal du siècle of 1820 does not take into account the tremendous impact of history (1789-1820) upon it. By 1820 romantic melancholy was already historicized.

17. Alfred de Musset, La Confession d'un enfant du siècle (Paris: Gallimard, 1960), p. 78. Musset was too young of course to have witnessed the events of 1783 and 1814 (he was born in 1810). He is talking of the legacy of history to his own generation. Although his credibility is weakened somewhat by the oratorical style of this chapter of La Confession, his ideas merit more reflexion than has been accorded to them by a number of literary historians. Musset is summarizing not only his own assessment but that of many of his contemporaries.

18. Peter L. Thorslev, The Byronic Hero (Minneapolis: University of Minnesota Press, 1962), p. 106.

19. René Jasinski, Histoire de la littérature française (Paris: Boivin, 1947), II, 324 ff.

20. Ridge, p. 7.

21. Ramon Guthrie and George E. Diller, French Literature and Thought since the Revolution (New York: Harcourt, Brace and Co., 1942), p. 9.

22. Ernst Robert Curtius, European Literature and the Latin Middle Ages (New York: Harper and Row, 1953), p. 98.

23. C. M. Bowra, Heroic Poetry (New York: St. Martin's Press, 1966), p. 96.

24. Otto Rank, The Myth of the Birth of the Hero (New York: Robert Brunner, 1957), p. 61.

25. Ibid., p. 93.

26. Ibid., p. 73.

27. For an interesting discussion of Michel Le Charpentier, see Grant Crichfield, "The Romantic Madman as Hero: Nodier's Michel Le Charpentier," The French Review, 51 (1978), 835-42. For a good discussion of Louis Lambert, see Ridge, pp. 10-11 and Barbéris, II, pp. 1726-62.

28. David Winter, introduction to Otto Rank's treatise on The Don Juan Legend (Princeton: Princeton University Press, 1975), p. 18.

29. Peter L. Thorslev, The Byronic Hero (Minneapolis: University of Minnesota Press, 1962), p. 178.

30. Edmond Estève, Byron et le romantisme français (Paris: Hachette, 1907), p. 4.

31. Elizabeth Longford, "Byron and Satanism," London News, Oct. 1977, p. 6.

32. Quoted by N. H. Clement, Romanticism in France (New York: Modern Language Association, 1939), p. 81.

33. For a good discussion of Ossianic poetry, especially as it relates to the romantic hero, see Paul Van Tieghem, Le Préromantisme (Paris: SFELT, 1948), I, especially pp. 279-84. Less important than Ossian but still operative as pre-romantic sources of romantic sensibility and melancholy were English poets like Thomson, Young and Gray. The elegiac tradition was continued, before Lamartine, by Parny, Chênedollé, Millevoye and in 1819 by the publication of Chénier's works.

34. Georg Wilhelm Friedrich Hegel, Lectures on the Philosophy of World History, trans. H. B. Nisbet (Cambridge: Cambridge University Press, 1975), p. 84. All subsequent references are to this edition.

35. A good example of this aspect of the romantic ethic is found in Mme de Staël's Corinne: ". . . no one can judge Corinne--but not because they do not know her well enough. Corinne cannot be judged because the rules and laws that govern the behavior or ordinary men do not apply to her. She is too extraordinary, too far above her society, to be expected to conform to the standards of that society" [Quoted by Maurice Z. Schroder, Icarus (Cambridge, Mass: Harvard University Press, 1961), p. 28].

36. Quoted by Clement, pp. 287-88.

37. Jean-Jacques Rousseau, Les Confessions (Paris: Garnier, 1964), p. 44. For a brief, but good discussion of Rousseau himself as romantic hero, see Schroder, pp. 26-30.

38. Clement, p. 421.

39. A.-F. Prévost, Histoire de Cleveland in OEuvres (Paris, 1810-1816; rpt. Geneva: Slatkine, 1969), IV, 233.

40. Armand Hoog, "Who Invented the Mal du Siècle?" Yale French Studies, 13 (Spring-Summer, 1954), 49. Paul Van Tieghem, Le Romantisme dans la littérature européenne (Paris: Albin Michel, 1948), I, 69.

41. Van Tieghem, ibid.

42. Cf. Pierre Barbéris's remark on romantic literature: "Jamais, sans doute, aucune littérature ne proclama avec plus de force son propre conditionnement par l'Histoire: "J'appartiens à cette génération . . ." (Balzac et le mal du siècle, I, 18).

chapter two

1. Quoted by Baldensperger, Le Mouvement des idées dans l'émigration française (1789-1815), (Paris: Plon, 1924), II, p. 77.

2. Quoted by Baldensperger, ibid, p. 19.

3. See Henri Peyre, What is Romanticism?, trans. Roda Roberts (University, Ala: University of Alabama Press, 1977), p. 39.

4. François-René de Chateaubriand, OEuvres romanesques et voyages (Paris: Gallimard, 1969), I, 49. All subsequent page references to Atala, René, and Les Natchez are to the same volume of this edition.

5. Pierre Barbéris, René de Chateaubriand (Paris: Larousse, 1973), p. 95.

6. Pierre Barbéris, A la recherche d'une écriture: Chateaubriand (Paris: Mame, 1974), p. 39.

7. Manuel de Dieguez, Chateaubriand ou le poète en face de l'histoire (Paris: Plon, 1963), p. 63.

8. Jean-Pierre Richard, Paysage de Chateaubriand (Paris: Seuil, 1967), p. 7.

9. Manuel de Dieguez, p. 72. See also his "Esquisse d'une psychanalyse orphique de la poésie," in Chateaubriand Today, ed. Richard Switzer (Madison: The University of Wisconsin Press, 1970), p. 280.

10. Jacques Barzun, Romanticism and the Modern Ego (Boston: Little, Brown and Co., 1947), p. 105.

11. For more details, see Armand Weil's critical edition of Atala (Paris: Corti, 1950), pp. xii-lxi.

12. Charles-Augustin Sainte-Beuve, Chateaubriand et son groupe littéraire (Paris: Garnier, 1948), I, 281.

chapter three

1. Etienne Pivert de Senancour, _Obermann_, critical edition by G. Michaut (Paris: Société Nouvelle de Librairie et d'Édition, 1912). The second volume of this edition was published by the Société des Textes Français Modernes (Paris: Hachette, 1913). All references are to this edition.

2. Alexandre Dumas, _Théâtre romantique_ (Paris: Firmin-Didot, n.d.), p. 126. Subsequent references are to this edition.

3. Henri Clouard, _Alexandre Dumas_ (Paris: Albin Michel, 1955), p. 161.

4. Ibid., p. 140.

5. Victor Hugo, _Théâtre complet_ (Paris: Gallimard, 1963), pp. 1029 and 1032. Subsequent references to Hugo's theater are to this edition.

6. Charles-Augustin Sainte-Beuve, _Vie, Poésies et Pensées de Joseph Delorme_, ed. Gerald Antoine (Paris: Nouvelles Éditions Latines, 1956), p. 103.

7. Alfred de Vigny, _OEuvres complètes_ (Paris: Gallimard, 1950), I, 153. All subsequent references to Vigny's work are to this edition.

8. Pierre-Georges Castex, "Les Destinées d'Alfred de Vigny (Paris: Société d'Édition d'Enseignement Supérieur, 1964), p. 113.

9. Vigny, II, p. 1001.

10. Ibid.

11. Jean-Paul Sartre, _L'Idiot de la famille_ (Paris: Gallimard, 1971), II, 1960.

12. "My soul is very sorrowful, even to death" (Mark 14:34 and Matthew 26:38). "And being in agony he prayed more earnestly; and his sweat became like great drops of blood upon the ground." (Luke: 22:44).

chapter four

1. Alfred de Musset, Poésies complètes (Paris: Gallimard, 1957), p. 275.

2. Alfred de Musset, OEuvres complètes, ed. Philippe Van Tieghem (Paris: Editions du Seuil, 1963), p. 113. Subsequent references are to this edition.

3. Alfred de Musset, La Confession d'un enfant du siècle in OEuvres complètes en prose, ed. Maurice Allem and Paul Courant (Paris: Gallimard, 1960), p. 88.

4. Several critics have noted the resemblances between Lorenzo and Hamlet. In the discussion that follows I am chiefly indebted to Jules Lemaître's Impressions de théâtre. Lemaître remains, in my opinion, one of the play's best critics. His contention that Lorenzaccio ranks with Hamlet and Faust in psychological and thematic richness merits reflection. For a more recent discussion of Lorenzaccio and Hamlet, see W. D. Howarth, Sublime and Grotesque--A Study of French Romantic Drama (London: Harrap, 1975), pp. 297-302.

5. Alfred de Musset, Lorenzaccio in Théâtre complet (Paris: Gallimard, 1958), pp. 80-81. Subsequent references are to this edition.

6. Jean Starobinski, "Note sur le bouffon romantique," Cahiers du Sud, no. 60 (Aug. 1966), 270-75. A belated but illustrious example of the romantic clown-hero is of course Cyrano.

chapter five

1. Henri Peyre, Literature and Sincerity (New Haven: Yale University Press, 1963), p. 141.

2. Sylvan Barnet et al, A Dictionary of Literary Terms (Boston: Little Brown and Co., 1960), pp. 51-52.

3. Henri Peyre, p. 141.

4. Raymond Immerwahr, "The Subjectivity or Objectivity of Friedrich Schlegel's Poetic Irony," Germanic Review, 26 (1951), 177.

5. Quoted by Morton Gurewitch, "European Romantic Irony," Diss. Columbia 1957, p. 61.

6. Robert Penn Warren, "Pure and Impure Poetry," The Kenyon Review (Spring, 1943), 252.

7. Lord Byron, Fragment on the back of the poet's manuscript for the first canto of Don Juan.

8. Alfred de Musset, Poésies (Paris: Gallimard, 1962), pp. 244-45. All subsequent quotations from Namouna are taken from this edition.

9. Jean Starobinski, L'Oeil vivant (Paris: Gallimard, 1961), II, 115.

10. Maurice Allem, Alfred de Musset, (Paris: Arthaud, 1947), p. 54.

11. For a similar appraisal see Maurice Allem, note 37 in Musset's Poésies, pp. 705-06.

12. Philippe Van Tieghem, Musset (Paris: Hatier, 1969), p. 47.

13. Ibid.

14. René Bourgeois, L'Ironie romantique (Grenoble: Presses Universitaires de Grenoble, 1974), p. 107. There is a brief discussion of romantic irony in Lucien Leuwen by Raymond Giraud in The Unheroic Hero in The Novels of Stendhal, Balzac and Flaubert (New York: Octagon Books, 1969), pp. 63-69.

15. Grahame C. Jones, L'Ironie dans les romans de Stendhal (Lausanne: Éditions du grand chêne, 1966), p. 80.

16. Ibid.

17. Bourgeois, p. 117.

18. Victor Brombert, Stendhal et la voie oblique (New Haven: Yale University Press, 1954), p. 164.

19. Ibid., p. 92.

20. Jones analyses Stendhal's ambivalence toward Julien in terms of identification vs. a sense of superiority, Brombert in terms of a paradoxical mixture of vengeance and compensation (for his own "déboires"), on the one hand, and self-punishment (since he is identifying with his autobiographical hero) on the other.

21. Morton Gurewitch, "European Romantic Irony," Diss. Columbia 1957, p. 188 ff. For Gurewitch, Innocence is the heroic imperative, and the susceptibility to wonder. Experience is Julien's "cunning care for his future" and revenge for imagined contempt. One could just as easily place these last two impulses under the heading of Inexperience, but at least Gurewitch has defined his terms.

22. Ibid., p. 188.

23. Stendhal, Romans et Nouvelles, ed. Henri Martineau (Paris: Gallimard, 1952), I, 257. All subsequent page references for Le Rouge and other novels of Stendhal are to this edition. For a more detailed analysis of Julien as "comic lover" and as comic hero in general, see Sandye Jean McIntyre, "The Comic Hero in Stendhal's Le Rouge et le Noir, diss. Case Western Reserve, 1974. Dr. McIntyre, does not claim, any more than I do, that Julien is fundamentally a comic hero, but this dissertation is the first serious attempt to study this aspect of Stendhal's hero in detail and in depth.

24. For a discussion of objective, subjective and naive irony, see above, p. 92.

25. See p. 611 for the "jeune philosophe" passage. Octave is also called "notre philosophe" (p. 75) precisely during a moment--rare for him--of intellectual frailty.

26. Georges Blin, Stendhal et les problèmes du roman (Paris: José Corti, 1953), p. 234.

27. Stendhal, op. cit, II, p. 124.

28. John Nist, "The Art of Chaucer: Pathedy," Tennessee Studies in Literature, 11 (1966), 2.

29. Alvin Eustis, "Introduction" to Le Rouge et le Noir (New York: Dell, 1963), pp. 17-18.

30. Théophile Gautier, Mademoiselle de Maupin (Paris: Garnier, 1966), p. 43. All subsequent references are to this edition.

31. Théophile Gautier, Poésies complètes de Théophile Gautier, ed. René Jasinski (Paris: Nizet, 1970) I, 157. Subsequent references are to this edition and will indicate stanza numbers.

32. P. E. Tennant, Théophile Gautier (London: The Athlone Press, 1975), p. 45.

33. The critic is Joanna Richardson and is quoted by Tennant, p. 46.

34. See Richard B. Grant, Théophile Gautier (Boston: Twayne, 1975), p. 35.

35. Vladimir Jankélévitch, L'Ironie ou la bonne conscience, (Paris: Presses Universitaires de France, 1950), pp. 22-23.

36. René Bourgeois, L'Ironie romantique (Grenoble: Presses Universitaires de Grenoble, 1975), p. 34.

37. Gustave Flaubert, Madame Bovary (Paris: Gallimard, 1972), p. 219.

38. Ibid., p. 202.

39. M. Boucher, "Ironie romantique," Cahiers du Sud, numéro spécial sur le Romantisme allemand (1937); réédition, 1947; p. 29.

40. Quoted by C. A. Hackett, Anthology of Modern French Poetry (New York: Macmillan, 1956), p. xv.

41. Paul Verlaine, OEuvres posthumes (Paris: Messein, 1913), II, 9-10.

42. Bourgeois, p. 47.

43. "L'Héautontimorouménos," Les Fleurs du Mal, ed. Jacques Crépet and Georges Blin (Paris: Corti, 1942), p. 85.

44. Hackett, p. 226.

45. Henri Peyre, "Laforgue among the Symbolists," in Jules Laforgue --Essays on a Poet's Life and Work, ed. Warren Ramsey (Carbondale, Illinois: Southern Illinois University Press, 1969), p. 45.

46. Jankélévitch, pp. 21-22.

47. Warren Ramsey, Jules Laforgue and the Ironic Inheritance (New York: Oxford University Press, 1953), p. 137.

48. The two critics are Michael Collie and J. M. L'Heureux in their edition of Laforgue's Derniers Vers (Toronto: University of Toronto Press, 1965), p. 85.

chapter six

1. George Ross Ridge, <u>The</u> <u>Hero</u> <u>in</u> <u>French</u> <u>Decadent</u> <u>Literature</u> (Athens, Ga.: University of Georgia Press, 1961), p. 48.

2. A. Boutet de Monvel, "Postérité du héros romantique," <u>Revue</u> <u>des</u> <u>Sciences</u> <u>Humaines</u>, no. 62-63 (April-September, 1951), 140.

3. Ridge, p. 49.

4. A. E. Carter, <u>The</u> <u>Idea</u> <u>of</u> <u>Decadence</u> <u>in</u> <u>French</u> <u>Literature</u> (Toronto: University of Toronto Press, 1958), p. 27.

5. <u>The</u> <u>Hero</u> <u>in</u> <u>French</u> <u>Romantic</u> <u>Literature</u>, p. 53.

6. François Livi, <u>J.-K.</u> Huysmans--<u>A</u> <u>Rebours</u> <u>et</u> <u>l'esprit</u> <u>décadent</u> (Paris: Nizet, 1972), p. 19.

7. Ibid.

8. Quoted by Mario Praz, <u>The</u> <u>Romantic</u> <u>Agony</u>, 2nd ed. (London: Oxford University Press, 1951), p. 361.

9. Ibid., p. 306.

10. Quoted by Praz, p. 307.

11. P. 316.

chapter seven

1. Jacques Barzun, Romanticism and the Modern Ego (Boston: Little, Brown and Co., 1947), p. 138.

2. From the statement of purpose ("Notre But"), Revue néo-romantique, no. 1 (February, 1907), 2.

3. Marcel Arland, "Un nouveau mal du siècle," Nouvelle Revue Française, 75 (1924), 149-58.

4. See Edmond Sée, Notre Epoque et le théâtre (Paris: Les Éditions de France, 1930), I, 204-36, for a discussion of neo-romanticism in the French theater from the end of the First World War to 1930.

5. Julien Benda, Trois Idoles Romantiques (Geneva: Éditions du Mont-Blanc, 1948), p. 9.

6. Armand Hoog, "Le Romantisme et l'existence contemporaine," Mercure de France, no. 1071 (November, 1952), 438.

7. Henri Peyre, "Romanticism and French Literature: 'Le Mort vivant'," Modern Language Quarterly, 15 (March, 1954), 81.

8. Marsi Paribatra, Le Romantisme contemporain (Paris: Les Éditions Polyglottes, 1954), p. 7.

9. Germaine Mason, A Concise Survey of French Literature (New York: Greenwood Press, 1959), p. 241.

10. R.-M. Albérès, Bilan littéraire du XXe siècle (Paris: Nizet, 1971), p. 39.

11. Germaine Brée, Littérature française--Le XXe Siècle (1920-1970) (Paris: Arthaud, 1978), II, 46.

12. Ibid.

13. R.-M. Albérès, Portrait de notre héros (Paris: Le Portulan, 1945), p. 203.

14. Ibid., pp. 115-16.

15. Ibid., p. 32.

16. Quoted by Richard W. B. Lewis in Malraux--A Collection of Critical Essays, ed. (Englewood Cliffs: Prentice Hall, 1964), p. 3

17. Cecil Jenkins, "Malraux the Romantic," London Magazine (March, 1961), p. 52.

18. "Postface" to the 1949 edition, p. 163.

19. André Malraux, Les Conquérants (Paris: Gallimard, 1947), p. 16. Subsequent page references are to this edition.

20. Edmund Wilson, The Show of Light (New York: Farrar, Strauss and Young, 1952), p. 567.

21. Quoted by Denis Boak, André Malraux (Oxford: Clarendon Press, 1968), p. 241.

22. Pierre de Boisdeffre, _Métamorphoses_ _de_ _la_ _littérature_ (Paris: Editions Alsatia, 1963), I, 462.

23. Boak, p. 241.

24. See Frédéric J. Grover's introductory chapter in _Drieu_ _La_ _Rochelle_ _and_ _the_ _Fiction_ _of_ _Testimony_ (Berkeley: University of California Press, 1958).

25. Quoted by Maurice Bruézière, _Histoire_ _Descriptive_ _de_ _la_ _littérature_ _contemporaine_ (Paris: Berger-Levrault, 1976), II, 203.

26. Pierre Drieu La Rochelle, _L'Homme_ _couvert_ _de_ _femmes_ (Paris: Gallimard, 1925), p. 44. Subsequent page references are to this edition.

27. Pierre Drieu La Rochelle, _Drôle_ _de_ _voyage_ (Paris: Gallimard, 1933), p. 189. Subsequent page references are to this edition.

28. Pierre Drieu La Rochelle, _Gilles_ (Paris: Gallimard, 1939), p. 260. Subsequent page references are to this edition.

29. M. Rieuneau, _Guerre_ _et_ _Révolution_ _dans_ _le_ _roman_ _français_ _de_ _1919_ _à_ _1939_ (Paris: Klincksieck, 1974), p. 550.

30. Robert Emmet Jones, _The_ _Alienated_ _Hero_ _in_ _Modern_ _French_ _Drama_ (Athens, Ga.: The University of Georgia Press, 1967), p. 4.

31. Ibid., p. 10.

32. Michael Goldman, "The Ghost of Joy: Reflections on Romanticism and the forms of Modern Drama," in _Romantic_ _and_ _Modern_, ed. George Bornstein (Pittsburg: University of Pittsburg Press, 1977), p. 54.

33. _Forces_ _in_ _Modern_ _French_ _Drama_ (London: University of London Press, 1972), p. 77.

34. Edward Owen Marsh, _Jean_ _Anouilh--Poet_ _of_ _Pierrot_ _and_ _Pantaloon_ (New York: Russell and Russell, 1953), p. 197.

35. See John Fletcher, pp. 87 and 89.

36. Jacques Guicharnaud, _Modern_ _French_ _Theatre_ (New Haven: Yale University Press, 1951), p. 114.

37. Asher Moore and Rollo Handy, "Existential Phenomenology," in _Philosophy_ _Today_, ed. Jerry H. Gill (New York: Macmillan, 1968), I, 193.

38. See for example Iris Murdoch, _Sartre:_ _Romantic_ _Rationalist_ (New Haven: Yale University Press, 1959) and Robert Champigny, _Stages_ _on_ _Sartre's_ _Way_ (Millwood New York: 1974).

39. Quoted by Robert D. Cumming, ed., _The_ _Philosophy_ _of_ _Jean-Paul_ _Sartre_ (New York: The Modern Library, 1965), p. 4.

40. Jean-Paul Sartre, _Les_ _Mains_ _sales_ _in_ _The_ _French_ _Theater_ _since_ _1930_, ed. Oreste F. Pucciani (New York: Blaisdell, 1954), p. 392. Subsequent page references are to this edition.

41. Victor Brombert, ed., _The_ _Hero_ _in_ _Literature_ (Greenwich, Conn: Fawcett, 1969), p. 258.

42. Hazel E. Barnes, _Sartre_ (Philadelphia: J. B. Lippincott, 1973), p. 117.

43. Ellin Horowotz, "The Rebirth of the Artist, in _On Contemporary Literature_, ed. Richard Kostelanetz (New York: Avon Books, 1969), p. 331.

44. Ihab H. Hassan, ibid., pp. 39–40.

45. Gore Vidal, ibid., p. 29.

chapter eight

1. Victor Brombert, ed., The Hero in Literature (Greenwich, Conn: Fawcett Publications, 1969), p. 21.

2. Walter L. Reed, Meditations on the Hero (New Haven: Yale University Press, 1974), p. 192.

3. Bowie, Malcom, Henri Michaux (Oxford: Clarendon Press, 1973), p. 7.

4. Ibid., p. 10.

5. Henri Michaux, "Le grand combat," L'Espace du Dedans (Paris: Gallimard, 1966), p. 14. Originally appeared in Qui je fus (1927).

6. Jean Pénard, "Une Approche d'Henri Michaux," Critique, 15 (1959), 946.

7. Henri Michaux, Plume (Paris: Gallimard, 1963), p. 143.

8. Ibid., p. 13.

9. David I. Grossvogel, The Self-Conscious Stage in Modern French Drama (New York: Columbia University Press, 1958), p. 16.

10. Ruby Cohn, Back to Beckett (Princeton: Princeton University Press, 1973), p. 145.

11. Samuel Beckett, Théâtre (Paris: Les Editions de Minuit: 1971), I, 145. Subsequent page references are to this edition.

12. A. Alvarez, Beckett (Fontana: William Collins Sons and Co., 1973), p. 60.

13. Samuel Beckett, "Breath," First Love and Other Shorts (New York: Grove Press, 1974), p. 91.

14. Alvarez, p. 115.

15. I believe it was Ruby Cohn who first used the term "nihilotropism" to describe Beckett's work.

16. Samuel Beckett, Théâtre, I, p. 99.

17. Jacques Guicharnaud, Modern French Theater (New Haven: Yale University Press, 1961), p. 204.

18. Beckett, op. cit., p. 24.

19. Lewis T. Cetta, Profane Play, Ritual, and Jean Genet (University, Alabama: University of Alabama Press, 1974), pp. 88-89.

20. Jean Genet, Journal du voleur (Paris: Gallimard, 1949), p. 278.

21. Ibid., p. 258.

22. Jean Genet, OEuvres complètes (Paris: Gallimard, 1951), III, 141. Subsequent references to Pompes funèbres are to this edition and will be cited hereafter as PF.

23. Richard N. Coe, The Vision of Jean Genet (New York: Grove Press, 1968), p. 155.

24. Lewis Cetta, p. 71.

25. Genet, OEuvres complètes, II, p. 408--my translation.   Subsequent references to Miracle de la Rose will hereafter be cited as MR.

26. Journal du voleur, p. 48.

27. See Claude Bonnefoy, Jean Genet (Paris: Editions Universitaires, 1965), p. 29.

28. OEuvres complètes, II, p. 62.   Subsequent references to Notre Dame des Fleurs will hereafter be cited as NDF.

29. Richard Coe, p. 76.

30. Jean-Paul Sartre, Saint Genet--Actor and Martyr (New York: New American Library of World Literature, 1952), p. 62.

31. Ibid., p. 60.

32. Coe, p. 49.

33. Ibid., pp. 313-14.

chapter nine

    1.   See   Joseph   Wood   Krutch,   The Modern   Temper   in   A   Krutch   Onmibus
(New York: William Morrow, 1970), p. 94.

appendix one

    1. Pierre Moreau, Ames et thèmes romantiques (Paris: Corti, 1965), p. 280.

    2. Robert B. Johnson, Henry de Montherlant (New York: Twayne, 1968), p. 28.

    3. Henry de Montherlant, Romans (Paris: Gallimard, 1959), p. 8. Subsequent page references are to this edition.

    4. Pierre Moreau, pp. 284-85.

    5. Romans, p. 182.

    6. Quoted by Pierre Moreau, p. 281.

appendix two

    1. Bruno Vercier, ed., Les Critiques de notre temps et Saint-Exupéry (Paris: Garnier, 1971), p. 8.

    2. Quoted by Vercier, ibid., p. 74.

    3. Michel Quenel, ibid., p. 145.

    4. Georges Moulin, ibid., p. 34.

    5. Jules Roy, "Fatalité de l'avion," France Libre, vol. 8, no. 48 (October, 1944), 418.

    6. Antoine de Saint-Exupéry, OEuvres (Paris: Gallimard, 1959), p. 61. Subsequent page references are to this edition.

    7. Jules Roy, p. 418.

    8. Quoted by Michel Quenel in Les Critiques de notre temps et Saint-Exupéry, ed. Bruno Vercier (Paris: Garnier, 1971), p. 145.

appendix three

    1. Julien Gracq, "Réflexions sur Chateaubriand," Cahiers du Sud, no. 357 (1960), 172.

2. Léon Roudiez, "Le Beau Ténébreux à l'ombre du Château d'Argol," in Julien Gracq, ed. Jean-Louis Leutrat (Paris: Editions de l'Herne, 1972), p. 76.

3. Julien Gracq, Un Beau Ténébreux (Paris: Corti, 1945), pp. 145-46.

4. Béatrice Didier in Julien Gracq, p. 342.

appendix four

1. See Christopher Robinson, French Literature in the Nineteenth Century (London: Davis and Charles, 1978), p. 31.

2. See Frank Thilly, History of Philosophy, rev. ed. (New York: Henry Holt, 1952), pp. 499-500.

3. The World as Will and Idea (1883), I, 415; quoted by Will Durant, The Story of Philosophy (New York: Pocket Library, 1954), p. 326.

4. Schopenhauer, The World as Will and Idea in The Works of Schopenhauer, ed. Will Durant (New York: The Philosopher's Library, 1931), p. 309.

appendix five

1. Durant, The Story of Philosophy, p. 439.

2. Friedrich Nietzsche, Thus Spake Zarathrustra, trans. Thomas Common (New York: Russell and Russell, 1964), p. 9.

3. Durant, p. 440.

4. H. G. Schenk, The Mind of the European Romantics (Garden City, NY: Doubleday, 1969), p. 241.

5. Anthony M. Ludovici, "Notes" to Thus Spake Zarathrustra (1964), p. 435.

Excursus one

1. Erich Fromm, Man for Himself (New York: Fawcett World Library, 1968), pp. 48–50.

2. Sigmund Freud, Civilization and its Discontents in the Standard Edition of the Complete Psychological Works of Sigmund Freud (London: The Hogarth Press, 1961), XXI, 143.   (Our emphasis)

Excursus two

1. César Graña, Bohemian versus Bourgeois (New York: Basic Books, 1964), pp. 184–85.

2. Ibid., pp. 187–88.

3. Max Weber, From Max Weber: Essays in Sociology (New York: Oxford University Press, 1958), p. 220.

4. Jacques Hardré, La France et sa civilisation (New York: Dodd, Mead, 1969), p. 274.

Excursus three

1. Erich Fromm, Man for Himself (New York: Fawcett World Library, 1968), p. 50.

2. See Frank G. Goble, The Third Force (New York: Grossman, 1970), p. 52.

3. For fuller information, see Goble, ibid., chapter 14.

4. Abraham Maslow, Toward a Psychology of Being, 2nd ed. (Princeton: D. Van Nostrand, 1968), p. 155.

5. Ibid., p. 159.

6. John Steinbeck, The Grapes of Wrath (New York: Bantam Books, 1972), p. 164.

BIBLIOGRAPHY

Primary Sources

Balzac, Honoré de. La Comédie humaine. Ed. Marcel Bouteron. Paris:
    Gallimard, 1952. Vol. IV.

Baudelaire, Charles. Les Fleurs du mal. Ed. Jacques Crépet and Georges
    Blin. Paris:, Corti, 1942.

_____. OEuvres complètes. Paris: Gallimard, 1975, Vol. I.

Beckett, Samuel. First Love and Other Shorts. New York: Grove Press,
    1974.

_____. Théâtre. Paris: Les Editions de Minuit, 1971.
    Vol. I.

_____. Malone meurt, Paris: Les Editions de Minuit, 1951.

Camus, Albert. L'Etranger. New York: Appleton Century-Crofts, 1955.

Chateaubriand, François-René de. Essai historique, politique et moral
    sur les Révolutions anciennes et modernes considérées dans leurs
    rapports avec la révolution française. Paris: Ch. Hingray, 1838.

_____. Le génie du christianism.

_____. René. Ed. Armand Weil. Paris: Droz, 1935.

_____. OEuvres romanesques et voyages. Ed. Maurice Regard.
    Paris: Gallimard, 1969.

Constant, Benjamin. OEuvres. Ed. Alfred Roulin. Paris: Gallimard, 1957.

_____. Adolphe. Ed. J.-H. Bornecque. Paris: Garnier, 1968.

Drieu L. Rochelle, Pierre. L'Homme couvert de femmes. Paris: Gallimard,
    1925.

_____. Drôle de voyage. 3rd edition. Paris: Gallimard,
    1933.

_____. Gilles. Paris: Gallimard, 1939.

Dumas, Alexandre, père. Théâtre romantique. Paris: Firmin-Didot, n.d.

Eliot, T.S. Collected Poems, 1909-1935. New York: Harcourt, Brace, 1936.

Flaubert, Gustave. Madame Bovary. Paris: Gallimard, 1972.

Gautier, Théophile. Mademoiselle de Maupin. Paris: Garnier, 1966.

_____. Poésies complètes de Théophile Gautier. Ed. René Jasinski. Paris: Nizet, 1970. Vol. I.

Genet, Jean. OEuvres complètes. Paris: Gallimard, 1951. Vols. II and III.

_____. Journal du voleur. Paris: Gallimard, 1949.

Gracq, Julien. Un beau ténébreux. Paris: Corti, 1945.

Laforgue, Jules. Derniers Vers. Ed. Michael Collie and J.M. L'Heureux. Toronto: University of Toronto Press, 1965.

Hugo, Victor. Théâtre complet. Ed. J.-J. Thierry and Josette Mélèze. Paris: Gallimard, 1963.

Huysmans, J.-K. A rebours. Paris: Fasquelle, 1974.

Malraux, André. Romans. Paris: Gallimard, 1947.

Michaux, Henri. Plume: précédé de Lointain intérieur. Paris: Gallimard, 1963.

_____. L'Espace du dedans. Paris: Gallimard, 1966.

Montherlant, Henry de. Romans et oeuvres de fiction non théâtrales. Paris: Gallimard, 1959.

Musset, Alfred de. Poésies complètes. Ed. Maurice Allem. Paris: Gallimard, 1957.

_____. Théâtre complet. Ed. Maurice Allem. Paris: Gallimard, 1958.

_____. OEuvres complètes en prose. Ed. Maurice Allem and Paul Courant. Gallimard, 1960.

_____. Poésies. Paris: Gallimard, 1962.

Nietzsche, Friedrich. Thus Spake Zarathrustra. Trans. Thomas Common. New York: Russell and Russell, 1964.

Prévost, A.-F. OEuvres. Paris, 1810-1816; rpt. Geneva: Slatkine, 1969. Vol. IV.

Rousseau, Jean-Jacques. Les Confessions. Ed. Jacques Voisine. Paris: Garnier frères, 1964.

Sainte-Breuve, Charles-Augustin. Vie, Poésies et Pensées de Joseph Delorme. Ed. Gerald Antoine. Paris: Nouvelles Editions Latines, 1956.

_____. Volupté. Paris. Garnier-Flammarion, 1969.

Saint-Exupéry, Antoine de. OEuvres. Paris: Gallimard, 1959.

Senancour, Étienne Pivert de. Obermann. Vol. I. Paris: Edouard Cornély, 1912. Vol. II. Paris: Hachette, 1913.

Shelley, Percy Bysshe. Prometheus Unbound. Ed. Lawrence John Zollman. New Haven: Yale University Press, 1968.

Steinbeck, John. The Grapes of Wrath. New York: Bantam Books, 1972.

Stendhal (Henri Beyle). <u>Romans</u> <u>et</u> <u>Nouvelles</u>. Ed. Henri Martineau. Gallimard, 1952.

Verlaine, Paul. <u>OEuvres</u> <u>posthumes</u>. Paris: Messein, 1913. Vol. II.

Vigny, Alfred de. <u>OEuvres</u> <u>complètes</u>. Ed. F. Baldensperger. Paris:
Gallimard, 1950. Vol. I.

* * *

274

Secondary Sources

Abraham, Pierre and Roland Desné eds. Histoire littéraire de France. Paris: Éditions Sociales, 1978. Vol. VII.

Adam, Antoine et al. Littérature française. Paris: Larousse, 1972. Vol. II.

Albérès, R.-M. Portrait de notre héros: Essai sur le roman actuel. Paris: Le Portulan, 1945.

_____. La Révolte des écrivains d'aujourd'hui. Paris: Corrêa, 1949.

_____. Bilan littéraire du XXe siècle. 3rd Ed. Paris: Nizet, 1971.

Allem, Maurice. Alfred de Musset. Rev. ed. Paris: Arthaud, 1947.

Alvarez, A. Beckett. Fontana: Williams Collins Sons, 1973.

Anderson, R. D. France 1870-1914: Politics and Society. London: Rutledge Kegan Paul, 1977.

Arland, Marcel. "Un nouveau mal du siècle." Nouvelle Revue Française, 75 (1924), 149-58.

Awad, Lewis. "The Theme of Prometheus in English and French Literature." Diss. Princeton 1967.

Babbitt, Irving. Rousseau and Romanticism. Boston: Houghton Mifflin, 1947.

Baillot, Louis. "La jeunesse et le mal du siècle." La Nouvelle Critique, 3e année, No. 30 (Nov. 1951), 23-34.

Baldensperger, Fernand. Goethe en France. Paris: Hachette, 1904.

_____. Le Mouvement des idées dans l'émigration française (1789-1815). Paris: Plon, 1924. Vols. I-II.

_____. La littérature française entre les deux guerres. Los Angeles: Lymanhouse, 1941.

Barbéris, Pierre. Balzac et le mal du siècle. Paris: Gallimard, 1970. Vols. I-II.

_____. René de Chateaubriand: un nouveau roman. Paris: Larousse, 1973.

_____. A la recherche d'une écriture: Chateaubriand. Paris: Mame, 1974.

Barnes, Hazel E. Sartre. Philadelphia: J. B. Lippincott, 1973.

Barnet, Sylvan et al. A Dictionary of Literary Terms. Boston: Little, Brown and Co., 1960.

Barrère, J.-B. Victor Hugo. Paris: Hatier, 1967.

Barzun, Jacques. Romanticism and the Modern Ego. Boston: Little, Brown and Co., 1947.

_____. Classic, Romantic and Modern. Chicago: University of Chicago Press, 1961.

_____. "Romanticism." Colliers Encyclopedia. 1975 ed.

Bauer, George Howard. Sartre and the Artist. Chicago: Chicago University Press, 1969.

Béguin, Albert. L'Âme romantique et le rêve. Paris: Corti, 1939.

Benda, Julien. Trois Idoles romantiques. Geneva: Éditions du Mon-Blanc, 1948.

Bersani, J. et al. La Littérature en France depuis 1945. Paris: Bordas, 1970.

Blin, Georges. Stendhal et les problèmes du roman. Paris: Corti, 1953.

Boak, Denis. André Malraux. Oxford: Clarendon Press, 1968.

Bois..deffre, Pierre de. Métamophoses de la litérature. Paris: Éditions Alsatia, 1963. Vol. I.

_____. Les Écrivains français d'aujourd'hui. Paris: Presses Universitaires de France, 1973.

Bonnefoy, Claude. Jean Genet. Paris: Éditions Universitaires, 1965.

Bonnefoy, George. La Pensée religieuse et morale d'Alfred de Vigny. Paris: Hachette, 1944.

Bornstein, George, ed. Romantic and Modern: Revaluations of Literary Tradition. Pittsburg: University of Pittsburg Press, 1977.

Boucher, Maurice. "Ironie romantique." Cahiers du Sud, numéro spécial sur le romantisme allemand (1937), 29-32.

Bourgeois, René. L'Ironie romantique. Grenoble: Presses Universitaires de Grenoble, 1974.

Boutel de Monvel, M.A. "Posterité du héros romantique." Revue des Sciences Humaines, 62-63 (April-Sept. 1951), 138-45.

Bowie, Malcolm. Henri Michaux. Oxford: Clarendon Press, 1973.

Bowra, C. M. Heroic Poetry. New York: St. Martin's Press, 1966.

Brée, Germaine. Littérature française: Le XXe siècle 1920-1970. Paris: Arthaud, 1978.

Brereton, Geoffrey. A Short History of French Literature. London: Penguin Books, 1954.

Brombert, Victor, ed. The Hero in Literature. Greenwich, Conn.: Fawcett, 1969.

_____. Stendhal et la voie oblique. New Haven: Yale University Press, 1954.

Bruézière, Maurice. Histoire descriptive de la littérature comtemporarine. Paris: Berger-Levrault, 1976. Vols. I-II.

Canat, René. Une forme du mal du siècle: du sentiment de la solitude morale chez les Romantiques et les Parnassiens. Paris: Hachette, 1904.

Carter, A. E. The Idea of Decadence in French Literature. Toronto: University of Toronto Press, 1958.

Castex, Pierre-Georges. "Les Destinées" d'Alfred de Vigny. Paris: Société d'Edition d' Enseignement Supérieur, 1964.

Cerný, Václav. Essai sur le titanisme dans la poésie romantique occidentale, entre 1815 et 1850. Prague: Editions Orbis, 1935.

Cetta, Lewis T. Profane Play, Ritual, and Jean Genet. University, Ala.: The University of Alabama Press, 1974.

Champigny, Robert. Stages on Sartre's Way 1938-1952. Bloomington, Ind: University Publications, 1959; rpt. Millwood: Krauss, 1974.

Clarac, Pierre. A la recherche de Chateaubriand. Paris: Nizet, 1975.

Clement, N. H. Romanticism in France. New York: MLA, 1939; rpt. Millwood: Krauss, 1966.

Clive, Geoffrey. The Philosophy of Nietzsche. New York: The New American Library, 1965.

Clouard, Henri. Alexandre Dumas. Paris: Albin Michel, 1955.

Coe, Richard N. The Vision of Jean Genet. New York: Grove Press, 1968.

Cohn, Ruby. Back to Beckett. Princeton: Princeton University Press, 1973.

Coppleston, Frederick. A History of Philosophy. Westminster, Maryland: The Newman Press, 1963, Vol. VII.

Chrichfield, Grant. "The Romantic Madman as Hero: Nodier's Michel le Charpentier." The French Review, 51 (May, 1978), 835-42.

Cumming, Robert D., ed. The Philosophy of Jean-Paul Sartre. New York: The Modern Library, 1965.

Curtius, Ernst Robert. European Literature and the Latin Middle Ages. New York: Harper and Row, 1953.

Dédéyan, Charles. Le Thème de Faust dans la littérature européenne. Paris: Lettres Modernes, 1955. Vol. II.

_____. Le Nouveau Mal du siècle: de Baudelaire à nos jours. Paris: Société d'Édition d'Enseignement Supérieur, 1968.

_____. Chateaubriand et Rousseau. Paris: Société d'Édition d'Enseignement Supérieur, 1973.

Dieguez, Manuel de. Chateaubriand ou le poète face à l'histoire. Paris: Plon: 1963.

Driver, Tom F. Jean Genet. New York: Columbia University Press, 1966.

Dumont, Francis. Naissance du romantisme contemporain. Paris: Calmann-Lévy, 1942.

Durant, Will. The Story of Philosophy. New York: Pocket Library, 1954.

Estève, Edmund. Byron et le romantisme français. Paris: Hachette, 1907.

Eustis, Alvin. "Introduction" to Le Rouge et le Noir. New York: Dell, 1963, 9-21.

Fletcher, John. Forces in Modern French Drama. London: London University Press, 1972.

Freud, Sigmund. The Standard Edition of the Complete Psychological Works of Sigmund Freud. London: The Hogarth Press, 1961. Vol. XXI.

Fromm, Erich. Man for Himself. New York: Fawcett, 1968.

Garber, Frederick K. "Self, Society, Value, and the Romantic Hero." Comparative Literature, 19 (1967), 321-33.

Gasset, José Ortega y. Meditations on Quixote. Trans. Evelyn Rugg and Diego Marín. New York: Norton, 1961.

Gautier, Théophile. Histoire du romantisme. Milan: La Goliardica, 1970.

George, Albert Joseph. The Development of French Romanticism: The Impact of the Industrial Revolution on Literature. Syracuse: Syracuse University Press, 1955.

Giraud, René. Mensonge romantique et Vérité Romanesque. Paris: Grasset, 1961.

Giraud, Raymond. The Unheroic Hero in the Novels of Stendhal, Balzac and Flaubert. New York: Octagon Books, 1969.

Goble, Frank G. The Third Force. New York: Grossman, 1970.

Grabo, Carb. Prometheus Unbound: An Interpretation. New York: Gordon Press, 1968.

Gracq, Julien. "Reflexions sur Chateaubriand." Cahiers du Sud, No. 357 (1960), 163-72.

Graff, Gerald. Literature against Itself. Chicago: Chicago University Press, 1979.

Graña, César. Bohemian versus Bourgeois. New York: Basic Books, 1965.

Grant, Richard B. Théophile Gautier. Boston: Twayne, 1975.

Grossvogel, David I. The Self-Conscious Stage in Modern French Drama. New York: Columbia University Press, 1958.

_____. The Blasphemers: The Theater of Brecht, Ionesco, Beckett, Genet. Ithaca: Cornell University Press, 1965.

Grover, Frédéric J. Drieu La Rochelle and the Fiction of Testimony. Berkeley: University of California Press, 1958.

Guerne, Armel. L'Ame insurgée: écrits sur le romantisme. Paris: Éditions Phébus, 1977.

Guicharnaud, Jacques. Modern French Theater. New Haven: Yale University Press, 1961.

Gurewitch, Morton L. European Romantic Irony. Diss. Columbia 1957.

Guthrie, Ramon and George E. Diller. French Literature and Thought since the Revolution. New York: Harcourt, Brace, 1942.

Hackett, C. A. Anthology of Modern French Poetry. New York: Macmillan, 1956.

Hardré, Jacques. La France et sa civilisation. New York: Dodd, Mead, 1969.

Hegel, Georg Wilhelm Fredrich. Lectures on the Philosophy of World History. Trans. H. B. Nisbet. Cambridge: Cambridge University Press, 1975.

Henriot, Émile. Les Romantiques. Paris: Albin Michel, 1953.

Hoog, Armand. "Le Romantisme et l'existence contemporaine." Mercure de France, No. 1071 (Nov. 1952), 436-48.

_____. "Who Invented the Mal du Siècle?" Yale French Studies, 13 (Spring-Summer, 1954) 42-51.

Howarth, W. D. Sublime and Grotesque: A Study of French Romantic Drama, London: Harrap, 1975.

Immerwahr, Raymond. "The Subjectivity or Objectivity of Friedrich Schlegel's Poetic Irony," Germanic Review, 26 (1951), 173-191.

Jankélévitch, Vladimir. L'Ironie ou la bonne conscience. 2nd ed. Paris: Presses Universitaires de France, 1950.

Jasinski, René. Histoire de la littérature française. Paris: Boivin, 1947. Vol. II.

Jenkins, Cecil. "Malraux the Romantic." London Magazine, March 1961, pp. 50-57.

Johnson, Robert B. Henry de Montherlant. New York: Twayne, 1968.

Jones, Grahame C. L'Ironie dans les romans de Stendhal. Lausanne: Éditions du grand chêne, 1966.

Jones, Robert Emmet. The Alienated Hero in Modern French Drama. Athens, Ga: University of Georgia Press, 1967.

Julleville, L. Petit de. Histoire de la langue et de la littérature françaises des origines à 1900. Paris: Colin, 1899; rpt. Millwood, Krauss, 1975.

Jung, Carl G. Modern Man in Search of a Soul. New York: Harcourt, Brace and World, 1933.

Kern, Edith. "The Modern Hero: Phoenix or Ashes?" Comparative Literature, 10 (1958), 325-34.

Kierkegaard, Søren. Either/Or. Trans. David F. Swenson and Lillian Marvin Swenson. Garden City: Doubleday, 1959.

Kostelanetz, Richard, ed. On Contemporary Literature. New York: Avon Books, 1969.

Krutch, Joseph Wood. The Modern Temper in A Krutch Omnibus. New York: William Morrow, 1970.

Lacretelle, Jacques de, et al. Victor Hugo. Paris: Hachette, 1967.

Langlois, Walter G., ed. André Malraux: visages du romancier. Paris: Minard, 1973.

Lasserre, Pierre. Faust en France. Paris: Calmann-Lévy, 1929.

Lenski, B. A. Jean Anouilh: Stages in Rebellion. Atlantic Highlands, N.J.: Humanities Press, 1975.

Leutrat, Jean-Louis, ed. Julien Gracq. Paris: Éditions de l'Herne, 1972.

Lewis, R. W. B., ed. Malraux: A Collection of Critical Essays. Englewood Cliffs: Prentice-Hall, 1964.

Livi, François. J.-K. Huysmans: A Rebours et l'esprit décadent. Paris: Nizet, 1972.

Longford, Elizabeth. "Byron and Satanism." London News, Oct. 1977, p. 6.

Lorris, Robert. Sartre dramaturge. Paris: Nizet, 1975.

Martino, Pierre. L'Époque romantique en France. Paris: Hatier-Boivin, 1944.

Marsh, Edward Owen. Jean Anouilh: Poet of Pierrot and Pantaloon. New York: Russell and Russell, 1953.

Maslow, Abraham. Toward a Psychology of Being. 2nd ed. Princeton: D. Van Nostrand, 1968.

Mason, Germaine. A Concise Survey of French Literature. New York: Greenwood Press, 1959.

Maurois, André. Chateaubriand. Trans. Vera Fraser, New York: Harper and Brothers, 1958.

McIntyre, Sandye Jean. "The Comic Hero in Stendhal's Le Rouge et le Noir." Diss. Case Western Reserve 1974.

McMahon, Joseph. The Imagination of Jean Genet. New Haven: Yale University Press, 1963.

Michaud, Guy and Ph. Van Tieghem. Le Romantisme. Paris: Hachette, 1952.

Miles, David H. "Portrait of the Marxist as a Young Hegelian: Lukács' Theory of the Novel." PMLA, 94 (1979), 22-35.

Milner, Max. Le Romantisme (1820-1843). Paris: Arthaud, 1973. Vol. I.

Moore, Asher and Rollo Handy. "Existential Phenomenology." Philosophy Today. Ed. Jerry H. Gill. New York: Macmillan, 1968, 184-199. Vol. I.

Moreau, Pierre. Le Romantisme. Paris: Del Duca, 1957.

_____. Ames et thèmes romantiques. Paris: Corti, 1965.

_____. Chateaubriand. Rev. ed. Paris: Hatier, 1969.

Monvel, A. Boutet de. "Posterité du héros romantique." Revue des Sciences Humaines, Nos. 62-63 (avril-septembre 1951), 138-45.

Muecke, D.C. Irony. London: Methuen, 1970.

Murdoch, Iris. Sartre: Romantic Rationalist. New Haven: Yale University Press, 1959.

Nadeau, Maurice. The French Novel since the War. New York: Grove Press, 1967.

Nelson, Hilda. Charles Nodier. New York: Twayne, 1972.

Nist, John. "The Art of Chaucer: Pathedy." Tennessee Studies in Literature, 11 (1966), 1-10.

Olivier, A. Richard. Charles Nodier: Pilot of Romanticism. Syracuse: Syracuse University Press, 1964.

Paribatra, Marsi. Le Romantisme contemporain. Paris: Les Éditions Polyglottes, 1954.

Pénard, Jean. "Une Approche d'Henri Michaux." Critique, 15 (1959), 943-51.

Peyre, Henri. "Romanticism and French Literature: Le Mort vivant." Modern Language Quarterly, 15 (March, 1954), 3-17.

_____. Literature and Sincerity. New Haven: Yale University Press, 1963.

_____. What is Romanticism? Trans. Roda Roberts. University, Ala: University of Alabama Press, 1977.

Picon, Gaëton. Panorama de la nouvelle littérature française. Paris: Gallimard, 1960.

_____. Malraux. Paris: Seuil, 1974.

Praz, Mario. The Romantic Agony. 2nd Ed. London: Oxford University Press, 1951.

Priestley, J. B. Literature and Western Man. New York: Harper and Brothers, 1960.

Pucciani, Oreste, ed. The French Theater since 1930. New York: Blaisdell, 1954.

Quinet, Edgar. Histoire de mes idées. Paris: Flammarion, 1972.

Radine, Serge. Anouilh, Lenormand, Salacrou: trois dramaturges à la recherche de leur vérité. Geneva: Editions des Trois Collines, 1951.

Ramsey, Warren. Jules Laforgue and the Ironic Inheritance. New York: Oxford University Press, 1953.

_____, ed. Jules Laforgue: Essays on a Poet's Life and Work. Carbondale: Southern Illinois University Press, 1969.

Rank, Otto. The Don Juan Legend. Trans. David G. Winter. Princeton: Princeton University Press, 1975.

_____. The Myth of the Birth of the Hero. New York: Robert Brunner, 1957.

Reboul, Pierre. Laforgue. Paris: Hatier, 1960.

Reed, Walter L. Meditations on the Hero. New Haven: Yale University Press, 1974.

Richard, Jean-Pierre. Paysage de Chateaubriand. Paris: Seuil, 1967.

Ridge, George Ross. The Hero in French Romantic Literature. Athens, Ga: University of Georgia Press, 1959.

_____. The Hero in French Decadent Literature. Athens: Ga: University of Georgia Press, 1961.

Rieuneau, M. Guerre et Révolution dans le roman français de 1919 à 1939. Paris: Klincksieck, 1978.

Robinson, Christopher. French Literature in the Nineteenth Century. London: David and Charles, 1978.

Roger, Jacques. Histoire de la littérature française. Paris: Armand Colin, 1970.

Roy, Jules. "Fatalité de l'avion." France libre, Oct. 1944, pp. 418-420.

Rudwin, Maximilien. Romantisme et satanisme. Paris: Les Belles Lettres, 1927.

_____. The Devil in Legend and Literature. La Salle: The Open Court Publishing Co., 1973.

Sainte-Beuve, Charles-Augustin. Portraits contemporains. Paris: Calmann-Lévy, 1876. Vol. I.

_____. Chateaubriand et son groupe littéraire sous l'Empire. Paris: Garnier, 1948. Vol. I.

Sartre, Jean-Paul. Saint-Genet: Actor and Martyr. New York: New American Library of World Literature, 1952.

_____. L'Idiot de la famille. Paris: Gallimard, 1971.

Saulnier, Verdun. La littérature française du siècle romantique. 8th ed. Paris: Presses Universitaires de France, 1966.

Schenk, H. G. The Mind of the European Romantics. Garden City: Doubleday, 1969.

Schopenhauer, Arthur. The World as Will and Idea in The Works of Schopenhauer. Ed. Will Durant. New York: The Philosopher's Library, 1931.

Schroder, Maurice Z. Icarus: The Image of the Artist in French Romanticism. Cambridge: Harvard University Press, 1961.

Sée, Edmond. Notre Époque et le théâtre. Paris: Les Éditions de France, 1930, Vol. I.

Shattuck, Roger. The Banquet Years: The Origins of the Avant-garde in France (1885 to World War I). Rev. ed. New York: Knopf and Random House, 1968.

Smith, Albert B. Ideal and Reality in the Fictional Narratives of Théophile Cautier. Gainesville: University of Florida Press, 1969.

Stanford, Raney. "The Romantic Hero and that Fatal Selfhood." The Centennial Review, 12 (Fall, 1968), 430-54.

Starobinski, Jean. L'Oeil vivant. Paris: Gallimard, 1961. Vol. II.

_____. "Notes sur le bouffon romantique." Cahiers du Sud, 60 (August, 1966), 270-75.

Switzer, Richard, ed. Chateaubriand Today. Madison: The University of Wisconsin Press, 1970.

_____. Chateaubriand. New York: Twayne, 1971.

Symons, Arthur. "The Decadent Movement in Literature." Harpers New Monthly Magazine, 87 (1893), pp. 858-67.

Tennant, P. E. Théophile Gautier. London: The Athlone Press, 1975.

Thilly, Frank. History of Philosophy. Rev. ed. New York: Henry Holt, 1952.

Thorslev, Peter L. The Byronic Hero: Types and Protypes. Minneapolis: University of Minnesota Press, 1962.

Trousson, Raymond, Le Thème de Prométhée dans la littérature européenne. Geneva: Droz, 1964. Vol. II.

Thomas, Jean. Quelques aspects du romantisme contemporain. Paris: Les Belles Lettres, 1929.

Turnell, Martin. The Novel in France. New York: Vintage Books, 1958.

Vandromme, Pol. Jean Anouilh: Un auteur et ses personnages. Paris: La Table Ronde, 1965.

Van Tieghem, Paul. Le Romantisme dans la littérature européenne. Paris: Albin Michel, 1948. Vol. I.

Van Tieghem, Paul. Le Préromantisme. Paris: SFELT, 1948. Vol. I.

Van Tieghem, Philippe. Musset. Paris: Hatier, 1969.

Vercier, Bruno. Les Critiques de notre temps et Saint-Exupéry. Paris: Garnier, 1971.

Warren, Robert Penn. "Pure and Impure Poetry." The Kenyon Review, Spring 1943, 228-54.

Weber, Max. From Max Weber: Essays in Sociology. Eds. Hans Gerth and C. Wright Mills. New York: Galaxy Books, 1958.

Weil, Armand, ed. Atala. Crit. ed. Paris: Corti, 1950.

Weinstein, Leo. The Metamorphoses of Don Juan. Stanford: Stanford University Press, 1959.

Werblowski, R. J. Zwi. Lucifer and Prometheus. London: Rutledge and Kegan Paul, 1952.

Wiecka, Edouard. "Roman et histoire: la composition thématique d'Oberman." Romantisme, 19 (1978), 25-40.

Wilson, Edmond. The Shores of Light. New York: Farrar, Strauss and Young, 1952.

Wright, Charles H. C. The Background of Modern French Literature. Freeport, NY: Books for Libraries Press 1926; rpt. 1971.

INDEX